"ANNA, WHERE ARE YOU? DO PLEASE WRITE. THOMASINA."

. . . read Miss Silver, while perusing the Agony Column in the *Times*. Then, soon afterwards, Thomasina Elliot, a beautiful young London heiress, hired her to find her best friend, Anna Ball, who had mysteriously disappeared.

Miss Silver, the resourceful ex-schoolmarm turned private eye, soon uncovers traces of the missing girl in a twisted trail that leads to the uncanny art colony of Deep End.

Here, against the excellent advice of Inspector Abbott of Scotland Yard, the fearless Miss Silver takes up the job Anna had briefly held as governess to the head family's three unruly children —and finds herself plunged into a sinister drama involving weird characters, ancient ghosts, and brand-new chicanery—a situation of mounting terror, in which a deadly killer who has struck once will strike again—soon. . . .

ABOUT THE AUTHOR

In the early years of this century the pseudonymous Englishwoman PATRICIA WENTWORTH began her writing career with an historical novel which immediately captured her a valued prize. It also launched her on a long and rewarding writing career.

In 1923 Patricia Wentworth wrote her first mystery, *The Astonishing Adventure of Jane Smith*, and proceeded to write over sixty mysteries in the next thirty-odd years.

"It is my aim," she wrote, "to portray ordinary, convincing human characters in extraordinary circumstances." As millions of happy readers will attest, she fulfilled her goal, creating Miss Maud Silver, one of the most popular of all fictional detectives, a paragon of refinement and good sense.

The mystery critic James Sandoe wrote in 1954, "The bountiful Miss Wentworth supplies a measure full to overflowing . . . agreeable, teasing, soothing."

A GREEN DOOR MYSTERY

DEATH AT DEEP END

(original title: "ANNA, WHERE ARE YOU?")

PATRICIA WENTWORTH

PYRAMID BOOKS • NEW YORK

DEATH AT DEEP END
(original title: "Anna, Where Are You?")

A PYRAMID BOOK

Published by arrangement with J. B. Lippincott Company

PRINTING HISTORY
Lippincott edition published September 1951
Pyramid edition published November 1963

Library of Congress Catalog Card Number 51-11189

Printed in the United States of America

Pyramid Books are published by Pyramid Publications, Inc.,
444 Madison Avenue, New York 22, New York, U.S.A.

DEATH AT DEEP END

PROLOGUE

AT HALF PAST TWO on a dark September afternoon Anna Ball came down the steps of No. 5 Lenister Square with a suit-case in her hand. Mrs. Dugdale's middle-aged parlourmaid stood at the open door just long enough to see that she turned to the left, a direction which would take her down to the roaring traffic at the end of the road. Lenister Square was still quiet, but it had been quieter. The tide of noise was coming in. If it rose too high, Mrs. Dugdale would be obliged to move.

Agnes went down into the basement kitchen and told Mrs. Harrison, the cook, that Miss Ball had gone, and a good riddance. Mrs. Harrison looked round from the kettle which she was taking off the fire.

"I didn't hear any taxi."

"She didn't have one—just went off down the road with her suit-case."

Mrs. Harrison began to pour boling water into a squat brown teapot.

"She'll be catching a bus. Well, it's the last of her, and thank goodness for that!"

Anna Ball walked on down the street. It was a dark afternoon, but it was not raining yet. There might be rain coming, or one of those creeping fogs. She was glad that she had not far to go, and very glad indeed to have seen the last of her job with Mrs. Dugdale. Whatever happened, she would never be a companion again. Children were bad enough, but nerve cases ought to be in a lethal chamber.

She came to the end of the street and waited for a Hammersmith bus. At this time of the day there was really nothing you could call a queue. She set her suit-case down on the pavement, and was glad that she had not to carry it any farther.

As she stood there behind a stout woman in navy blue and a poking old woman in black, no one would have given her a second glance. Her dark grey coat and skirt were not so much shabby as badly cut and badly worn. She had no looks, no style, no special height or breadth to mark her out from the thousands of other young women who have their living to earn. She might have been of any age between twenty and thirty. She was, in fact, singularly well qualified to pass unnoticed in a crowd.

When the bus stopped, the two other women got on to it, and she followed them. It is safe to assume that neither of them would have known her again. The stout woman was on her way to spend the afternoon and evening with a married daughter. She was taken up with how pleased the children were going to be when they saw what she had brought them Ernie's birthday, and such a big boy. But you couldn't leave little Glad out—she had to have her present too.

The old woman was crouched forward over her knees. Ten years now since she had had any place she could call her own. Three months with Henry, and three with James, three with Annie, and three with May. Henry's wife wasn't so bad, but that girl James had married! Annie's husband was too grand for her. Schoolmasters were all the same—laying down the law. Poor May did her best. She shouldn't have married the man, but she wouldn't listen. She nodded forward over her knees and thought of the days when she had her own little place and the children were small. She'd brought them up right, but they didn't want her now.

Anna Ball was thinking of the new job she was going to. She was going to see how it suited her. She might stay, or she might not. She wasn't going to put up with anything she didn't like. Three children was rather a lot, but anything was better than an only child. Spoiled. And for ever wanting something done to amuse it. Whereas three played with each other.

At the first stop beyond the Broadway she got out and stood waiting by the kerb. Presently a car drew in, stopped briefly, and picked her up. The door shut on her and her suit-case. The car slid into the line of traffic and was gone.

CHAPTER 1

It is a truism that dangers and difficulties do not always present themselves in that guise. A violent thunderstorm may be heralded by a cloud so small and distant as to arise unseen. When Miss Maud Silver took up her *Times* on a January morning and, having perused the Births, Marriages and Deaths, turned with interest to those personal and private messages in what is known as the Agony Column, she had no idea that she was about to make her first contact with one of her most disturbing and dangerous cases. It was now many years since she had abandoned what she herself called the Scholastic Profession in favour of a career as a private detective. It was this career which had provided her with her flat in Montague Mansions and the modest comfort with which she was now surrounded. There had been years when she had hoped for nothing more than a life in other people's houses, and in the end a bare existence on such sparse savings as could be wrung from her salary. She had only to look about her to be filled with feelings of devout gratitude to the Providence which, as she most firmly believed, had directed her energies into other channels. She took her new profession very seriously indeed. She was the servant of Justice and of the Law, she played her part in restraining the criminal and protecting the innocent, she made many devoted friends, and all her needs had been met. The photographs which covered the mantelpiece and the top of the bookcase, and which had their place amongst other things upon several small tables, proclaimed the fact that a great many of these friendships were with the young. Young men and girls, and babies of all ages, smiled from the frames of an earlier day—Victorian and Edwardian survivals in plush, in silver, in filagree silver on plush. If they were out of keeping with their present occupants they went very well with the peacock-blue curtains, the carpet in the same shade with its bright flowery garlands, the chairs with spreading laps and curly walnut frames. The carpet was a new one, but it maintained the Victorian tradition. Upon such wreaths had the gaslight of that famous age shone down. Miss Silver esteemed herself most fortunate in having been able to repeat a favourite colour, and a pattern which she could remember in her girlhood's home. The price had shocked her, but the carpet would last for years. Above the photographs from three of the walls reproductions of famous nineteenth-century paintings gazed upon the contemporary scene—Millais' "The Huguenot," "The Soul's Awakening," "The Stag at Bay."

Miss Silver herself completed the scene in a garment of sage green fastened at the neck with a heavy gold brooch which displayed in high relief the entwined initials of her parents and contained the treasured locks of their hair. She had neat, small features, a clear skin, and a good deal of mouse-coloured hair worn in a plait behind and a formal fringe in front, the whole very strictly confined by a net. Her trim ankles and small feet were encased in black woollen stockings and rather worn black slippers with beaded toes. She might have stepped out of a group in any family album and been instantly identified as governess or spinster aunt.

She allowed her eyes to travel slowly down the Agony Column:—

"Lady wishes to be received as guest in comfortable home. Social amenities. Slight help in return. No rough work, no cooking."

She reflected that a great many people still appeared to think that they could get something for nothing. A further illustration of this fact presented itself a little way down:—

"Most comfortable home offered to gentlewoman. Share household duties. Cat lover. Should be able to drive car. Fond of gardening. Some knowledge of bee-keeping. Early riser."

Miss Silver said, "Dear me!" and continued to peruse the column. Two-thirds of the way down an unusual name caught her eye. Anna—one did not often come across the name in that form—

"Anna, where are you? Do please write. Thomasina."

She did not remember that she had ever encountered a Thomasina. Pleasant to find these old-fashioned names coming back into use again. Ann, Jane, Penelope, Susan, Sarah—they had roots in English life, in English history. She approved them.

Beyond this approval there was nothing to hold her attention. There was nothing to tell her that a first faint contact had been made with a case which was to call forth all her courage and test to the uttermost the qualities which had brought her success.

She went on to one of the breezier appeals.

"Be a sport! Young man, 25, no money, no qualifications, needs job urgently. Will you give him one?"

Having finished the Agony Column, she folded the *Times* and laid it aside. The news had already reached her through a somewhat lighter medium. To the articles, correspondence, etc. she would give serious attention in a more leisured hour. At the moment her correspondence claimed her. She went over to a plain, solid writing-table and began a long affectionate letter to her niece Ethel Burkett, who was the wife of a bank manager in the Midlands.

Each member of the family was touched upon. Dear John, so kind, so hardworking—"I hope he has quite shaken off the cold you mentioned." The three boys, Johnny, Derek and Roger, now all at school and doing well. And little Josephine, who would soon be four years old—"She is, I know, everybody's darling, but you must be careful not to spoil her. The spoiled child is seldom happy or well, and is the cause of constant unhappiness in others."

Having reached this point, she could pass by an easy transition to the disquieting affairs of Ethel's young sister, Gladys Robinson. Her small, neat features took on a shade of severity as she wrote.

"Gladys is a case in point. Her thoughtlessness can no longer be excused on the ground of extreme youth, since she passed her thirtieth birthday a year ago. Her behaviour is increasingly selfish and indiscreet, and I am very much afraid of an open breach with her husband. Andrew Robinson is a worthy man, and has been exceedingly patient. Gladys should have discovered that she found him dull before she made her marriage vows. She really thinks of no one but herself."

There was a good deal more about Gladys. Thomasina Elliot's appeal to Anna Ball had passed completely from Miss Silver's mind.

CHAPTER 2

"I CAN'T THINK why you bother about the woman," said Peter Brandon.

Thomasina Elliot replied with simplicity,

"There isn't anyone else."

Peter gave her one of his loftier glances.

"Do you mean she hasn't anyone else to bother about her, or you haven't anyone else to bother about? Because in that case—"

Thomasina interrupted him.

"She hasn't anyone else to bother about her."

They were sitting side by side on a rather hard bench in one of those small galleries which specialize in winter shows. The walls were covered with pictures from which Thomasina preferred to avert her gaze. She had already changed her seat once because, without being prudish, she found the spectacle of a bulging woman stark naked and apparently afflicted with mumps embarrassing. On reflection she thought she had better have remained where she was, since she was now confronted by an explosion in magenta and orange and a quite horrible picture of a woman without a head holding an enormous frying-pan in her skeleton fingers. She was therefore more or less obliged to go on looking at Peter. She would have preferred not to do so, because he was being superior and interfering, which meant that she would have to be very firm and go on snubbing him, and it is very much easier to snub someone when you can present them with a cold profile. She was, of course, perfectly well aware that she had not been favoured with the best kind of profile for snubbing purposes. It was not regular enough. It was not in fact regular at all, though it had been considered agreeable.

Peter Brandon considered it a waste of time. He preferred her full face because of her eyes. Thomasina's eyes were really quite undeniable. Unusual too, though more so in England than in her native Scotland, where wide grey eyes with black lashes are by no means out of the way. Thomasina's eyes were of the bright clear grey which has no shade of blue or green. Peter had once remarked that they matched his flannel trousers to a hair. What distinguished them from other grey eyes was the fact that the bright grey of the iris was rimmed with black. Set off by very dark lashes and a skin which glowed with health, they were very well worth looking at. Peter looked at them from a superior height and repeated his original remark.

"I can't see why you want to bother about her."

Thomasina had not exactly a Scotch accent, but her voice lifted a little. She said,

"I've told you."

"Was she the one with the squint, or the one who breathed very loud through her nose? Being frightfully conscientious about it—like this—" He was a personable young man, but all in a moment he managed to produce a pop-eyed stare and a heavy snuffle.

Thomasina repressed a giggle.

"That was Maimie Wilson. And it's too bad of you, because she couldn't help it."

"Then she should have been drowned in infancy. Well, which was this Anna female—what did you say her surname was?"

"Ball," said Thomasina in a depressed voice. "And you've seen her quite often."

He nodded.

"Yes—your school leaving party—flowing cocoa and stacks of girl friends. Anna Ball—I'm getting there. . . . Dark girl with an oily skin and a 'Nobody loves me—I'll go into the garden and eat worms' kind of look."

"Peter, that's horrid!"

"Very. Fresh air and exercise strongly indicated. Outside interests lacking."

"Oh, no, you're wrong there—absolutely. It was one of the things that made people not like her very much. She didn't take too little interest in other people's affairs. It was quite the other way round—she took a great deal too much."

Peter cocked an eyebrow.

"Nosey Parker?"

"Well, yes, she was." A kind heart prompted her to add, "A bit."

"Then I don't see why you are bothering with her."

"Because she hasn't got anyone else. I keep telling you so."

Peter stuck his hands in the pockets of his raincoat, a gesture equivalent to clearing the decks for action.

"Now look here, Tamsine, you can't go through life collecting lame ducks, and stray dogs, and females whom nobody loves. You are twenty-two—and how old would you be when I first patted your head in your pram? About two. So that makes it twenty years that I've known you. You've been doing it all the time, and it's got to stop. You started with moribund wasps and squashed worms, and you went on to stray curs and half-drowned kittens. If Aunt Barbara hadn't been a saint she would have blown the roof off. She indulged you."

Properly speaking, Barbara Brandon was a good deal more Thomasina's aunt than Peter's, because she had been born an Elliot and had only married John Brandon, who was Peter's uncle. She had not been dead for very long. A bright shimmer of tears came up in Thomasina's eyes. It made them almost unbearably beautiful. She said with a little catch in the words,

"It—was nice."

Peter looked away. If he went on looking at her he might find himself slipping, and it was no time for weakness. Discipline must be maintained. He was helped on this rather arid path by the fact that Thomasina almost immediately tossed her head and said with complete irrelevance,

"Besides, I don't believe you ever patted my head in my pram."

"Besides what?" Women were really quite incapable of reason.

Thomasina's dimple showed. It was rather a deep one, and very becomingly placed. She said,

"Oh, just besides—"

Peter now felt superior enough to look at her again.

"My good child, I remember it perfectly. I was eight years old—in fact I was getting on for nine. You needn't imagine it was a caress, because it wasn't. You had a lot of black curls all over your head, and I wanted to see if they felt as stiff as they looked."

"They did not look stiff!"

"They looked as stiff as wood shavings, only black."

The dimple reappeared.

"And what did they feel like?" Thomasina's voice had that undermining lilt.

Quite suddenly Peter had the feel of those soft springing curls under his hand. She had them still. He said firmly,

"They felt like feathers. And that's enough about that. You

just brought it up to change the subject, and I'm not changing it. This is not a conversation about your hair, it's a conversation about Anna Ball. She was one of your lame dogs when you were at school, and you've kept on propping her ever since. Now that she has apparently faded out, instead of thanking your lucky stars you go looking for trouble and trying to hunt her up again."

"She hasn't got anyone else," said Thomasina obstinately.

Peter produced the frown which meant that he was really beginning to get angry.

"Thomasina, if you go on saying that, I shall lose my temper. The girl has made other friends, and she has faded. For heaven's sake, let her go!"

Thomasina shook her head.

"It isn't like that. She doesn't make friends—that's always been the bother. It was horrid for her in the war, you know, being half German, and she got an inferiority complex. Her mother was a morbid sort of person—Aunt Barbara knew her. So I don't think Anna had much chance."

"Well, she got a job, didn't she?"

"Aunt Barbara got her one with a Major and Mrs. Dartrey, to look after their child."

"Unfortunate child."

"It wasn't a frightful success, but she went to Germany with them, and stayed for more than two years. She used to write very grumbling letters, but she did stay. And then they went out east and left the little girl in a nursery school near Mrs. Dartrey's mother, and Anna went to some kind of a cousin of theirs who wanted a companion. But she only stayed a month. The cousin was a rich nervous invalid, and of course they wouldn't have suited a bit. Anna wrote to me and said she was leaving as soon as the month was up. She said she had got another job and she would write and tell me all about it when she got there. And she never wrote again. You see, I can't help worrying."

"I don't see why."

"I don't know where she is."

"The woman she was with, the Dartreys' cousin, would know."

"She says she doesn't. She says Anna never told her anything. She's the vague, ineffectual sort of person who gets a headache the minute you ask her to remember things like names and addresses. I tried for half an hour, and if she had been a jellyfish she couldn't have taken less interest in anyone except herself."

"Do jellyfish think?"

"Mrs. Dugdale doesn't—she just drifts. Anyhow I couldn't get anything out of her about Anna. Peter, I really am worried. Anna has written to me at least once a week for years. I mean, she always wrote in the holidays, and all the time she was with the Dartreys."

"To say what a poisonous time she was having, and how foul everyone was!"

"Well, it was rather like that. I was an outlet. You must have someone you can say that kind of thing to. And then all of a sudden she stops dead. It's four months since she left Mrs. Dugdale, and she hasn't written a line. Don't you see there's something odd about it?"

"She may have gone abroad."

"That wouldn't stop her writing. She always wrote when she was with the Dartreys, and she said she was going to write. Peter, don't you see that there must be something wrong?"

"Well, I don't see what you can do about it. You put that silly advertisement in the *Times*, and nothing came of it."

"And why was it silly?"

"Asking for trouble," said Peter briefly. "You don't know when you are well off. Take my advice and leave well alone."

Thomasina's colour deepened.

"I wouldn't mind leaving it alone if I knew that it was well. But suppose it isn't. Suppose—" She stopped because she didn't want to go on. It was like coming to a corner and being afraid of what you might find if you went any farther. The colour drained away.

Peter said stubbornly,

"Well, I don't see what you can do."

"I can go to the police," said Thomasina.

CHAPTER 3

IT WAS ABOUT a week later that Detective Inspector Abbott was taking tea with Miss Maud Silver, whom he regarded with a good deal of the fondness of a nephew together with a respect not always accorded to the spinster aunt. Spinster, Miss Silver certainly was and had never desired to be otherwise. With a most indulgent heart towards young lovers, and a proper regard for the holy estate of matrimony, she never regretted her own independent position. Aunt to Frank Abbott she was not, but the tie between them was a strong one. His irreverent sense of humour was continually delighted by her idiosyncrasies, the primness of her appearance, her fringe, her beaded slippers, her quotations from Lord Tennyson, the rapid play of the knitting-needles in her small competent hands, her moral maxims, and the inflexibility of her principles. But with and behind all this there was an affection, an admiration, and a respect very rarely displayed, but always there to be reckoned with. From their first encounter down to this present day these feelings had continued to increase and to be the source, as he once informed her, of both pleasure and profit.

He had done full justice to the three kinds of sandwich, the scones, and the layer-cake which Hannah Meadows had produced for his benefit. Ordinary visitors did not get scone, as well as sandwich, nor did Hannah produce for them the honey sent up from the country by Mrs. Randal March, but Mr. Frank would always be welcomed with the best of everything. Not that Hannah approved of the Police as a profession for a gentleman any more than she considered private detection to be a suitable occupation for a lady, though in the course of years she had become enured to the social changes which made such a state of affairs possible.

No one could have looked less like a policeman than the young man now passing his cup to be filled for the third time. From his very fair hair, slicked back and mirror-smooth, to the well-cut shoes polished to an equal brilliance, he presented a most elegant picture. The suit, the handkerchief, the socks, the tie—all had a touch of distinction. There was an effect of slender height. The pale complexion, the long nose, the pale blue eyes, imparted a fastidious air. The hand stretched out to take his cup was noticeably well kept and of the same long, thin shape as the foot in the shining shoe.

He talked discursively and enjoyed his tea. Crime it appeared was booming, and the criminal elusive. There were some very tricky forgeries on the market. One of the few privately owned services of gold plate had been lifted, and had apparently vanished into thin air. At the moment he was being rueful over a bank hold-up.

"There are too many of them, and that's a fact. Small branch on the London fringes. Sort of place that has forgotten to be a village without quite managing to be a town. In fact, what Tennyson had in mind when he wrote, 'Standing with reluctant feet, where the brook and river meet.' "

Miss Silver's partiality for the Victorian poet laureate being notorious, this was a challenge. She accepted it mildly.

"It was not, as you know, intended to have that application, the subject of the poem being maidenhood."

He reached for a sandwich.

"Another good quotation wasted! Anyhow, the place is Enderby Green, and the bank manager was held up and shot dead, poor chap, just before closing time yesterday afternoon. A young clerk got a bullet through his shoulder and is lucky to be alive. There had been some big sums paid in that day—all the shops were having sales—and the chap got away with fifteen hundred pounds. Now everyone wants to know what the police are doing. Funny for us! I expect you've seen about it in the papers."

Miss Silver inclined her head.

"Was he not seen? Did nobody hear the shot?"

"There was a pneumatic drill working outside. I don't suppose anyone would have noticed a machine-gun, let alone a couple of revolver shots! The clerk's description wouldn't fit more than about two or three hundred thousand people—except for red hair which nobody would go out gunning with unless as a disguise for the occasion. The lad did one rather bright thing though. He was making an entry in red ink at the time the hold-up occurred, and he managed to smear some of the notes they made him hand over. He says he doesn't think the chap noticed."

"The clerk will recover?"

"Oh, yes. The other poor chap was shot down in cold blood—he hadn't a chance. Somebody saw a car drive off and was able to describe it. But of course it was stolen, and got rid of as soon as possible—found abandoned not half a mile away. The bother is there have been too many of these shows, and a tendency to ask what the police are paid for. You may yet see me playing a barrel-organ on the kerb and holding out my cap for coppers. Or I might do a great disappearing act on my own. 'Well Known Detective Inspector Vanishes. Loss of Memory, or Murder?' It would make very good headlines. And then when I turned up again I could sell my life story to the Sunday papers—'A Blank World. What It Feels Like To Be Lost.' Quite a tempting prospect."

Miss Silver smiled.

"My dear Frank, you really do talk very great nonsense."

He took another sandwich and said,

"I wonder how many of the missing people whose husbands and wives, and fathers and mothers, and brothers and sisters, and cousins and aunts come clamouring to Scotland Yard are really lost?"

Miss Silver was filling her own cup. She said in a noncommittal tone,

"I suppose there are statistics."

"I don't mean that sort of thing. I mean, how many of them cut loose because they have got to the point where they feel they can't go on any longer? The husband has had one girl friend too many, or got drunk just once too often. The wife has nagged until the man thinks he had better get out before he does her in. The boy or the girl just can't stand being asked all the time, 'Where did you go—what did you do—whom did you see?' The routine of the shop, or the office, or the factory just gets them where they feel they are going to smash things up unless they clear out. Statistics only give you the facts—lost, stolen, or strayed—so many human cattle. They don't give you the reasons behind the facts."

Miss Silver gave a gentle meditative cough.

"Loss of memory is too often advanced as an explanation to be a very credible one. That there are such cases, I do not doubt, and they must, I fear, be the cause of a great deal of suffering—the sudden shock of disappearance, the continued strain, the anguish of longing so beautifully expressed by Lord Tennyson in two of his best known lines—'But O for the touch of a vanished hand, and the sound of a voice that is still!' But it is only too easy an explanation when a missing person has been traced and desires to avoid the social and domestic consequences of a voluntary disappearance."

Frank laughed.

"Do you remember a case which was in all the papers a few years ago? A young woman disappeared in the neighbourhood of a large garrison town. She had a father, a stepmother, and the usual quota of friends, but no one seems to have bothered. There had been rows with the stepmother, and everyone seems to have taken it for granted that she had just got herself a job somewhere else. Until—" he paused and reached for a sandwich—"until rather over a year later a young soldier in a regiment which had moved to the Midlands up and confessed that he had murdered the girl in a fit of jealousy and buried her body on a sandy common. He mentioned pine trees and gorse bushes. Since the whole of the neighbourhood was fairly littered with sandy commons, pine trees, and gorse bushes, it became necessary to take the murderer down there and ask him to indicate the spot. He walked them over umpteen miles of pinewood and heath, with refreshing intervals when he stood and watched whilst they dug holes in the landscape, and every time they didn't find a corpse he just said these places were all so much alike, and led them to another spot. They went on for about a fortnight. And then the girl turned up—very sorry and all that, but she had only just seen about it in the papers. She didn't know the soldier from Adam. She had got fed up with her stepmother and went and got a job in London, and she'd been married for a year and had a baby of two months old."

Miss Silver said,

"I remember." And then, "An aunt of mine used to tell the story of a woman who had a very bad husband. He drank, he beat her, and he went after other women. She had to go out charing to support herself and her children—people had very large families in those days. When the youngest child was two years old she felt that she could not bear it any longer. The man came home one night, and he was drunk. There was no sign of his wife or of the children. He went into the bedroom, and there were the children's seven straw hats perched on the knobs of the big brass bedstead, and a note to say they had gone to Australia. My aunt said they did very well there. The children never saw their father again, but twenty years after, when he was old and ill, the wife came back and nursed him until he died."

Frank raised a sarcastic eyebrow.

"Incredible!"

"She was a good woman, and she considered it to be her duty."

He set down his cup, and found her regarding him thoughtfully.

"You are concerned about the case of some missing person, Frank?"

He leaned forward and put a log on the fire, which sent up a shower of sparks.

"Oh, not really."

Miss Silver smiled.

"Are you going to tell me about it?"

"Well, as a matter of fact there isn't anything to tell. The girl had an unusual name and a pair of unusual eyes, that's all."

She leaned sideways and picked up her knitting. The first few rows of what was to be a cardigan for her niece Ethel Burkett, were in a deep and particularly pleasing shade of blue.

"Really that sounds as if it might be interesting."

He laughed.

"Not a hope! The name is Thomasina, and the eyes are a quite extraordinarily bright shade of grey, with black lashes and a dark ring round the iris—very arresting. But as for anything else—"

Miss Silver coughed.

"Did you say Thomasina?"

He nodded.

"Unusual—isn't it?"

Miss Silver's needles clicked.

"And she wants to trace a girl called Anna?"

Frank Abbott stared.

"And who told you that, ma'am? You know, a few hundred years ago you would have been in very serious danger of being indicted for witchcraft."

"My dear Frank!"

There was a teasing gleam in his eye.

"There are moments when old Lamb isn't at all sure about it himself. Officially, of course, he doesn't believe in witches, but I've seen him look as if he expected you to fly out of the window on a broomstick."

Miss Silver rebuked this flippancy.

"I have the highest possible respect for the Chief Inspector, and I hope that the sentiment is to some extent reciprocated."

"Oh, he respects you all right. But he gets his back up wondering just how the trick is done. The quickness of the hand deceives the eye, and the Chief doesn't like having his eye deceived. He likes to take things decently and in order, with plenty of time to think everything out a step at a time. When you get there in a flash of lightning he begins to suspect the unlawful arts."

She smiled indulgently.

"When you have finished talking nonsense, Frank, you will perhaps let me tell you that my information about Thomasina and Anna was derived from nothing more supernatural than the Agony Column of the *Times*. I was struck by the two old-fashioned names, and when you mentioned one of them I naturally remembered the other."

He laughed.

"Things are always so simple when they have been explained! She did mention that she had put in an advertisement. I didn't see it myself. What did it say?"

Miss Silver pulled on the large ball which lurked in a knitting-bag of gaily flowered chintz.

"'Anna'—that is how it began. And then, I think, 'Where are you? Do please write.' And it was signed, 'Thomasina.' Perhaps you will now tell me a little more."

"The names are Anna Ball and Thomasina Elliot. Thomasina is the one with the eyes. Anna sounds as dull as ditch-water, but she has disappeared, and Thomasina wants to find her. When I say disappeared I am quoting Thomasina. She apparently thinks herself responsible because Anna hasn't any relations. School friendship. Pretty, popular girl taking up the cudgels for dreary, unpopular one. Three years' intensive post-school letter-writing on Anna's part. Generous response by Thomasina. A last letter saying Anna was going to a new job and would write when she got there. And then finish. No address. No hint of any destination. Previous jobs, nursery governess for over two years, and companion for one month. No clue as to new job. Might be anything from a housemaid to a henwife—and I rather gather she was likely to be a washout at whatever it was—"

He broke off suddenly to enquire, "Why are you looking at me like that? You can't possibly be interested. I can assure you that nothing can be duller than the whole affair."

She gave him her charming smile.

"Yet you have introduced the subject with care, and you are quite unable to let it drop."

He had a half-laughing, half-rueful expression which took years off his age.

"You always see right through one. The case is dull, and Anna sounds deadly. I keep on telling myself that she has probably just got fed up with writing to Thomasina, or she has taken a huff about something—that sort does. Or she has found herself a young man—which doesn't sound the least likely, but the oddest specimens do—in which case she wouldn't have any more use for the girl friend."

Miss Silver shook her head in a very decided manner.

"Oh, no, it would not have that effect at all. She would be pleased and excited, and her letters to Thomasina would be long and full. It did not happen like that."

"Then the only possible spark of interest expires."

"Yet you are interested."

"I can't imagine why I should be. There's nothing to it—just a girl who has stopped writing."

Miss Silver echoed his words in a very thoughtful manner.

"Just a girl who has stopped writing."

CHAPTER 4

A COUPLE OF DAYS had passed, when Miss Silver looked up from the letter she was writing and lifted the receiver of the table telephone. Inspector Abbott's voice greeted her by name.

"Hullo! Here we are! Marvellous and beneficent instrument the telephone—except when it wakes you in the middle of the night and you wish that the progress of science had stopped short at rubbing two sticks together to make a fire. But, as you are about to remark, that isn't what I rang you up to talk about. 'Hail, vain deluding joys!' and all the rest of it. Business before pleasure."

"My dear Frank!"

"I know—I'm getting there. In the matter of Thomasina Elliot—"

Miss Silver coughed.

"You are not speaking from Scotland Yard."

A suspicion of a laugh came to her along the wire.

"How right you are! The official style is more restrained. I am in a call-box. In the matter of Thomasina we appear to have got to a dead end. To start with, there isn't any evidence that the girl Anna really has disappeared, and no clue as to where to begin to look for her. In fact, as I said, a dead end. There were just two chances. One, that an advertisement would produce something. Well, Thomasina has advertised, and we have had a wireless appeal put out. We had to strain a point there, but a string or two was pulled and we got it done. No response. The second chance was that Mrs. Dugdale, the last employer, or someone in her household, might know something. A girl who is going to a new job is practically bound to say something about it to somebody. She asks for a reference—she leaves an address for letters to be forwarded. Well, according to Mrs. Dugdale and her household Anna didn't do any of these things. Jackson went round to see them and he says they were most unco-operative. Mrs. Dugdale appeared to be threatened with a nervous collapse every time she was asked to remember anything. He opined that it really was nerves, and not a guilty conscience. He said he had an aunt who was just the same, and she fairly wore everyone out. Getting sense out of her was like trying to get water out of an empty well—no matter how often you sent the bucket down it would always come up dry. From which you may deduce that our Sergeant Jackson grew up in a village which still pumped its water from its native springs."

"And Mrs. Dugdale's household?"

"Impenetrability, as Humpty Dumpty remarked! There is a personal maid who sounds like a cross between a steel trap and an oyster. The other two—there really are two more—are both elderly, and wouldn't demean themselves by getting mixed up with the police. Jackson opined they didn't know anything but wouldn't have talked if they did. And that is where you come in."

Miss Silver coughed in a deprecatory manner.

"May I ask in what capacity?"

She heard him laugh.

"Oh, strictly professional. Thomasina is coming to see you. She has come in for quite a lot of money from an aunt, and no expense is to be spared. I told her that if anyone could charm an oyster into speech, it was you. Seriously, you know, someone in that Dugdale lot must know something. Thumbscrews being out of date, there doesn't seem to be any way of making them talk. Anna left them—alive and in her right mind—"

"How did she go?"

"By bus, with a single suit-case which was all she brought with her. She had only been there a month, you know. She sent a box to Thomasina in Scotland and said she would write for it later. Well, she didn't write."

Miss Silver asked a pertinent question.

"Where was the bus going to?"

"That's just what nobody knows. Anna walked to the end of the road and took a bus. Six buses pass there. No one knows which one of them Anna took. Nice simple little problem, isn't it? She could have gone to King's Cross, Waterloo, Victoria, Baker Street, Holborn, or the Tottenham Court Road. She could have got off her bus and travelled by tube. She could have gone to Scotland by motor coach. She could have taken a taxi and driven down to the docks. Anybody's guess is as good as anybody else's."

Miss Silver said, "Dear me!"

An hour or two later Thomasina Elliot sat in one of the curly walnut chairs and gazed at Miss Silver. She had been sitting there for not more than twenty-five minutes, but she had already told this dowdy little ex-governess quite a number of things which she had not seen fit to impart to Peter Brandon or to Detective Inspector Abbott.

Things about Anna Ball—"She depended on me. People oughtn't to depend on each other like that. I did my best to stop her, but it wasn't any use, and she just hadn't got anyone else. That is how I am quite sure she didn't just get bored and stop writing. She hasn't got any family, and she hasn't got any friends. She hasn't got anyone except me. I've got to find her."

Things about herself—"Aunt Barbara left me quite a lot of money. I'm twenty-two, and I can do anything I like with it. It really is a lot, because she had a frightfully rich godmother—rather queer but very kind. She was about a hundred, and she left everything to Aunt Barbara, and Aunt Barbara left half to me and half to Peter. I used to be taken to see her." Thomasina's gaze became one of artless interest. "She had curly chairs just like yours, and the exact twin of your bookcase. You don't mind my saying that, do you? It made me feel as if I knew you the minute I came in."

She received the smile with which Miss Silver had won not only the confidence but the affection of many clients. It prompted Thomasina to discourse about Peter Brandon.

"Aunt Barbara married his uncle. He is about ten years older than I am. Aunt Barbara wanted me to marry him, but she didn't put it in her will. He asks me every now and then, but I don't suppose he really wants me to. You see, he knows all my faults and I know his, and it might be dull not having anything to find out about each other. Of course one would know the worst—"

Miss Silver looked at her kindly.

"There is much to be said for a steady affection as a foundation for marriage."

Thomasina sighed.

"That is what Aunt Barbara used to say." She sighed again. "Peter has a very domineering disposition. He writes books, you know. I suppose when you get accustomed to pushing characters about just the way you want to, it makes you think you can do the same thing with real people. Peter is being very domineering about poor Anna. He keeps saying, 'Let her alone and she will turn up.'"

Miss Silver knitted in silence for a moment. Then she said, "That last letter you spoke of—I should like to see it."

Thomasina opened her bag.

"Inspector Abbott said you would. It's very short. Here it is."

A folded sheet was handed over—notepaper with an embossed heading, 5 Lenister Square, S.W., and a telephone number, obviously Mrs. Dugdale's. Under the heading a few lines in a scrawled downward-sloping hand with no set beginning:

"I shall be out of here by the time you get this, and *thank goodness!*" Heavy underlining. "How I have *borne* it! I shan't tell you about my new job until I get there—no time—all very sudden. I'm sending you a box of things to keep for me in case I don't stay.

Love,

Anna."

Miss Silver handed the letter back.

"Have you seen this Mrs. Dugdale, Anna Ball's late employer?"

Thomasina's eyes kindled.

"If you can call it *seeing!*" she said in an indignant voice. "Flat on a sofa in a dressing-gown, with all the blinds down and a bottle of smelling-salts in her hand! And all she would say was, Anna didn't leave an address and she didn't know anything about her, and please would I go away, because her head was too bad to talk. And a most frightful prison wardress sort of maid gave me a look and told me to go. Oh, Miss Silver —you will do something about it, won't you? Inspector Abbott said if anyone could get something out of her, it would be you."

CHAPTER 5

IT WAS BY GOOD MANAGEMENT and not by mere good fortune that Miss Silver penetrated the defences of 5 Lenister Square in the late afternoon of the following day. As a result of her cases she had acquired a number of useful social contacts. With the information supplied to her by Scotland Yard and a judicious employment of the telephone she arrived at a friend of a friend of Mrs. Dugdale's. A little kindly pressure, some expressions of regard and gratitude, and the desired introduction had been achieved.

Miss Silver rang the bell, was admitted by a middle-aged maid of a most sedate and respectable appearance, and was by her conducted to a first-floor drawing-room where a single shaded lamp diffused a wan green light. Very depressing—very depressing indeed. And the temperature must be at least seventy. No wonder Mrs. Dugdale was troubled with nerves.

The well-trained maid had murmured her name and vanished. The room being crowded with small gimcrack tables and spidery chairs, there was some danger of being tripped up. Miss Silver's advance towards a distant sofa was therefore a cautious one.

Arrived, she touched a faint extended hand, and was aware of a smothered growling note from beneath the embroidered coverlet.

"No, Chang!" said Mrs. Dugdale in an exhausted voice. "Do please sit down, Miss Silver. Mother's Boy is a very, very naughty boy. No, Chang—*no!*"

The coverlet heaved, the growl passed into a snarl, and the snarl into a furious bark. Mother's Boy emerged—a tough, belligerent Pekinese with a tawny coat and a black mask from which there glowered a pair of vindictive eyes. Mrs. Dugdale pressed the small electric bell which lay to her hand upon one of the spidery gimcrack tables. Two long rings and a short one produced, not the maid who had admitted Miss Silver, but a severe-looking female whom Miss Silver was able at once to identify as the prison wardress of Thomasina Elliot's description. Mrs. Dugdale addressed her in a voice which she had perforce to raise in order to compete with Chang, who continued to bark.

"Oh, Postlethwaite, please take him away! My poor head! No, Mother's Boy! Naughty—*naughty!* He dislikes strangers so very much."

Watching the reluctant removal of Chang, Miss Silver reflected that the feeling was probably mutual.

"And oh, Postlethwaite—my smelling-salts. I had them just now, but I don't seem to see. . . . Oh, thank you—how very kind!" This to Miss Silver who had detected and restored the missing bottle.

But the maid had barely reached the door again when Mrs. Dugdale discovered that her handkerchief had gone astray. There was a search during which Chang made so much noise that even Miss Silver felt inclined to put her hands to her ears. When the door finally closed upon his protests she experienced a good deal of relief. Accustomed by this time to the green twilight, she was able to give her whole attention to Mrs. Dugdale, now lying back in a swooning attitude amongst a great many cushions. She saw a small fair person who had probably been extremely pretty some thirty years ago. There was still a profusion of light hair which had not been allowed to go grey, a pair of rolling blue eyes, and features which might still have been pleasing if it had not been for their fretful expression.

"He is so high-spirited," said Mrs. Dugdale in a sighing voice. "And *so* devoted. He will hardly leave me."

"I believe they are very intelligent."

"*Human,*" said Mrs. Dugdale—"*positively* human. And so handsome—like a little lion. And of course they are as brave as lions too. You have no idea how venturesome he is."

Miss Silver not only permitted but encouraged several anecdotes in illustration of the charm, the courage, and the fidelity of Chang. Mrs. Dugdale became quite animated as she narrated them, finishing up with,

"And he came in all covered with blood where that horrible cat had scratched him. But his spirit was as high as ever. You could tell when he was thinking about the cat, because his tail curled up and he growled, and he actually bit Postlethwaite when she was washing off the blood. She is devoted to him of course, but she really didn't quite like it."

Miss Silver considered that the time had come to introduce the name of Ball. She did so firmly.

"Was Miss Ball attached to him? She was with you for a short time, I believe."

"Oh, *no!*" said Mrs. Dugdale. "Attached! She was quite callous! A most unfeeling girl. When she trod on him and he bit her, she was much more upset about the hole in her stocking and the mark of his poor little teeth than about anything else. Why, as I said to her, she might have lamed him for life, my precious boy—treading on his poor little foot with her great clumping one! And she was most rude, most offensive. I had one of my worst headaches after it, and my nerves were upset for days."

Miss Silver coughed.

"A most trying experience."

"I was *thankful* when she left. Postlethwaite can tell you how thankful I was. She came to me from my cousin, Lilla Dartrey. Most inconsiderate of her to recommend such an unsuitable person. I only kept her a month, and you would think once she was gone I might be allowed to have a little peace. But no—would you believe it, the police—the *police* have come here wanting to know about her!"

"It must have upset you very much."

Mrs. Dugdale had opened her smelling bottle. The atmosphere became tinged with aromatic vinegar. She sniffed.

"I was prostrated. My nerves are not strong enough for that sort of thing. I told Sergeant Jackson so. 'It is no use your asking me,' I said, 'I cannot help you at all. She was only here for a month, and she went away without leaving any address. I found her a most unsympathetic character, and I was thankful to see the last of her. I cannot help you in any way, and I really must decline to be mixed up in her affairs.' Don't you think I was *right?*"

"The police are so very pertinacious," said Miss Silver in tones of regret. "I fear they may trouble you again."

"I shall refuse to see them."

Miss Silver let that go. She said,

"It seems strange in these days when there are so many undesirable people about that anyone should be willing to employ a young woman without taking up her references. Miss Ball had not, I suppose, the temerity to ask you for one, though I believe you would be legally obliged to pass on the reference you had with her if she did not stay with you for longer than a month."

Mrs. Dugdale became quite animated.

"Nothing could be more unfair, and so I told the person who rang me up. I had a very good reference from my cousin, and how she could bring herself to deceive me as she did, I really do not know. I couldn't have done it! I told the person who rang me up that Miss Ball had been with a cousin of mine for a year or two—*in Germany.*" She pronounced the words as if they indicated a highly suspicious background. "I said that I had not found her congenial and could not recommend her personally, but I had no reason to suppose that she was not honest and respectable. I do not see that I could have said any more."

Miss Silver coughed.

"The police could take no exception to that."

A little colour had come into Mrs. Dugdale's face.

"Oh, I didn't tell the *police.* It had nothing to do with them one way or the other."

"So inquisitive—" sighed Miss Silver. "I wonder how long a girl such as you describe would satisfy any employer. This person who rang up—what did you say the name was?"

Mrs. Dugdale had recourse to the smelling-salts.

"I never *can* remember names—I find it a strain upon the nerves." She paused, sniffed, and added in a doubtful tone, "It wasn't Cadbury?"

There appeared to be no reason why it should have been Cadbury.

Mrs. Dugdale continued in a musing tone,

"Or Bostock—or Cadell—or Carrington. . . . Such a curious voice too—very deep. Really, I thought it was a man speaking, but what she wanted was a nursery governess for her children. There were three of them, and I felt it my duty to tell her of Miss Ball's callous behaviour to my precious boy, but she said her children could look after themselves, so my conscience is clear."

"And the name was?"

"Chelmsford—or Ruddock—or Radford—I really cannot say which," said Mrs. Dugdale in a drifting voice.

Miss Silver had produced pencil and paper from a shabby black handbag. She added these names to those which she had already written down.

"I have a young friend who is anxious to find Miss Ball. It appears that she left a trunk in her keeping, and she does not know what to do about it."

Mrs. Dugdale sniffed at her aromatic vinegar.

"Most inconsiderate," she said—"but only what one would expect from Anna Ball. I remember my husband's sister doing the same to me—a box of clothes, taking up room and collecting moth. But he was deplorably weak where his family was concerned."

Miss Silver allowed herself to be told all about Miss Mary Dugdale. It was a theme upon which her sister-in-law became quite animated.

"Such a domineering person, and really terribly fatiguing. Breezy, her friends called it—'Mary is so *breezy!*' " She shuddered. "I really don't think my nerves have ever quite got over it. She stayed for three months, and always opened a window whenever she came into the room."

The atmosphere was so oppressive, so heavily impregnated with aromatic vinegar, a strongly-scented face-powder, and an occasional whiff of moth-ball that Miss Silver could not help feeling some sympathy with the breezy Miss Dugdale. Not that she had any partiality for draughts—on the contrary—but an invalid's room should be regularly aired.

When the last drop of self-pity had been distilled, and not till then, did a slight cough re-introduce the subject of Anna Ball's employer.

"I felt sure that you would sympathize with my young friend's predicament. Perhaps your maid—what is her name—ah, yes, Postlethwaite—perhaps she can help us."

Mrs. Dugdale's animation ceased. She closed her eyes and said she doubted it. But after a little tactful persuasion Miss Silver was allowed to ring the bell.

"Two long and one short. And I am really afraid that I must not talk very much more. It has been very pleasant, but I shall pay for it. My *head*—"

A description of the expected symptoms was still not complete when it was interrupted by the appearance of Postlethwaite, more like a wardress than ever, but mercifully not accompanied by Mother's Boy. Even Miss Silver's tact failed to penetrate the armour-plating. Postlethwaite made it perfectly plain that she had no intention of either remembering or attempting to remember anything to do with Miss Ball. As far as she was concerned, Anna Ball no longer existed.

Mrs. Dugdale's attitude was hardly a helpful one.

"We don't know Miss Ball's address—do we, Postlethwaite?"

"No, madam."

"Or where she has gone?"

"No, madam."

Mrs. Dugdale closed her eyes.

"Then I am afraid I must not talk any more."

The interview was plainly at an end. It was disappointing—very disappointing indeed. Miss Silver had perforce to take her leave.

A faint hope arose at the discovery that it was no part of Postlethwaite's duties to speed the departing guest. A single long trill of the electric bell summoned the middle-aged parlourmaid to discharge this task, and it was while discoursing to Agnes with bright amiability on her young friend's predicament with regard to Miss Ball's trunk that Miss Silver produced a five-pound note from her shabby bag. Telling Mrs. Harrison the cook about it afterwards, Agnes could hardly get the words out fast enough.

"Well, I thought, it only just shows what I've always said, you never can tell. Mind you, I know a lady when I see one, and a lady she was. But old-fashioned—well, I ask you! One of those black cloth coats that don't look as if they'd ever been anything else, and the sort of fur tie you'd expect to see in a second-hand clothes shop. Black wool stockings, and a hat the very moral of the one we saw in that film—now what was it called? You know, the one where the girl has that awful governess that wants to poison her."

Mrs. Harrison opined that governesses were always a trouble in the house, but there weren't so many of them nowadays, and a good thing too.

"Well, that's what she looked like—one of those old-fashioned governesses, and when she took a five-pound note out of her bag you could have knocked me down with a feather. 'My young friend,' she says—that's the one she'd been telling me about all the way down the stairs, not mentioning any names but just 'My young friend,' like that—'well she's very anxious to get rid of this trunk Miss Ball left with her, so she wants to know where she is, and if you or the cook can give her any help, there's a reward offered, and another note like this to come.' Well, she puts it into my hand and stands there looking at me very pleasant. So what I thought was, it wasn't anything to do with Miss Postlethwaite, and I said we'd be very pleased to help, and I'd talk it over with you, and would leave her address, which she wrote it down on a piece of paper, and here it is."

The five-pound note and the piece of paper lay side by side on the kitchen table. Mrs. Harrison stared at them and said,

"Well, I never!"

CHAPTER 6

"MRS. HARRISON AND ME, we talked it over," said Agnes. "And what we thought was, we didn't see that it had got anything to do with Miss Postlethwaite." She sat on the edge of one of Miss Silver's more upright chairs, her hands gripping a new shiny black handbag with a gilt clasp. Her gloves were new too and of a good quality, and her black cloth coat had cost a great deal more than Miss Silver would have dreamed of paying.

As she paused, and apparently expected some comment, Miss Silver coughed and said,

"Quite so."

Agnes opened the shiny black bag, took out a clean folded white handkerchief with an initial A lurking in a wreath of forget-me-nots, dabbed the tip of her nose with it, and having returned the handkerchief still folded to the bag, proceeded to emphasize her last remark.

"We didn't see that it had got anything to do with her."

Miss Silver finished a row and turned her knitting. About ten inches of the back of Ethel Burkett's cardigan now showed upon the needles. If she had not interrupted her work upon it to knit a pair of baby's bootees, it would have been still farther advanced. She understood perfectly that the five-pound note already received and the one which Agnes was now hopefully expecting would be shared between herself and Mrs. Harrison, and that Postlethwaite would have no part in it. She smiled in an encouraging manner, and Agnes proceeded.

"Such being the case, we thought it would be best if I came to see you, Mrs. Harrison's feet being a trouble to her."

"It was quite the best thing you could do."

"That's what we thought. Not that there's a great deal to say, but your friend being so kind—and a reward offered—we thought it would be best if I came along."

The encouraging smile was repeated.

"That is very frank of you. And now what have you to tell me?"

A little colour came into the long, sallow face.

"Well, it was this way. There's the telephone in the drawing-room, but except it's for a special friend it's kept switched through to the front hall so that I can do the talking—Mrs. Dugdale being troubled with her nerves."

"Yes?" said Miss Silver on an enquiring note.

Agnes took out the handkerchief and dabbed again.

"It was about a week before Miss Ball left. I was in the dining-room putting away my silver, when the telephone went. 'Well,' I thought, 'you can wait till I get these spoons out of my hand.' I wasn't a minute, but just as I got to the door, there was Miss Ball taking off the receiver, which is a thing she hadn't any call to do. She didn't see me, and I thought I'd find out what she was at. Regular spying, creeping ways she'd got, and I thought if I could catch her out, it would give her a lesson. I wouldn't have listened, not if it had been anyone else, but she'd no call to be answering the telephone in that way, so I did."

"Yes?"

Agnes was warming to it. She had another dab with the handkerchief and went on.

"Well, she said at once, 'Yes, that's right—it's Miss Ball speaking. . . . Yes, yes, of course—you can speak to Mrs. Dugdale. I'll put you through to her. She isn't at all pleased about my leaving, you know, but she can't help handing on the reference from Mrs. Dartrey—I do know that.' "

Miss Silver said thoughtfully,

"I see—she was talking to her future employer—"

"It seemed like it. She was listening for a bit, and then she said, 'What sort of place is it? The country is all very well in the summer, but that's a long way off still, and we don't always get one. Sounds as if it might be the depths of the country, a name like Deep End, doesn't it?' And she gave a silly kind of a laugh, as if she had make a joke. There was a bit of listening again, and then she said, 'All those houses? Sounds funny to me. What do they call themselves a *colony* for?' Well, I hadn't the patience to listen to any more of it. I come out into the hall and I said, 'If that's a message, I'll take it, Miss Ball, and if it's anyone for Mrs. Dugdale, you'd better put them through.' Of course if I'd known—"

An apposite quotation occurred to Miss Silver, but she kept it to herself—"Evil is wrought by want of thought, as well as want of heart." She deplored the impatience which had made Agnes interrupt Anna Ball's telephone conversation, but there was nothing to be done about it now. She said,

"You are sure the name you heard was Deep End?"

Agnes brightened.

"Oh, yes, I'm quite positive about that, because one of my sister's children was born at a place with a name like that. Her husband was gardener to a titled gentleman."

"And where was this place?"

"Lincolnshire—a damp part of the world, my sister used to say—Deeping St. Nicholas. And they called the baby Nick, which isn't a name I'd care about. Seems silly too, because the old gentleman died and they moved right down to Devonshire no more than six months after."

"But the name mentioned by Miss Ball was not Deeping, but Deep End. You are really sure about that?"

"Oh, yes, I'm sure. It just put me in mind of my sister and the baby."

"Was there any place called Deep End in the neighbourhood? Or did your sister ever mention anything in the way of a 'colony' in connection with the place?"

Agnes shook her head.

"I can't call anything like that to mind. But she wasn't there more than eight or nine months—and the best part of thirty years ago, so there's no saying what there might be by this time."

Miss Silver's needles clicked.

"A great deal has come and gone in thirty years," she said.

Agnes nodded mournfully.

"My brother-in-law for one, and that poor boy Nick for another—killed at Alamein, and a young wife at home with a twin of little girls. Nice children they are too—ever so bright. And I've nothing against her marrying again, but it don't give my sister back her boy."

The interview, having been warmed by this human touch, came to an end in a manner very satisfactory to Agnes, who went away with another five pounds to divide between herself and Mrs. Harrison.

Miss Silver also was not dissatisfied. If she had not got all she hoped for she had at least got something, which was more than the police had. She proceeded to call up Scotland Yard, and was fortunate enough to be put through to Inspector Abbott without delay. To his "Hullo, ma'am—what can I do for you?" she replied with reticence.

"In the case of the missing person to which you introduced me—"

"The elusive Anna? Yes?"

"I have some information. There is reason to believe that she went from Mrs. Dugdale to a place called Deep End. To my informant this name suggested Deeping, there being some family connection with Deeping St. Nicholas in Lincolnshire. She overheard Miss Ball in conversation on the telephone with her prospective employer. Deep End was mentioned, and she is sure that she made no mistake about the name. I thought at once of the Deeping in Ledshire where I spent such a very interesting time with Colonel and Mrs. Abbott. There is not, I suppose, any spot called Deep End in that vicinity? I know that you spent a good deal of your time there when you were a boy."

"No, there's no Deep End."

"From the context it would seem to be a country place, but there is a suggestion Miss Ball was told that its solitude would be mitigated by the presence of a *colony*—" She paused.

"Is that all?"

"I fear so."

"How extremely cryptic! She is sure the place named was Deep End, but it reminded her of Deeping! Well, I suppose it might. And I suppose it might really have been Deeping, even if she thinks it wasn't, in which case there could be a fairly wide choice. I'm pretty sure it wouldn't be the one where my uncle and aunt lived, but I've got a sort of idea that there's another Deeping, even in Ledshire. Of course Deep End sounds to me like the sort of name that might be given to almost any huddle of houses which has gone and got itself built in a bog. Sounds damp. Sounds as if there might be a good few of it—one per county, all over the place. I'll see how many I can collect and come round this evening with the catch, if any. If that will be all right for you?"

The catch proved to be a small one, which, as Frank observed, was better luck than they had any right to expect. Produced over some excellent coffee, it amounted to this, Besides Deeping St. Nicholas in Lincolnshire, which was a sizable place, and the village in the north of Ledshire where Colonel and Mrs. Abbott lived, there was another Deeping in the southwest corner of the same county.

"As a matter of fact I think we've struck it lucky. Deeping St. Nicholas doesn't fit into the picture, and I think we can leave it out. Also our family Deeping. But I think the other one may be what we're looking for. I've been on to Randal March about it. He says this second Deeping is just on the county border and used to be called Deeping-in-the-Marshes, but after most of the land had been drained they rather dropped the end of the name. It's just a village, with some big nursery gardens which serve the Ledlington market, and there's a kind of off-shoot called Deep End which is just over a mile away. There was a big house there which was bombed during the war. Grounds now a building estate. That might be be your 'Colony.' March said he'd find out and let me know."

Miss Silver beamed.

"It might indeed. Is your coffee sweet enough? . . . . Whilst you are drinking it I will tell you about my interview with Mrs. Dugdale's parlourmaid."

Frank Abbott leaned back in one of the wide-lapped chairs and listened whilst with meticulous accuracy she repeated the account which Agnes had given of Anna Ball's conversation on the telephone. When she had finished he said,

"And you think she can be depended upon?"

"Oh, yes—an old-fashioned type, conscientious and accurate."

"A pity she didn't get the employer's name."

Miss Silver coughed.

"The only person who seems to have heard it is Mrs. Dugdale, and she, I fear, can hardly be described as either accurate or conscientious. One of those vague, straying minds, and too much occupied with herself to give any but the most passing attention to the affairs of others."

"Did you get anything out of her at all? Jackson couldn't."

Miss Silver handed him a half sheet of paper.

"She showed no reluctance to talk, but produced all these names one after the other, beginning with the remark that it wasn't Cadbury."

He raised his eyebrows.

"Had you suggested that it might be Cadbury?"

"I had made no suggestion of any kind."

He read aloud from the paper.

"Cadbury – Bostock – Cadell – Carrington – Chelmsford – Ruddock – Radford—" He gave her an enquiring look. "Well?"

"What do you make of it?"

"Not very much, I'm afraid, except—" he went back to the list—"Cadbury, Cadell, Carrington, Chelmsford—there are rather a lot of C's. Anything else? Let me see—Bostock, Ruddock—those are both unusual names. Cadbury, Cadell, Carrington, Radford—a definite similarity about the first syllables."

"That is what occurred to me. I could not help the feeling that all these names were suggested by the one which she had heard but had not troubled herself to remember."

"You think it began with a C?"

"I think it possible that it did. And that it ended in *ford* or *ock*. Probably the latter, since Bostock and Ruddock are both uncommon names and not very likely to occur unless there had been some strong association, whereas *ford* is an extremely common suffix."

He looked at her with a quizzical smile.

"And what does that suggest to you?"

"It suggests that one of these names may really be the name of Anna Ball's employer. I do not think so, but it is possible. Or that if we are to look for another name, it may be Craddock."

"And how do you arrive at that—no, let's see—*ad* three times—*ock* twice—a sprinkling of *r's* and a lot of *c's*—it might be. Or—" The smile became definitely provocative—"perhaps you are just being a great deal more ingenious than Mrs. Dugdale. That kind of mind is capable of almost any degree of irrelevance, and the name may turn out to be plain Smith or Jones."

She looked across her deep blue knitting.

"That is quite possible. Meanwhile perhaps you would make some enquiries about the Deeping in Ledshire, and its offshoot, Deep End. I think we may leave Deeping St. Nicholas on one side. But Deep End with its new building estate would fit the case. What we have to look for is someone with three children who is known to have engaged a governess or a nursery-governess between four and five months ago. The one thing that Mrs. Dugdale seems to remember about Miss Ball's prospective employer is that her voice was so deep she thought at first that it was a man who was speaking. It may really have been a man. If she had no help the mother might have been unable to leave her children. I suggest that enquiries should be made at Deep End. It would be known whether the building estate was commonly alluded to as the Colony. It would be known whether there was a family such as I have described, and whether the name has any resemblance to those we have considered. If this is so, you will agree that some enquiry should be made with regard to Miss Ball. If she took up the post for which she appears to have been in treaty, it would be known. She may be still there, or she may have left, in which case Mrs. Craddock may have her address."

Frank Abbott laughed.

"Craddock?"

Miss Silver coughed.

"Or Smith, or Jones, or Robinson."

CHAPTER 7

FRANK ABBOTT CALLED UP THE NEXT DAY.

"Look here, I caught the Chief in a melting mood, and he says I can run down, and make some enquiries. The usual trimmings about mare's nests and what not, but all in good part. So expect me tomorrow on my way back. Will it matter if I'm late? . . . . All right then—we'll say any time up to midnight."

It was not nearly so late as that when Hannah let him in. As she opened the sitting-room door, her voice could be heard telling him that his sandwiches were waiting, and that the coffee wouldn't be a moment.

Miss Silver smiled.

"Hannah is always sure you must be starved when you go out of town."

"Well, I did have some ghastly kind of a meal, but I'm trying to forget about it." He pulled a chair in to the fire and spread out his hands to the glow. "Brr—it's cold! And I've had my journey for—well, not quite nothing, but about as near as makes no difference."

He thought, not for the first time, how comfortable and restful the room was, with its out-of-date furniture and its reminders of an age untroubled by the aeroplane and the bomb. Security—that is what the Victorians had, and what perhaps they paid too high a price for. They had slums and child labour, and culture was only for the few, but at least their children were not dragged from their beds to take refuge in underground shelters, and their slums were not blasted into rubble. There were times when the blessings of education appeared a little over-rated, since it seemed only to enable the nations to quarrel with greater fluency in some modern Tower of Babel.

Miss Silver, smiling at him from the other side of the hearth, her hands busy with her knitting, remained a stable point in an unsettled world. Love God, honour the King; keep the law; be kind, be good; think of others before you think of yourself; serve Justice; speak the truth—by this simple creed she lived. *Si sic omnes!* . . . .

His sense of humour tripped him up. Miss Silver at the council board—at the Admiralty, the War Office, the Air Ministry. An infinite procession of Miss Silvers running everything everywhere. John Knox's *Monstrous Regiment of Women.* No, no, it wouldn't do. There was only one Maudie—let her remain unique.

Hannah came in with the coffee, poured him out his first cup, fussed over him with sandwiches, and departed. Then, and not till then, Miss Silver said,

"So you had your trouble for nothing?"

"Well, not quite. To start off with, Craddock it is—and I take off my hat to you, though I suppose you will admit that it was a very long shot."

She was knitting demurely.

"They do occasionally hit the mark. So you found Mrs. Craddock?"

"Mr. Craddock, Mrs. Craddock and young, as stated. The young have to be seen to be believed. I am not surprised that Anna didn't stay."

Miss Silver said, "Oh?" and stopped knitting. "She had been at Deep End with the Craddocks?"

"And left before the end of the second week. But I expect you would like me to begin at the beginning."

"It would be as well. But pray do not hurry yourself. Hannah's liver sandwiches are really very good indeed. I find them difficult to distinguish from *pâté de foie gras.*"

"She is a genius. I warn you that I shall probably eat them all."

"That is what they are there for, my dear Frank. And pray do not let your coffee grow cold."

He lay back in his chair with a feeling of being at home.

"Well, Deep End used to be three cottages and a cow, with one of those overgrown Big Houses which have started Tudor and finished up Victorian. No, it was the war that finished it—direct hit right in the middle of the Great Hall, and consequent wreckage of most of the principal rooms. Rather appropriate, because the old family that had been there for donkey's years had just petered out. Well, after standing derelict until three years ago it was bought for a song and patched together. That is to say, the middle block where most of the damage had been was tidied up, but there has been no attempt to make it habitable."

"Was it Mr. Craddock who bought it?"

"It was. He lives in one of the wings, and has let the other. And—prepare for a shock—he has changed the name from Deepe House to Harmony!"

Miss Silver coughed.

"The intention of such names is no doubt laudable, but in practice they attract invidious criticism."

"Like the miserable little shrimps who get christened Gloria, and all the dark Italian girls who are called Bianca! Well, Craddock called the place Harmony and proceeded to start the Colony by letting out a lodge and the stables to assorted cranks, after which he got a permit and began to build."

"And Miss Ball?"

"She was engaged as mother's help to Mrs. Craddock, but she only stayed a fortnight. If you saw the children you wouldn't be surprised. They are being brought up in a state of nature."

"In this weather? My dear Frank!"

"No, not nudist—they just do what they like, and if they wanted to go about without any clothes on, of course no one would stop them. You just let the natural tastes develop untrammelled and unchecked. I had a long and earnest talk with Mr. Craddock about it. Children must never be thwarted, or they'll get complexes, and they must never be punished or told anything is wrong, because of course a guilt complex is about the worst of the lot. I felt sorry for the unfortunate Anna Ball."

"I feel sorry for the children. Fancy going out into the world under the impression that you can always have your own way! Would anything be more likely to lead to disaster? But let us return to Miss Ball. If she left Deep End at the end of a fortnight, where did she go? Did she again leave no address?"

Frank nodded.

"According to the Craddocks she just burst into tears one day and said the children were too much for her and she would like to go at once. So she packed her bag, and he drove her in to Dedham, where she took a third-class ticket for London, and that was that. She didn't leave any address, because she said she hadn't made up her mind what she was going to do, and she would write to her friends when she had.

He said he pressed her, but she wasn't very co-operative. From which I gather she had given him to understand it wasn't his business. I got the impression that they hadn't liked Anna any more than she liked them. But having seen the children, I don't imagine they will find it at all easy to replace her."

"Are they trying to replace her?"

"Mr. Craddock said so."

Miss Silver knitted in silence for a moment or two.

"Had Mrs. Craddock nothing to say?"

He laughed.

"Very little. I should say that the spirit was more or less broken. One of those little tired women."

"And Mr. Craddock?"

"An eye like Jove to threaten and command. Very Jovian altogether. A brow and a good deal of hair. Looks like a tall man till he stands up. Quite a presence. The serious crank with Views and a belted blouse. Mrs. Craddock merely wrapped in the common domestic overall."

After a slight pause Miss Silver said,

"Life must be very hard for her, poor woman. Has she no help at all?"

"A daily was spoken of."

"They should certainly try to get someone who would live in. You say Mr. Craddock mentioned that they were trying to do so?"

"He said they were advertising, but it was so difficult to get someone to come to the country." He hesitated for a moment, and then went on. "As a matter of fact they seem to have had someone since Anna Ball, but she didn't stay."

"They would not, I imagine, advertise under their name. A box number would be more usual. Mrs. Dugdale takes the *Daily Wire.* If a previous advertisement appeared in that paper and was answered by Anna Ball, it is quite likely that they will use the same medium again. It would, I suppose, be possible for you to ask the *Daily Wire* to let you know if they receive any advertisement from the Craddocks, and to supply you with the box allotted to it."

His lazy gaze became a very direct one.

"You mean we might send someone down there?"

"I mean that I might go myself."

No one who knew Frank Abbott would have suspected him capable of the vehemence with which he said,

"No!"

"My dear Frank!"

The vehemence persisted.

"Why on earth should you? The whole thing is dead and done with. Anna Ball went there in November, and stayed less than a fortnight. She didn't leave an address, and she hasn't written to Thomasina. Repetition of her conduct when she left Mrs. Dugdale."

"She meant to write to Thomasina Elliot. She left a trunk with her. Miss Elliot informs me that it contains all her winter clothes. She had only a suit-case with her, and we are now in the third week of January. I should like to satisfy myself that she really did leave Deep End."

Frank made an impatient gesture.

"Oh, she left all right. I didn't only see the Craddocks, you know. I went the round of the Colony, just in case Anna had told anyone what she was going to do. They had all seen her, but it doesn't seem to have got much farther than that. The Misses Tremlets, who do folk dancing and handicraft, said she was very unresponsive. Miss Gwyneth Tremlett, who has a hand-loom, offered to teach her weaving, but she would have none of it. One Augustus Remington, a piece of whimsy who embroiders pictures on satin, stigmatized her as aloof. A florid and exuberant lady who calls herself Miranda—only that and nothing more—assured me that Anna had one of the gloomiest auras she had ever encountered, which, I imagine, was her way of saying the same thing. They seem to have taken a kindly interest. Rather a matey crowd. And they took it as a sign of grace when she drove over to Ledlington with the Craddocks and came back with a red hat. They thought the colour a little crude, but definitely a step in the direction of expressing joy, which the Miss Tremletts are tremendously keen about."

Miss Silver coughed.

"Why did she buy a red hat?"

"The Craddocks gave it to her. 'Dear Mrs. Craddock, always so kind, so overburdened. And Mr. Craddock—' I really can't do justice to the spate of words about Craddock."

Miss Silver had a very thoughtful expression. She said,

"Why did they give Miss Ball a red hat?"

"A desire to spread sweetness and light."

"And why are you telling me about it?"

He was watching her between narrowed lids.

"Because it is proof positive that Anna went away. Both the Miss Tremletts saw her go by with Craddock. So did Miranda and Augustus, who were having a cosy little confab over their mutual fence. You remember he drove her to Dedham, where she took a London ticket. And she really did, because I went to Dedham, and the stationmaster remembers Craddock seeing her off—a dark young woman in a red hat. He says she seemed a good deal upset, and Mr. Craddock told him she had been having trouble with her nerves, and they were glad to be quit of her. So you see!"

In a tone as firm as it was mild, Miss Silver said,

"I think I will go down to Deep End."

He sat up with a jerk.

"As mother's help to Mrs. Craddock?"

"I think so."

"You will do nothing of the sort!"

"Why should I not?"

"Because it's absurd—because I won't have it! Because—"

Miss Silver coughed gently.

"And since when have you dictated my movements, Frank?"

"You can't do it without me! The *Wire* won't let you have that box number."

He had the sensation of being looked through and through.

"You are very heated, my dear Frank. What is behind it?"

"There isn't anything behind it. I just don't want you to go there."

"And pray why not?"

"It's quite irrational— I just don't want you to go."

After a moment she said in her temperate way,

"Either there is nothing behind Anna Ball's disappearance, or there is something which requires investigation. In the former case, I should take an early opportunity of terminating the engagement. In the latter, I have undertaken an obligation towards Thomasina Elliot, and I shall endeavour to discharge it. You cannot prevent me from going to Deep End. You can merely withhold the assistance which would make my task easier and safer."

He threw out a hand.

"All right—you win—you always do. But there's something —I didn't mean to tell you. On the face of it, it's quite irrelevant, but—"

"Yes, Frank?"

"Eighteen months ago a young woman was found drowned between Deep End and Deeping. I told you the road flooded. Well, there's a boggy bit of ground on either side of it. It was a very wet night, and the girl must have got off the road in the dark. There are some sizable pot-holes. She was found lying face downwards in one of them. Not the slightest indication of anything but a purely accidental death. She was mired up to her knees, and she had slipped and fallen forward into the pot-hole. You see, it's all purely irrelevant."

Miss Silver's needles clicked.

"But she was employed by the Craddocks? Is that what you were trying not to say?"

He gave her an exasperated look.

"She came over by the day from Deeping. She had been doing it for some months. There was no suggestion of anything wrong. I didn't think it would be fair to mention it."

"But you have mentioned it now."

He said in a shame-faced way,

"I don't want you to go there."

CHAPTER 8

IT WAS ABOUT TEN DAYS LATER that Miss Silver went down to Deep End in the capacity of mother's help to Mrs. Craddock. There had been a short preliminary interview with Mr. Craddock in the lounge of a private hotel, for which occasion the Jovian gentleman had discarded the belted blouse of Frank Abbott's description for a suit of clerical grey in which he might very well have been taken for a clergyman of what used to be known as Broad Church views. He certainly had a very fine head of hair. For the rest, Mr. Craddock would pass for a handsome man, with a fresh complexion and eyes of a shade between blue and grey. It was obvious that he considered himself to be a person of importance and expected to be treated as such. He had the deep resonant voice and assured manner of a man who is accustomed to having his utterances received with respect.

Miss Silver demeaned herself accordingly. She had no need to play a part. She had only to go back to her old self and be the modest, tactful governess.

On Mr. Craddock's side, he was able to congratulate himself upon her complete suitability. She was elderly, it was true, but elderly women who work for their living are often extremely tough and active, and if she obtained the post she would be anxious to keep it. He had had enough of girls—

restless, emotional, always wanting something they couldn't have. He expounded his views on the bringing up of children for twenty minutes, observed Miss Silver's respectful attention with approval, and engaged her as mother's help to Mrs. Craddock at a salary of two pounds a week, subject to her references being satisfactory.

As she gave the names of Mrs. Charles Moray and Mrs. Garth Albany, Miss Silver found herself filled with the deepest gratitude. It might well have been that this was the kind of post which she would by now have had to accept. The lot of the ageing governess is not an enviable one. She had indeed much to be thankful for.

A few days later she was taking a familiar train journey to Ledlington, where she changed and embarked upon one of those branch lines which pursue their leisurely course through rural England. The nearest station to Deep End was Dedham, five miles away, where she found that a rickety taxi had been ordered to meet her. The afternoon being by now well advanced, and an early mist having turned to a weeping rain, the drive gave her no more idea of the scenery than that it appeared to be of a flat and agricultural nature. But as the rain increased, the road began to follow a downward course. They went over a hump-backed bridge, the hedges ceased, there was a boggy emptiness on either side. And then a slight rise, until they turned in between tall stone pillars and followed an over-shadowed drive to what had once been Deepe House and was now, at Mr. Craddock's instance, Harmony. It was so nearly dark that Miss Silver could see nothing except a vague central mass flanked by two jutting wings.

The taxi drove into the courtyard and drew up at what had once been a side door opening from the right-hand wing. Miss Silver alighted, rang the bell, and paid her fare, after which the driver, who had not troubled to get out, started up the engine and rattled off down the drive.

Since Miss Silver, like Anna Ball, had not encumbered herself with too much luggage, she was not unduly disconcerted. Her two suit-cases stood beside her on the step. At a pinch she was prepared to carry them herself.

As she rang for the third time, there was the sound of a noisy rush, the door was flung back, and a cacophony of tooth-combs met her ear. It really seemed hardly possible that a combination of three children, three combs, and some toilet-paper could produce so much din. If there was a tune, it was not discernible—the impact on the ear was just pure noise.

Miss Silver picked up her suit-cases, walked in, and found herself in an uncarpeted passage paved with stone and lighted only by a very low-powered bulb at the far end. Like shadows against this insufficient light there danced, shrieked, howled, and blew upon their cobs, a long thin girl of twelve whom she knew to be Jennifer, and the two boys of seven and four who were Maurice and Benjy.

Miss Silver walked past them without paying any attention to their antics, upon which the performance on the combs passed into a loudly shrieked-out "Dilly, dilly, dilly, come and be killed!" But before there had been more than half a dozen repetitions of this rather sinister invitation a door on the left was flung open and Mr. Craddock appeared, very Olympian in a belted blouse of white wool. In the dusk of the passage this was as much as could be seen, but as the children vanished with loud quacking noises and he ushered her into the room from which he had emerged, Miss Silver perceived that his costume was completed by corduroy trousers of a rich shade of crimson, and that the blouse itself was a work of art embroidered with a number of figures which she presently discerned to be the signs of the Zodiac.

The room into which they had come was warm and well lighted. There were book-lined walls, a large writing-table, thick curtains, and some comfortable chairs. A wood fire burned pleasantly on the wide, deep hearth. Advancing towards it, Miss Silver remarked upon its cheerful glow.

"Really quite a chilly afternoon."

Mr. Craddock beamed.

"There is no welcome like a fire," he said in the resonant voice which gave an air of importance to the words and an almost ecclesiastical flavour to a passing reference to the children's noisy greeting. "Such high spirits. The privilege of youth."

She was replying in a noncommittal manner, when the door was opened and there came in a little woman carrying a loaded tray. The sound of scattering footsteps suggested that it was one of the children who had opened the door.

Mr. Craddock waved a majestic hand.

"My wife, Mrs. Craddock. Emily, this is Miss Silver who is going to be so kind as to help you. This is most opportune—she will be glad of some refreshment after her cold journey."

He made no effort to help his wife, and she was too much encumbered to do more than murmur a few breathless and rather unintelligible words before setting down the heavy tray. Since there was no table ready to receive it, it had perforce to be accommodated on the writing-table, a circumstance which called forth a rebuke from Mr. Craddock.

"My dear Emily, would it not be as well to have the tea-table in readiness before you bring in the tray? A little forethought, my dear—a little forethought."

If it did not occur to him that he might have exercised this forethought himself, it certainly did not occur to Mrs. Craddock. A nervous start, an indistinguishable murmur of apology, and she was busying herself with dragging forward a gate-legged table and setting the tray on it. Her surprised, "Oh, thank you!" as Miss Silver hastened to assist her showed how little she was accustomed to being helped. The tray was a great deal too heavy for so frail a person. Mr. Craddock found Miss Silver regarding him in a manner so little suggestive of admiration as to cause him some annoyance.

Looking back afterwards, she was to consider her first impressions of the Craddocks. That he was desirous of producing an effect, she was at once aware. There was nothing very strange about this. A man with a fine exterior and some natural advantages may readily be tempted to assume a part which he is not really qualified to play. To look like Jove does not imply a power to wield the thunder. As for Mrs. Craddock, she was, as Frank Abbott had said, quite literally wrapped in the domestic overall, a garment of faded print which hung limply on her small, thin frame. She was very thin and a good deal bent. Her little pinched face was deeply lined. A pair of faded blue eyes looked nervously from her husband to Miss Silver, and then as a matter of habit back again to her husband. She admired him, she was afraid of him, she made haste to do his slightest bidding.

Over what she now discovered to be health tea with an odd lingering flavour of camomile, Miss Silver began to talk to her about the children. Jennifer was twelve, Maurice was seven, and Benjy four.

"They have so much energy," said Mrs. Craddock in the soft tired voice which seemed to slur the words because it really had not strength enough to sustain them. "I hope you will not find them too difficult to manage."

Mr. Craddock cut himself a large slice of home-made cake.

"There must, of course, be no coercion," he said. "That is understood, is it not? The free expression and development of individuality is a cardinal point. Freedom to express, freedom to develop, freedom to come face to face with the Ultimate and fulfil its purpose—these are essentials. I can rely on you to give them full scope?"

Replying that she would do her best, Miss Silver could not help wondering which of these freedoms had fallen to Mrs. Craddock's share.

"Emily," said Mr. Craddock in his deepest tones, "you are neglecting Miss Silver. Her cup is empty." He turned a benignant gaze upon the guest. "My own special herbal tea—healthful and invigorating. I experimented for months before I satisfied my exacting taste. The gathering of the herbs is in accordance with the dictates of astrological science—those under the moon's influence to be gathered at the full of the moon, those under Venus and the other planets at the appropriate times. There is a vast mass of accumulated lore on the subject. But there are fields still unexplored. It is in connection with these that I hope my name may yet go down to posterity. Meanwhile my health tea is a humble offering to progress."

Miss Silver coughed.

"I am afraid I am very ignorant about such matters. They must require a great deal of study."

Since Mrs. Craddock had filled up her cup, she had perforce to drink a second and stronger infusion of the health tea. Considered as an offering to progress, it appeared to her inadequate, since its only merit was that it was hot, and this might have been achieved by the simple boiling of a kettle. She could not help reflecting that Mr. Craddock's labours had involved a sad waste of time.

In the course of the next half hour she heard a good deal more about those labours. Mr. Craddock, it appeared, was engaged upon a Great Work. He required perfect quiet, both for the preliminary meditations which such a task required and for the actual literary work involved. There were also, it appeared, experiments of so delicate a nature that the least interruption would be fatal to their success. To this end he reserved for himself what he alluded to as a Retreat in the otherwise unused central block of the house.

"It is not generally habitable, and parts of it are far from safe. As regards the children, I have been obliged to lay an embargo on it. Much as I dislike rules or any attempt to curtail their perfect freedom of action, you will, I am sure, understand that in this case there is no alternative." He was helping himself to strawberry jam as he spoke and spreading it thickly upon the current slice of cake.

"Mr. Craddock must have perfect quiet," said Mrs. Craddock in a faint twittering voice. "He must never be disturbed."

When Miss Silver was presently conducted to her room, it was by Mrs. Craddock. No one, least of all Mr. Craddock, having attempted to do anything about her suit-cases, she picked up one herself and saw Mrs. Craddock stoop for the other. Since the farther door had been closed, there was nothing to restrain her from saying in a decidedly disapproving manner,

"It is really too heavy for you. Perhaps Mr. Craddock—"

Emily Craddock shook her head.

"Oh, no—I am quite used to carrying things. We have taken up too much of his time already."

Four slices of buttered toast, three slices of cake and jam, and half a plate of biscuits had taken up a very fair share of the time alluded to, but it was certainly not the moment to remark upon it. Each carrying a suit-case, they turned to the left, and came into a small square hall from which a staircase ran up to the second floor. But before they could set foot on it there was a sound of flying footsteps behind them and, all in a rush, there was Jennifer with an arm about her mother's shoulders, shaking her, snatching the suit-case away with her free hand, and scolding in a rapid undertone.

"I won't have it—you know perfectly well I won't! Why does she let you? She's come here to help you, hasn't she? At least that's what she's supposed to have come for. Why doesn't she do it? I'd put up with her if she did. *You!*" She stared across Mrs. Craddock's shoulder at Miss Silver. "What's the good of you if you can't stop her carrying things?"

There was an unchildlike fury in the dark eyes. Miss Silver met it steadily. She said,

"I hope to be able to do so, Jennifer. If you will carry the case and show me my room, there will be no need for your mother to come up."

There was a moment of hostility, a moment of fading antagonism, a moment when Jennifer stood frowning and uncertain. Then she gave Mrs. Craddock quite a rough push, said, "Be off with you!" and ran up the stairs without waiting.

Miss Silver followed at leisure. She was perfectly able to carry her suit-case, but she had no intention of hurrying. She wondered a little whether Jennifer would be in sight when she reached the landing which corresponded with the hall below. It was crossed by a long passage upon which rooms opened to either side. A faint light illuminated the stair-head, but the passages were dark, and Jennifer had vanished in the darkness.

Miss Silver took a chance and walked down the right-hand passage. She was nearing the end of it, when a door flew open and light streamed out, to the accompaniment of Jennifer's mocking laughter. It broke off suddenly.

"You didn't scream!"

"I could see no reason to scream."

"Do you always see reason?"

The child's voice accused her of something—she wondered what? She said in her most equable tones,

"It is a very good plan."

As she came into the room, Jennifer backed away from her, tall and thin in old patched shorts and a faded scarlet jersey. The long bare legs were brown, the long thin feet were naked in their sandals. Miss Silver was reminded of a startled foal. There was the same mixture of awkwardness and grace, the toss of the head with which a straying forelock was shaken back. There was no timidity, but an alert wariness. From a safe distance Jennifer said,

"Do you always plan things?"

Miss Silver gave her the smile which had won the heart of many a reluctant client.

"Do you not do so?"

"Sometimes I do. Sometimes my plan isn't the same as someone else's plan. It mightn't be the same as yours—it might be a very opposite plan indeed. What would you do then?"

Miss Silver appeared to give this question as much serious attention as if it had been put to her by a grown-up person. Then she said,

"One can really only make plans for oneself. When they come into conflict with the plans of other people one has to consider to what extent each can accommodate his plan to another's. It is a problem that arises constantly. People who are successful in dealing with it will also make a success of their lives."

She had caught the child's attention. The dark eyes had a sudden bright spark of intelligence. Under the overhead light she saw that they were not brown as she had thought at first, but a sombre grey heavily shaded by black lashes. The spark flashed and was gone. Jennifer stood poised with her weight on one foot, as if ready to fly off at a tangent. She said,

"You planned to come here. So did the others. They didn't

stay. Perhaps you won't stay either. Do you think you will?"

Miss Silver was removing her black cloth coat. As she hung it up in the cheap plywood wardrobe she said in her temperate way,

"That will depend a good deal upon you. I should not care to stay where I was not wanted. But I think your mother needs someone to help her."

Jennifer stamped her foot. She said with sudden passion,

"If she doesn't have someone she'll *die!* I told him so! That's why he got you! He wouldn't like her to die! Because of the money! But she will if someone doesn't help her!" She came at Miss Silver with a rush, not touching her but coming up close, her dark head on the same level, her eyes full of angry tears. "Why do you make me say things?"

"My dear—"

The child stamped again.

"I'm *not!* And you needn't think you can make me do things I don't want to! Nobody can!" There was tragic intensity in the words.

Before Miss Silver could make any reply, one of those quick rushes took Jennifer across the floor and out of the room. She was as light on her feet as a kitten, the darting flight was soundless. The door clapped to with a bang.

Miss Silver said, "Dear me!" After which she removed her hat, changed into indoor shoes, and remembered that she had not ascertained the whereabouts of the bathroom. She was tidying her hair—an entirely superfluous action, since it was always perfectly under control—when the door was flung open again. Jennifer stood beyond the threshold, her head up, her look defiant.

"The bathroom is next door. I thought I'd make you look for it—and then I thought I wouldn't. Are you coming down?"

Miss Silver coughed.

"I thought that I would put my things away first."

Jennifer backed. She remained poised for a moment in the patch of light from the doorway. She said with a jerk in her voice,

"You won't stay—they never do!"

And was gone.

CHAPTER 9

SEEN IN THE LIGHT of a grey January morning, Deepe House had a very desolate and ruined look. The main block of the house showed plainly the bomb damage which it had sustained. Of the ornamental balustrade which had run the length of the roof only a few fragments survived, and no more than three of the windows in the whole façade still kept their glass, the rest had been roughly boarded up. These three windows, all on the ground floor, imparted a curious furtive look, as if the house were peering up from under the clogging weight of its two blind storeys. The courtyard between the two wings was slippery with moss. When the wind stirred, fallen magnolia leaves and droppings of ivy whispered against the stone flags with which it was paved.

Even in the Craddocks' wing not all the windows had glass in them.

"It is too big for us," Mrs. Craddock explained. "We could not furnish or keep so many rooms. But it will be nice when we can get the windows mended."

On the other side of the courtyard in the opposite wing all the windows were boarded up, the tenant using only those rooms which looked upon what had once been a garden. He was a Mr. Robinson, and Miss Silver gathered that he preferred seclusion and was addicted to bird-watching and nature-study. He could not be said to have a very extensive view, but if he desired privacy he had it. Dead grass stood knee-high amongst unpruned fruit trees. Roses gone back to briar contended with the wild raspberry and currant. Evergreens, some half dead, ran riot, with here and there a cypress grown to an immense height. There were dark patches of the churchyard yew. Miss Silver could see only the outer fringe of this wilderness, but the signs of ruin and neglect were unmistakable.

At lunch she made bright conversation about the house.

"A very interesting old place. It is sad to think how much

irreparable damage was done during the war, but perhaps it is better to reflect with gratitude upon what has been spared."

Mrs. Craddock said, "Oh, *yes.*" Mr. Craddock, partaking of a lentil cutlet, said nothing at all. The children said nothing.

Miss Silver, who was never at a loss for meal-time conversation, continued her remarks. An enquiry as to whether Mr. Craddock had had any difficulty with the plumbing—men generally took so much interest in this subject—elicited, not from him but again from Mrs. Craddock, an assurance that it was all that could be desired, and that though the new bathroom and hot water system had been a great expense, they were certainly a comfort.

It was not until he had absorbed four lentil cutlets and an inordinate amount of greenstuff that Mr. Craddock emerged from his philosophic abstraction. That he happened to do so at the moment when Miss Silver was remarking upon the ruins of what appeared to be a chapel at some little distance from the house was no doubt a coincidence. She had asked if the damage had been caused by the same bomb which wrecked the house, and was surprised to receive a decided negative.

"Oh, no. The old church had been a ruin for thirty or forty years before that. And by the way, the place is not safe. There is a danger of flying masonry."

With striking lack of tact Benjy chose this moment to say, "We play hide-and-seek there. It's a very good place for hide-and-seek."

Parental displeasure descended.

"It is not at all a safe place for you to play. If one of those big stones fell—"

"Would it cut my head off?"

There was a gasp of "Benjy!" from Mrs. Craddock, and a calm "It might," from Mr. Craddock.

"Right off?" enquired Benjy with interest. "And my hands? And my feet? Like the stone man inside the church?"

"Benjy!"

Jennifer, sitting next to him, slid a hand under the table and pinched hard. His outraged roar effectually changed the conversation, since he howled at the top of his voice until he discovered that the pudding was apple dumpling.

It was over the washing-up that Jennifer, washing whilst Miss Silver dried, said defiantly,

"Benjy is a damfool."

It was beyond Miss Silver to let this pass.

"My dear, you should not use such words."

Jennifer looked at her calmly.

"I shall use any words I like. If you interfere with my self-expression you will do something to my psyche. You ask *him* if you won't!" She broke into an angry laugh. "He talks that way, but when we do anything he doesn't like, a lot he cares about our psyches!" Then, still with the utmost aggressiveness of voice and manner, "Don't you hate, and loathe, and abominate, and *detest* washing-up?"

Miss Silver decided that it would be better to reply only to this last sentence.

"No, I really do not dislike it at all. With two of us it will be quickly done, and a great help to your mother. Do you not think that she might be persuaded to take a little rest while you and I go out for a walk with the boys?"

Jennifer said, "I don't know!" in an angry voice, but this time the anger was not for Miss Silver. She washed up at an incredible pace, neither chipped nor broke anything, and darted out of the room whilst Miss Silver finished the drying, to return a moment later with the triumphant announcement that Mrs. Craddock had promised to lie down.

Miss Silver, having donned the black cloth coat, the elderly fur tippet, the felt hat with a purple starfish on one side, and the black woollen gloves, her invariable wear in winter except when the occasion demanded her best hat and the kid gloves reserved to go with it, they set out, Benjy and Maurice running ahead, Jennifer hatless in her scarlet jumper, not walking with Miss Silver but making short excursions here, there, and everywhere, yet always coming back after the manner of a puppy or any young thing for whom the pace of its elders is too slow.

They were out of sight of the house and had come to the edge of a wide sloping common, when Benjy came running back.

"Are we going there now?" he said, the words tumbling one over the other. "I want to show her the man what had his head broke off, an' I want a piece of stone for my ruin I'm making in my garden, an' I want a snail for my other snail to run races with, an' I want—"

Jennifer came up with him and caught his hand.

"You want a lot, don't you?"

"I want a snail, an' a white spider, an' a little green spider, an' put them in a cage and see if they eat each other. An' I want a big fir cone—"

Jennifer said, "All right, Toad—come along!" She waved with her free hand to Miss Silver. "We shall be about an hour. We don't want you, and you don't want us. You can meet us where the ruined chapel is and make sure we don't get hit by flying masonry like he says."

She gave Benjy a tug, and they raced away together, gathering up Maurice as they went.

It being no part of Miss Silver's plan for the afternoon to pursue three wild children over country strange to her and perfectly well known to them, she merely remarked "Dear me!" and having watched them out of sight, retraced her steps until the ruins came in sight, and made her way towards them.

The church must have been a very tiny one. The chancel arch still stood, with parts of two others. Fallen stone lay confusedly amongst a prickly growth of bramble, whilst all around were the half-obliterated mounds and sunken headstones of a disused cemetery, the whole enclosed by a low wall. As this was in the same condition of disrepair as the church itself, it could not longer serve to keep anyone out.

Miss Silver walked through a gap and made her way cautiously amongst faded grass and fallen stones. The place was desolate in the extreme. With Deepe House behind her, there was not a human habitation in sight. All who had used this place for worship, for the christening of their children, for the marriage of their young people, for the burial of their dead, were gone. David's words came into her mind—"For the wind passeth over it and it is gone, and the place thereof shall know it no more."

In what had been the nave she came upon Benjy's man without a head, a tomb with the recumbent figure of a knight in armour. The head was gone, and so were the feet. The hands, much weathered, were crossed upon a sword, and the legs crossed at the knees, showing that he had been upon two crusades—the only information which the tomb could now afford, since the inscription which had once set forth his name and virtues could no longer be deciphered. A little nearer to what had been the entrance a stone slab lay slightly raised above the ground. She made out that it would have been just within and to the right of the west door, and that there was an inscription now so much defaced that it could no longer be read.

After observing it for some minutes Miss Silver prepared to

go. She was not very strongly addicted to ruins. Benjy's remarks about the snails and spiders lingered unfavourably in her mind. If a sense of duty compelled her to wait here for the children, she felt it would be more agreeable to do so on the other side of the wall. Turning from the stone slab, she saw that the ruins had another visitor, and a striking one. A very tall and very large woman in a voluminous dark cape was standing just beyond the gap through which she herself had entered. The cape billowed out on every side, giving in spite of her bulk the impression that it might at any moment spread into wings and carry its wearer away. She had blunt, ugly features, a pair of rolling eyes, and an immense bush of the dark red hair which is usually a product of the dye bottle. Miss Silver found herself quite unable to believe that it was natural, though, being old-fashioned in her taste and preferring the more conventional shades, she was at a loss to imagine why anyone should wish to dye her hair such a distressing colour.

A large hand let go of the cloak to wave at her and then clutched it again. A deep voice hailed her.

"That place isn't safe. The masonry flies."

This inversion of Mr. Craddock's phrase had a very peculiar sound, a peculiarity which was intensified when the stranger continued,

"Other things too perhaps. You had better not linger."

Declaimed in that contralto manner, the words were arresting. Miss Silver, having reached the gap in the wall, was arrested. The cloak flapped loose again. Her hand was grasped.

"You are Emily Craddock's new governess. I am Miranda! We must know each other! You are psychic?"

Miss Silver coughed a little primly.

"I do not think so."

The cloak threatened to engulf them both. Her hand was released.

"Many people do not know their own powers. We must talk. This place interests you?"

"It is very desolate."

"Ah—you are a sensitive." The words were pronounced in a pontifical manner. "The burial place of an extinct family. There are emanations from such places. They affect the sensitive. The Everlys once owned all this land. They were rich, they were powerful. They are ruined, they are gone. *Sic transit gloria mundi.*"

She rolled out the words with the air of making an original

statement. A sharp gust of wind blew the cloak right up over her head, disclosing the fact that she wore beneath it a curious short purple garment resembling a cassock which has been cut off at the knees. Comfortable for walking, no doubt, but most unsuitable for so large a figure. When the cloak was under control again the owner went on as if there had been no interruption.

"That stone—the one over which you were bending—it covers the entrance to their family vault. You could not read the inscription. It has been obliterated for years. Only a letter here and there remains. On my first visit I pored over it. Without success. Later, in trance, I read it clearly." She intoned the words: "'Here I—Ever Lye.' Spelt with a Y, you know! A play upon the name Everly. Strange mixture of the Pun and the Funeral Pall!"

"Strange indeed—"

Miss Silver's murmured words may not have referred entirely to an Elizabethan partiality for punning. Miranda's eyes, brown and rather prominent, stopped rolling and contemplated her in a fixed manner.

"You will stay with the Craddocks, I hope. Peveril is Marvellous—an inspiration to all Seekers. You will find it a Privilege to belong to his household. I may say a Great Privilege. Dear Emily, of course, is earthbound. One wonders why—" She shook her head with the air of a warning Sybil. "But he cannot fail to raise her."

Miss Silver coughed again.

"Mrs. Craddock is all that is kind."

"Oh, kind—" Miranda let go of the cloak with a free gesture which was obviously intended to dismiss Mrs. Craddock's kindness as irrelevant. By the time she had recaptured it the question of dear Emily's exact spiritual status or the lack of it had gone down the wind. She reverted to her original theme. "You will stay. They will need you. She is frail. And the children—sadly uncontrolled. Peveril believes in the self-expression of the Ego, but I do not follow him all the way. *Not* with children. For the adult, yes! Undoubtedly! Entirely! But for the untrained child intelligence, no! There must be Leading, Guiding—even at times Discipline. You agree with me?"

"I do indeed."

Miranda waved hand and cloak together.

"We must talk of it. Peveril must be made to see reason. His work must not be disturbed. And Emily requires relief. The young girls whom she has had were useless—no experience, no authority. Miss Dally left after a week because Maurice put a spider down her back and Benjy poured the ink over her hair, and all she did was to burst into tears and pack her bag. Fluffy fair hair and pale blue eyes—most unsuitable! Miss Ball equally so, but a different type. A morose girl. She stayed for a fortnight, and I told Emily at the time that she was a good riddance. I saw her go by to the station, and the words sprang unbidden to my lips. I spoke them aloud. Not to Emily Craddock, because she was not there, but to Augustus Remington. He lives next door to me. You must meet him. A gentle soul—he does exquisite needlework. Have you met Elaine and Gwyneth Tremlett yet?"

"Not yet. I only came yesterday."

"You will do so. Rather earthbound, but pleasant neighbours. They adore Peveril, but it would have been better if they had stayed at Wyshmere. Elaine had a folk-dancing class there—she misses it. Gwyneth, of course, can go on with her weaving. But it would be better if they had not come—I have told them so frankly. I always say just what I think. If it is not received in the same spirit, that is not my fault. What made you come here?"

"I answered Mr. Craddock's advertisement. Do you know, I believe I hear the children. They undertook to meet me here."

With a sweeping gesture Miranda folded her arms and her cloak across her capacious bosom.

"Then I will leave you. But we must meet again. Together we will see what can be done to help Emily. Goodbye!" She went off with a swinging stride, her dark red hair waving in the wind.

As soon as she was at a safe distance, the children came tumbling down hill out of a patch of scrubby woodland which looked as if it might harbour primroses in the spring. They were in high spirits, laughing and shouting.

"Did the masonry fly at you?"

"I'd like to see it fly— I want to see it fly!"

"I haven't got any spiders! They go somewhere in the winter!"

"They climb up drain-pipes and drown themselves in your bath!"

"Don't want spiders in my bath!"

Jennifer said,

"That was Miranda. She thinks we want discipline. Maurice

put an earwig in her tea, and she poured the whole cup down the back of his neck."

"It's better to leave her alone," said Maurice gloomily. "Is it tea-time yet? Shall we go home? I'm hungry."

They went home.

CHAPTER 10

THERE WAS A COLD WIND blowing in the park. Leafless trees made a pattern against the lowering sky. There was a kind of prickle in the air, which generally means that it may begin to snow at any moment. It was not the sort of day to tempt anyone to linger, but Thomasina Elliot and Peter Brandon were not only lingering, they were actually sitting on one of the green park seats. There is, of course, nothing so warming to the blood as a good brisk quarrel. Not that either Peter or Thomasina would have admitted that they were quarrelling. Thomasina was merely refusing to be bullied, while Peter was engaged in pointing out the folly of her ways. In an atmosphere of pure reason no doubt, and without any undignified heat, but he had no right to be doing it. After all, at twenty-one you are of age. You can record a vote or make a will, you can get married without anyone's leave. You are, in fact, an adult human being. And Thomasina was twenty-two. She had been an adult human being for thirteen months and ten days. It was outrageous of Peter to behave as if he was a Victorian parent, or the sort of guardian that you come across in old-fashioned books. She said so.

"Thank you— I don't feel in the least like a parent! And thank God I'm not your guardian!"

Rightly considering that she had scored a point, Thomasina produced an odiously complacent smile.

"It was rather clever of me really."

"Clever!"

"Well, it was, you know. I don't suppose I'd heard their names for years and years and years. Well, at least five, because that is when Aunt Barbara was down at that folk-weaving place, Wyshmere. She wanted to learn how to do it so as to teach Tibbie."

"Tibbie?"

"Jeanie's sister—the one that was crippled in an accident. She got her a little hand-loom, and she made scarves and did quite well with them."

"Who got who a loom, and who did quite well with it?"

She exercised an exasperated patience.

"Aunt Barbara gave Tibbie a loom of course. She never got very good at it herself, but Tibbie did."

Peter said in the tone of one who wouldn't agree with himself if he could help it, let alone with anyone else,

"I don't remember a thing about it."

"Because you were abroad. But that's where she met the Miss Tremletts—"

"Tibbie?"

The patience vanished, the exasperation became a good deal more evident.

"No, of course not! Aunt Barbara—at Wyshmere—I told you! And the minute Inspector Abbott mentioned their names—"

"Why on earth should he mention their names?"

"He was telling me about Anna going to Deep End and there being an arty-crafty colony there. As soon as he said two Miss Tremletts who did weaving and folk-dancing and their names were Gwyneth and Elaine, something went off in my head like striking a match, and I remembered Aunt Barbara and Wyshmere. So I thought supposing they were the same—"

"Supposing who were the same as what?"

Thomasina's eyes became considerably brighter. Some young men would have been alarmed, but Peter had a good deal of natural resistance.

"Peter, you are doing it on purpose!"

"My good girl, if you keep flinging about she's and who's and what's—"

"I am not your good girl!"

"Agreed."

"You are simply pretending not to understand. I thought if these Miss Tremletts were the same as Aunt Barbara's ones—and they were practically bound to be, because you simply couldn't imagine two families giving names like Elaine and Gwyneth—"

"I don't see why not."

Thomasina felt very much as she did on the occasion when she took off a shoe and threw it at Peter. The heel had cut his forehead and left a small white scar, and Aunt Barbara had talked to her about Cain, and being a murderess. All very horrifying when you were eight years old. She was twenty-two now, and they were in a public park, so she controlled herself.

"You just don't want to see—that's all. But I did, so I sent Jeanie a wire for Aunt Barbara's address book, and there they were—Elaine and Gwyneth Tremlett, Wyshcumtru, Wyshmere."

Peter laughed in a superior way.

"I don't believe it. No one could possibly have an address like that."

"Elaine and Gwyneth did. So I wrote and said I had just come across their names in Aunt Barbara's address book, and were they still there, and a bit about Tibbie and the handloom, and this morning I got a letter from Gwyneth, who is the weaving one, and she said they had moved and gone to this place, Deep End. A 'Colony of Seekers' she called it, with oh, such a wonderful man at the head of it. And she could never forget dear Mrs. Brandon, and they did sometimes take a paying guest, so if I ever wanted a country holiday, perhaps I would give them the great pleasure of making my acquaintance and renewing what had been very pleasant memories. There was a lot more like that, all underlined and gushing."

"Now look here, Thomasina—"

"It's no good, Peter—I'm going down."

"You can't possibly!"

"Oh, but I am. I wrote off at once and said I was *yearning* for a country holiday."

"If you will stop to think for a single instant—"

"Yes, darling?"

He said with extraordinary violence,

"Don't call me darling!"

"Well, I don't really want to."

"Then don't do it! What I want you to do is to listen. You are paying this Miss Silver of yours to try and trace Anna Ball—she has gone down to Deep End for that specific purpose. If you go butting in, the odds are you will queer her pitch. To start with, there's your name. Anna Ball may quite easily have talked about you when she was down there."

"Anna never talked about anybody. That was what was wrong with her—she was all shut-up and tight. I don't see her having a heart-to-heart with Gwyneth and Elaine."

"She probably had a photograph of you."

"Well then, she didn't—at least it wasn't with her. She only had one, and it was in the top of the trunk she sent to me."

Peter leaned forward and put a strong gripping hand on her wrist.

"If you don't make a mess of it one way, you will another. You'll be going down there under false pretences for one thing, and you'll be a serious embarrassment to Miss Silver for another. The whole thing is probably a complete mare's nest. Anna went there and came away again, and just hasn't bothered to write. But if there is anything wrong about the place—I don't say there is, but supposing there was—you might be running into something that would make you wish you had listened to reason."

Thomasina was only waiting for him to take breath. When he did she was more than ready.

"Why should I be going down under false pretences? I never heard of such a thing! I'm not calling myself Jane Smith or Elizabeth Brown, am I? They *did* know Aunt Barbara, and I *am* her niece, and if they want a paying guest and I want to learn folk-weaving and have a holiday in the country, why shouldn't I?"

"Because you don't want anything of the sort. You wouldn't go within twenty miles of these Tremletts if you didn't want to go snooping round about Anna Ball."

Thomasina went quite pale with anger.

"You just said that because it was the nastiest thing you could think of!"

"Perfectly correct."

"And it isn't true!"

"You wouldn't be so angry if it wasn't."

"Yes, I would! I don't like lies and unfairness! I don't suppose there's anything wrong with Gwyneth and Elaine. Aunt Barbara wouldn't have been friends with them if they hadn't been all right. She *liked* them, and Gwyneth called her 'Dear Mrs. Brandon.' So why shouldn't I go and be a paying guest? If they are all right, and everything is all right, then I just learn a little folk-weaving and come away again. You are not going to pretend there is anything wrong about that, I suppose."

"And if everything isn't all right?"

"Then the sooner it's found out about the better!"

There was quite a long pause. Thomasina's colour came back rather brightly. She had reduced Peter to silence, a thing which had practically never happened before. This was extremely pleasing. But when the silence had gone on for quite a long time it didn't feel so good. A small cold wind blew about them. The clouds were lower and had the rather horrid leaden look which is a presage of snow. She became aware that her feet were frozen, and that it would be much nicer to go and have tea somewhere instead of sitting mouldering on a park bench without even the satisfaction of saying how much you hated it. She looked sideways at Peter, who was staring gloomily at nothing at all, and was just going to look away again, when he turned with one of his abrupt movements and caught both her hands in his.

"Tamsine—don't go!"

It was always dreadfully hard not to weaken when he called her Tamsine, but if you didn't keep your end up with Peter you would be a trodden slave before you could turn around. The spirit of all the Border Elliots rebelled. She smiled right into his eyes and said,

"Darling, of course I'm going."

CHAPTER 11

AFTER A WEEK at Deep End Miss Silver had seen no reason to modify her first impressions. What she called her scholastic career had come to an end so many years ago that she might have expected to find it strange to be teaching children again, yet it was not strange at all. By what arts she had brought Jennifer, Maurice and Benjy to accept her teaching was just one of those things which cannot be explained. There are people who can manage children, and people who can't. There are qualities which compel respect. When they are present they are respected. Miss Silver possessed these qualities. In return she respected the children under her charge—their privacy, their confidence, their rights. These things, though never put into words, are deeply felt. They establish a sense of security and evoke a responsive trust.

It is not to be supposed that the Craddock children became orderly and disciplined in a day or two. Jennifer remained aloof, with flashes of interest. Maurice, sturdy and literal-minded, was discovered to have a passion for trains. His attention was captured and his heart won by the fact that Miss Silver had had the forethought to provide herself with a book which displayed upon its cover the picture of an enormous engine very strikingly coloured in Prussian blue and scarlet, and inside, in addition to many other illustrations of trains and engines all duly named and numbered, a quite extraordinary amount of information about railways. Margaret Moray, who had a boy of the same age, had assured her that nothing in trousers between four and eight could possibly resist its lure. Little girls would find it dull, but any normal boy would eat it and ask for more. The number of miles between London and Edinburgh, the number of miles between Edinburgh and Glasgow, the history of the *Flying Scotsman* and the *Coronation Scot,* innumerable and solid facts about bogies, about fuel, about taking in water—these were meat and drink.

Mrs. Charles Moray was perfectly right. From his first sight of the blue and scarlet engine Maurice simply never looked back. He could be heard murmuring the names of favourite engines in his sleep. With a maddening persistence he imparted technical details during the family meals, a circumstance particularly obnoxious to Mr. Craddock, who considered himself to be the fount of knowledge and had no desire to receive instruction from a child of seven. A frown descended upon the Jovian brow, a ponderous displeasure filled the room. When Mrs. Craddock's faint attempts to change the subject were disregarded her hands shook nervously. On one particularly trying occasion she dropped the teapot, scalding her wrist and flooding the table, but during the ensuing disorder Maurice could still be heard reciting the stations between London and Bristol, with Benjy chirping behind him and getting half of them wrong.

All this was trying, but both little boys now submitted to having their nails cut, and to washing their hands before meals, a practice previously considered to be sissy. Miss Silver found this expression intriguing, as it could not by any possibility have derived from Mr. Craddock. A conversation with Mrs. Craddock enlightened her. It appeared that they had been less than two years at Deep End. Mr. Craddock had been there a little longer, getting the place ready for them and for the Colony.

"You see we used to live at such a pretty little place called Wyshmere—at least I and the children did. My husband travelled a lot. He was an artist. There were several artists in Wyshmere, and when he was killed in an air crash we just stayed on. Of course the children had to go to the village school. I was not nearly clever enough to teach them myself, and there wasn't any money until my old cousin Francis

Crole left me quite a lot. It was so very kind of him, because I only saw him twice. He came down after my husband died and paid for everything. And he came again a year later and said I hadn't got any sense and the children were running wild, and I'd better marry someone who would look after them and me. He was killed in an accident about a month later, and he had made a new will and left me a lot of money. So I married Mr. Craddock."

Miss Silver was remembering Jennifer's "He wouldn't like her to die—because of the money." She found herself hoping that Cousin Francis had tied it up securely. Aloud she said,

"Then Mr. Craddock is the children's stepfather?"

A faint flush came into Emily Craddock's face.

"Oh, *yes*. It is a marvellous thing for them having a man like him. He came down to Wyshmere for a holiday after Cousin Francis died. Everybody thought him wonderful. The Miss Tremletts lived there too, you know. They quite worshipped him, and so did Jennifer." She paused, drew a long sighing breath, and added the one word, "*Then.*"

"Children take these fancies."

Emily Craddock sighed again.

"Yes, they do, don't they? But he was so good to them. He took such an interest. He gave Jennifer lessons in saying poetry. He said she really had talent—but I don't think I want her to go on the stage." She drew another of those deep tired breaths. "Oh well, you never know how things will turn out, do you?"

They were sitting in the large shabby ground-floor room which served as schoolroom and playroom for the children, Mrs. Craddock at her everlasting task of mending, Miss Silver winding pale blue wool for a baby's coatee. Her niece by marriage, Dorothy, the wife of Ethel Burkett's brother, was expecting her third child. Since there had been a dozen childless years before the first was born, everyone in the family was very much interested. A boy was hoped for, hence the pale blue wool.

Miss Silver looked compassionately at the small figure bent over a much patched pair of shorts and said,

"Sometimes they turn out better than we expect. Your boys are strong and healthy, and Jennifer is very intelligent."

"She is like her father. He had the artistic temperament. She has it too." She spoke rather as if it was a malady of some sort.

Miss Silver wound her wool in silence for a little. Then she said,

"Have you not thought that it would be better for her to be at school?"

Mrs. Craddock looked up in a startled manner.

"Oh—yes—I did—"

"It would be good for her to have the companionship of girls of her own age. She is too sensitive, too intense. She needs to be taken out of herself."

Emily Craddock shook her head.

"Mr. Craddock wouldn't let her go. He doesn't approve of boarding schools, and they are very expensive. You see, we had to buy this place. And then there have been the alterations. It cost quite a lot to convert the stables for the Miss Tremletts. And the lodge, and the two new cottages. It was a wonderful thing to do of course. Mr. Craddock has such very high ideals. I don't understand them all of course. He says I am very earth-bound, but when you have so many things to do in the house—and I've never been very good at them—it doesn't seem to leave you much time for anything else, does it? But of course I do feel that it was wonderful of him to want to marry me. Everyone at Wyshmere felt that —and it's a great privilege for the children."

Miss Silver wrote a letter that evening. It was addressed to Mrs. Charles Moray, and it ran:

My dear Margaret,

This is an interesting old place. Such a pity that it was bombed, but the Craddocks' wing is most comfortable. The children are a little out of hand, but I have very good hopes of them. You were quite right about the book of trains, which has been a great success with the little boys. Mr. and Mrs. Craddock are being all that is kind. He is a most interesting man, and very goodlooking. I understand that he is engaged upon an important book. She, I fear, is not very robust, and I am glad to feel that I can spare her some fatigue. I hope that all is well with you.

With my love,

Yours affectionately,
Maud Silver.

P.S. Pray let me know whether you are able to get the wool I mentioned.

This letter she stamped and placed upon a small table in the hall. There was only one incoming post a day, and the man who delivered the letters cleared the two post-boxes—the one at the gate of what he still called Deepe House in defiance of Mr. Craddock and the Colony, and the other amongst the cluster of cottages at the foot of the rise. The Colony corresponded voluminously, Deep End practically not at all. The Miss Tremletts in particular received letters, magazines, and periodicals from all over the world, and wrote reams in reply. Miranda's mail was also very extensive but mainly home-produced. The postman, a very respectable man of the name of Hawke, regarded it with disapproval. "Stands to reason a woman's bound to have two names same like anyone else, and stands to reason she's bound to be Miss or Mrs. Indecent it looks to me, having nothing but her Christian name on the envelopes. Miranda—just like that—for all the world like going about without her clothes on! Stands to reason she's bound to have a name! Same as anyone else! And why don't she use it?" There being no answer, and the sentiment being generally approved, he was able to repeat it until by force of custom the subject lost its interest.

Instead of leaving her letter on the hall table Miss Silver might have gone down to the gate and posted it. Or, if she preferred the longer walk, she could have gone as far as Deep End and pushed Mrs. Charles Moray's letter into the red slit which brightened the wall of old Mr. Masters' cottage. Rain or shine, snow, hail or thunder, Mr. Masters would be out in his porch at ten o'clock to have a word with Mr. Hawke. During the war years, when it was Mrs. Hawke who had taken round the letters and cleared the boxes, he had felt bitterly deprived. Most days it would be no more than "Morning, postman" and a brief bulletin about his rheumatism, with perhaps a word or two in return about Mr. Hawke's grandfather-in-law who was going to be a hundred on his next birthday, whereas Mr. Masters was only ninety-five, and no use trying to slip in an extra year or two, because everyone knew his age, and his daughter-in-law, still known as young Mrs. Masters though she was turned fifty, wouldn't have it. She was a large and in the main silent person, but in matters like how old you were and how many times you'd got the prize for the best marrows over at Deeping she would speak up very awkward. Downright unfeeling, old Mr. Masters considered. For the rest, she was a hard-featured woman who kept him and the cottage like a new pin and found time and energy to put in three hours a day up at Deepe House, which neither she nor anyone else in either Deep End or Deeping could bring themselves to call Harmony.

As Mr. Masters put it:

"Might as well start giving *me* a new name at my time o' life! And who's Craddocks to go giving names and taking of them away—you tell me that! Ignorance and imperence, that's what I call it! Why, that there old house bin standing there since Queen Elizabeth's time, and if you haven't got a right to your own lawful name after all that time, when have you got a right to it—you tell me that!"

CHAPTER 12

MARGARET MORAY received Miss Silver's letter at breakfast on the following day. It was a dark morning, and she took it to the window to get a better light. Then, still without opening it, she put it down before her husband.

"What do you make of it, Charles?"

He gave it his frowning attention, asked to have the light switched on, and slanted the envelope towards it, flap uppermost.

"Well, I should say it had been opened."

"So should I."

She slit it carefully at the bottom end and read the innocuous missive aloud.

Charles Moray looked up from his porridge.

"What were you to do about it?"

"Let Frank Abbott have it, and send her a postcard to let her know whether we think it's been tampered with. The postscript about the wool is the cue. If I was quite sure, I was to say, 'How much of the wool do you want? I can get it all right.'" She hesitated a moment. "I don't know that I can make it as definite as that."

"Perhaps not."

"Well, I thought I might say, 'I think I can get the wool you want. Will find out for certain and let you know.' I suppose they will be able to make sure at the Yard. Do you know, Charles, I do wish she hadn't gone down there. I don't like it a bit."

Charles Moray didn't like it either, but he wasn't going to say so. Instead, he unfolded the rather lively newspaper with which he preferred to cheer his porridge and remarked in a carping tone that Beauty Queens got plainer every year.

Margaret came to look over his shoulder.

"Darling, what a frightful bathing-dress!"

"If you call it a dress! I shouldn't! I wonder how much more she could leave off without getting arrested!"

She kissed the top of his head.

"I don't know, darling—I've never thought it out. I do hope Michael isn't being late for school. Betty *will* cut it too fine."

Mrs. Moray's postcard was duly delivered by Mr. Hawke next day. He was naturally aware that the new governess up at Deepe House was an indefatigable knitter, but he found himself unable to take a passionate interest in whether she could or could not get some particular kind of wool. And why write to London about it? Miss Weekes at the Fancy Stores at Dedham had a very good selection.

Meeting Miss Silver on his way up to the house, he imparted this information, adding,

"And Mrs. Hawke says it's the best she's seen for ever so long—quite pre-war, as you might say."

He bicycled on to Deep End, pleased with his own kind thought and with Miss Silver's pleasant response. And no harm in doing Miss Weekes a good turn neither, her sister Grace being married to a cousin of his own at Ledstow.

Miss Silver went rather thoughtfully back to the house with her postcard, which she made a point of showing to Mrs. Craddock.

"This special shade of pink is sometimes a little difficult, and it must be an exact match. Mrs. Moray was so kind as to say that she would do her best to get it for me."

It was a little later that Jennifer came into the room. Since this was considered to be holiday time, Miss Silver had not attempted regular lessons, but was endeavouring to find things that would interest the children to hear about or to do. Maurice was working on a model engine, and what Maurice did Benjy of course must copy. In Jennifer she discovered a quick and sensitive response to poetry and drama. Some short one-act plays had been obtained, and all three children were rehearsing one of them. Already some pattern had been introduced into their days, and the first beginnings of order and punctuality instilled.

Jennifer came in now, said briefly, "Mrs. Masters wants to

see you before she goes," and then stood staring out of the window as Mrs. Craddock put down her mending and hurried out of the room.

Jennifer did not speak. She looked out at a graceful leafless tree, tracing its outline on the glass with the tip of her finger. Miss Silver, watching, was aware of the moment when she stopped thinking about the tree and the pattern which it made against the sky. Until that moment Jennifer's thoughts had been lifted into an atmosphere of pure enjoyment—this lovely line and that, the way they crossed, the way through all the crossing and turning that they sprang upward towards the light. And then all at once she didn't see the tree or the sky any more. She saw her own hand spread out against the glass—a long, thin hand with the shape of the bones just showing through because a gleam of wintry sun was on the pane and its light made the flesh translucent.

It was when the sun came out that Jennifer stopped seeing the tree and began to stare at her hand. Looking on with interest and concern, Miss Silver was aware of a stiffening, a tension, an extraordinary concentration of the child's whole being. She might have been looking at something repulsive, something horrible.

Miss Silver laid her knitting down upon her knee and said in her most matter-of-fact tone,

"Is there anything wrong with your hand, my dear?"

Jennifer whipped round, startled, angry.

"Why should there be?"

"I thought perhaps—you looked as if you were not very comfortable."

"It's just a hand, isn't it? It's just my own hand. Why shouldn't I look at it if I like? There's nothing wrong about looking at your own hand, is there?"

Miss Silver had taken up her knitting again. She said with a smile,

"Sometimes if you look too long at a thing it gets out of focus. It may even look like something else."

Jennifer tossed back her dark untidy hair.

"Well then, it didn't! It looked like a hand. It just looked like my own hand—see?"

When she turned round she had put her hands out of sight behind her back. Now she thrust them out at Miss Silver, staring not at them, but at her.

"They're just my hands—they couldn't be anything else. I

don't know what you are talking about. They're just my hands."

Miss Silver continued to smile.

"And sadly dirty ones, my dear. It would be much easier for you to keep the nails clean if they were cut a good deal shorter. Your hands are a very nice shape. If you will allow me to cut your nails, you will not only find them much easier to keep clean, but a great deal pleasanter to look at."

She thought there was the beginning of a shudder, but it was controlled. With an abrupt movement Jennifer turned away and went over to the bookshelf, where she stood fingering the books, pulling one out a little way and pushing it back again, taking another down and fluttering the pages. Presently she said in a discontented voice,

"They're all as old as the hills. They belonged to the house. Did you know that? And the house used to belong to the Everlys. There aren't any of them left now. Miss Maria Everly was the last of them, and she died before the war. She was ninety-six years old. This was her schoolroom, and these were her books. There aren't any more Everlys. Old Mr. Masters told me about them. He's Mrs. Masters' father-in-law—he lives in the cottage with the post-box on the wall. He remembers Miss Maria Everly. He says she was a terror, but a real lady for all that. He says there aren't any left now—only bits of girls in breeches, and some that are old enough to know better. He's a very interesting person to talk to—I like going down there and talking to him. Only sometimes—" She frowned and broke off.

"Sometimes what, my dear?"

"Oh, nothing, He won't talk to everyone, you know—not about the Everlys. He says least said, soonest mended. You won't say I talked about them, will you? Did you know all the furniture in this room belonged to the house? It was the schoolroom, and nobody bothered to have things taken away. The good things were all sold, but *He* bought the rest when he bought the house."

Since Jennifer never gave Mr. Craddock any name, the pronoun no longer surprised Miss Silver. She let it pass without comment.

Jennifer pulled out another book. "*Ministering Children!*" she said in a tone of scorn. "I hate them!"

Miss Silver, who was familiar with this pious classic, remarked mildly that there were fashions in books just as there were fashions in clothes.

"They talked differently a hundred years ago, just as they dressed differently, but I do not think that they were at all different in themselves."

Jennifer rammed the *Ministering Children* back into their place.

"I hate them!" she said with emphasis. Then with a sudden and complete change of manner she turned round and came out with, "I saw Miss Tremlett, and I wasn't quick enough, so she saw me. She says they've got a paying guest coming. And why can't she just say lodger and have done with it? Paying guest is just nonsense, isn't it? If you're a guest you don't pay, and if you pay you're not a guest. That's all there is about it, and I shall just go on saying lodger. Every time I meet them I shall say it—'How is your lodger today, Miss Elaine? How do you like your lodger, Miss Gwyneth?' I wish I had said it to Elaine this morning. The lodger comes this afternoon, and they are going to give a party for her to meet everyone tomorrow. Gwyneth is taking the bus into Dedham this afternoon to buy cakes for it, and Elaine is going to make drop scones. And *He* will go, and I suppose you will too, but my mother won't, because I shall make her lie down on her bed and rest. And I think it would be a good plan if I locked her in."

Miss Silver shook her head.

"I do not think I should do that. It might alarm her very much."

Something like a shadow went across Jennifer's face. Her imagination had been pricked. She was thinking of being shut in—alone—in the dark. The scene sprang into view—hands beating on a locked door, shaking a fastened window—a voice sending out terrified screams—and at first they would be loud, and then choking, and then just a horrid whisper. And loud or soft, nobody would hear them. She stared at Miss Silver with dilated eyes and said in a shuddering voice,

"No—no—I won't lock her in. Nobody ought to be locked in—*really*. It's wicked!"

CHAPTER 13

IT WAS THAT EVENING after the children had gone to bed that the name of Mr. Sandrow emerged for the first time. Mr. Craddock was not present. His absence did not surprise Miss Silver, since he nearly always went away as soon as a meal was over, and often did not join the family at all. Sometimes Mrs. Craddock would load a tray and take it through to the main block where he had his study. The doors, one on each floor, which shut it off from the inhabited wing were kept locked, a precaution rendered necessary by the bombed state of the building. Mrs. Craddock would permit Jennifer, Maurice or Miss Silver to come with her as far as the locked door, but as soon as the key was turned and it had swung open she would take the tray and go through alone. The piece of passage disclosed was dark, dusty, and without other furniture than a small rough table upon which she could stand the tray whilst she locked the door behind her. Sometimes she merely put the tray down and returned immediately. Sometimes the door would be locked, and she would be absent for ten minutes or so. Every now and then she would repeat what she had said on the day of Miss Silver's arrival—"Mr. Craddock is engaged upon a great work. He must not be disturbed."

On this particular evening, as the two women sat by the schoolroom fire, the house was still and peaceful. Mrs. Craddock was patching Benjy's shorts, whilst Miss Silver, her knitting laid aside, was engaged in filling up two gaping holes in one of Maurice's jerseys. There had been a companionable silence for a time, when Mrs. Craddock gave a little sigh and said,

"It makes such a difference when there is someone to share the mending."

Miss Silver gave her small prim cough.

"Did not Miss Ball or Miss Dally help you with it?"

"Oh, no." There was another sigh. "They really were not

very much help. Miss Dally had no idea—she liked young men and parties. Of course she was quite young, so I suppose it was natural. And Miss Ball—I really was quite glad when she went. She seemed to dislike me, and that is a very uncomfortable feeling."

"And quite uncalled for, since I am sure you were all kindness to her, as you have been to me."

Mrs. Craddock sighed again.

"Oh, I don't know. Of course it was dull for her. But then there was Mr. Sandrow— I have always wondered if anything came of that. But of course he didn't come again, and she never wrote—"

With no more than an absent-minded interest in her voice, Miss Silver said,

"Mr. Sandrow?"

Emily Craddock said, "Yes." Her fingers smoothed the grey flannel patch, her needle took a stitch and halted. "I sometimes wondered whether we ought to have mentioned him, but Mr. Craddock said it wasn't our business. I don't know how old she was—but not a very young girl—she may have had her own reasons. Mr. Craddock thought we had no right to interfere."

"Had you any reason to suppose that she went away with this Mr. Sandrow?"

Emily looked startled.

"Oh, no—of course not. I only thought— She didn't write, but then why should she? She was only here for such a short time, and she didn't like us—there was really no reason. But she didn't write to her friends either. Someone came down only the other day to make enquiries. She hadn't any relations, I believe, but there was a friend who was worried at not hearing from her. Only people don't always write, do they, and she may not have wanted to keep up with her friend. She was a moody sort of girl."

"The friend was trying to trace her?"

"Oh, yes. Someone came by—from the police, I think, only not in uniform. But of course there wasn't anything we could say."

Miss Silver was picking up run-down stitches on Maurice's left sleeve, using a darning needle in a very expert manner. She paused for a moment to look at Emily Craddock and say,

"And now you feel that you ought to have spoken of Mr. Sandrow?"

"There was so little to say," said Emily in a distressed

voice. "I only saw him once—quite at a distance, and it was getting dark. There was a car at the gate, and I just saw him stop and drive on again. She had been out for the afternoon, you know. We walked up the drive together, and she had that excited way with her, but when I asked her whether her friend wouldn't have come in she changed and said no, he didn't like a crowd."

"How extremely rude."

"Yes, I thought so. And then she laughed and said quite angrily, 'Two is company, isn't it?' She didn't say any more, and I didn't like to. Her tone was really quite rude."

"But she told you his name?"

Emily had her startled look.

"No—no—I don't think she did. I think it must have been somebody else—perhaps one of the children."

"She spoke of him to the children?"

"I think she must have done—because of the name. . . . Yes, it was Jennifer, because I thought it sounded as if it might be Italian—Sandro, you know. But she said it wasn't. She said it was R O W."

Miss Silver remarked in a meditative voice,

"If Miss Ball was so reserved about her affairs, it seems strange that she should have talked to Jennifer."

"Oh, I don't know. We had a governess when I was twelve, and she told me all about being engaged to a young man who was a missionary in China. When you are in love with someone you do want to talk about them. I think the children may have teased her about his being Italian, and that made her explain that he wasn't and tell them how the name was really spelt."

"Did they ever see him?"

"I don't think so. Jennifer did say he was very goodlooking, but I think that was only what Miss Ball had told her. I think Elaine Tremlett saw him once or perhaps it was Gwyneth. She said he had red hair, which doesn't sound at all Italian, does it?"

"Did Miss Ball see much of him?"

"Oh, I don't know. She used to slip out in the evenings—it was one of the things I didn't like. And people talked."

Miss Silver reflected that they had not talked to Detective Inspector Abbott. It became apparent that Emily Craddock had told all she knew about Mr. Sandrow. Anna Ball had neither said where he came from or how long they had known each other. After that momentary outburst in the dark drive she had gone back into her silent antagonism, and a few days later had taken her departure, a good deal to Emily Craddock's relief.

"I did try to be nice to her," she said in her plaintive voice. "We didn't like her, but we did try. We gave her a red hat."

"A red hat?"

"Mr. Craddock thought it would cheer her up," said Emily.

CHAPTER 14

THE MISS TREMLETTS were very proud of their converted stable. By knocking down partitions between the stalls a large living-room had been contrived, with a kitchenette and a bathroom beyond, whilst a staircase ran up with what they considered a most decorative effect to three bedrooms above.

"So nice to have room to give a party," as Miss Elaine said. "Our cottage at Wyshmere was *most* picturesque, but so very small and so very dark. Leaded panes, you know—and quite authentic, so it would have been impossible to replace them, but they let in so *very* little light. And though, of course, candles or even rushlights would be more in character, we cannot help feeling *most* grateful for the supply of electricity from dear Peveril's installation."

Miss Silver found the room a little too suggestive of a barn. Its plain whitewashed walls did not appeal to her. What she admired was a nice wallpaper with a satin stripe or bunches of flowers. She did not think that the chairs looked as if they would be comfortable. They had angular armchair shapes and were entirely destitute of upholstery. Hand-made rugs strewed the floor. Miss Gwyneth's loom stood by one of the windows.

Miss Elaine, small and thin in a pea-green smock, and Miss Gwyneth, larger and inclined to billow in a sacklike garment of peacock-blue, were both all that was welcoming and kind. That the welcome was more particularly directed towards Mr. Craddock did not at all surprise Miss Silver, since from the first moment of her arrival in Deep End it had been made perfectly plain to her that everything in Harmony revolved round him. The sisters were polite to her and affectionate to "dear Emily," but their deference, their enthusiasms, their flutterings centred upon Peveril. They fluttered a good deal, assisted by a flowing of scarves and a jingle of beads. With her pea-green smock Miss Elaine wore a necklet of blue and silver beads from Venice and a long string of Chinese amber, whilst Miss Gwyneth's peacock curves supported a short row of cornelians and two longer strings, one of pink coral and the other filagree silver and amethyst. Miss Elaine had fair, faded hair in a pre-Raphaelite knot on the nape of her neck. Miss Gwyneth wore hers, which was grey and rather sparse, in a long straight bob to the shoulder which gave her an odd resemblance to some French abbé of the eighteenth century.

Miss Silver's hand was pressed by Miss Elaine.

"We hope you are going to like being here. We are a friendly Community."

It was pressed by Miss Gwyneth.

"It is not the best time of the year for the country, but each season has its beauty. Are you a nature-lover?"

It being her private opinion that the country was a cold and draughty place and only too apt to be lacking in modern conveniences, Miss Silver found it best to make a noncommittal reply. She was able to say with truth that she had spent a good deal of time in country places.

"And if one is interested in one's work, surroundings are of secondary importance."

Miss Elaine said vaguely,

"Ah, yes—the children. They interest you?"

Miss Elaine fidgeted with her amber beads.

"They are a little uncontrolled, but of course, as Peveril says, one can only guide, never thwart the expression of the ego. But if you are *interested,* that is the great thing. And such a privilege to work with *him!*"

A little later on it was Miss Gwyneth who, in a louder voice and with greater freedom of gesture, emphasised the privilege alluded to by Miss Elaine.

"I hope you appreciate it, but I am sure you do. Those two girls did *not*—Miss Ball and Miss Dally. Not the right type at all, either of them—Miss Dally so thoughtless, and Miss Ball so wrapped up in herself. The real teacher must be ready to *give*—my sister and I feel that so strongly. Now I am sure *you*—But let me introduce you to Miranda."

Miss Silver's hand was taken and held in a clasp which became oppressive

"We have met!" said Miranda in her deepest voice. She drew Miss Silver aside. "We will not say where. It is not an auspicious spot. You have not brought the children? Perhaps it is as well. The harmony of a social gathering is so easily disturbed. I find Boys a disturbing element. They are crude and violent. But something might be made of Jennifer. There are points of interest, but she is in revolt against her circumstances. Even against Peveril. Strange! He is very patient, very forbearing. He will not thwart her. But his friends cannot help being indignant on his behalf. Such a marvellous opportunity for the child and she does not appreciate it! Adolescence? Perhaps! It is a time of ferment and revolt! Very trying for poor Emily. The maternal instinct is strong in her, but she is devoted to Peveril."

Under these rather odd phrases Miss Silver discerned a homely desire to gossip about the Craddocks. Encouraging this, she found herself on a comfortless oak settle with Miranda. The subject of Emily's maternal instinct was pursued. It appeared that she had been in the habit of going upstairs to kiss her children good-night, and that Peveril had put a stop to it as likely to result in a mother-fixation.

"I do not know that I agree. These psychological terms! A little extreme! And Benjy is only four. It is at these times that a mother wins her children's confidence."

It was not in the least necessary for Miss Silver to reply, since Miranda was always ready to go on talking. This was fortunate, because she had no desire to be quoted as disapproving of Mr. Craddock. She listened with interest to a description of his aura, and to the assertion that he was intensely psychic.

"Had he given his mind to it he would have been a wonderful medium. But he resists. I have told him so plainly. I have said, 'Peveril, you resist,' and he has not denied it. His work lies in other directions—he has told me so. You know, of course, that he is engaged upon a Monumental Work. It was very good of him to come this afternoon. Most gratifying for Gwyneth and Elaine, but they should not expect him to waste his time at social functions. They adore him of course. Gwyneth wove the stuff of that white smock, and Elaine embroidered it with the Signs of the Zodiac. It is very becoming, but I do not know that Emily was pleased. She is no needlewoman, and does not rise above the mending-basket."

Miss Silver coughed.

"There is a good deal of mending."

Miranda was attired in a long black velvet robe. It was low in the neck, and the hanging sleeves disclosed a pair of strong white arms. Her red hair had been combed and was partially confined by a purple fillet. It threatened to break loose now as she made a vigorous gesture.

"There should not be so much. The children wear nothing but shorts and jerseys. Jennifer should do her own mending. Even Maurice could learn to use a darning-needle. Emily has the slave mentality. She allows herself to be Put On." She contrived to invest this homely phrase with a gloomy significance which persisted through an enumeration of other weak points in Emily Craddock's character.

"She cannot cook." Miranda's tone was tragic. "I have tasted lentils there which were not fit for human consumption. I will not say that I have eaten them. That was Impossible! The position was serious—we feared for Peveril's health. But Mrs. Masters now prepares the meals before she leaves. She cannot, of course, do the housework as well, and since it is beyond Emily's strength, I fear that much of it remains undone. Marriage makes more demands upon women than it did. They should learn to cook and to make use of labour-saving appliances. But when I suggested a vacuum-cleaner, Emily asserted that it would use too much current. Now I happen to *know* that the electric light installation is an extremely powerful one. I said to her, 'Emily, you are being obstructive,' and she could not deny it. She is one of those people who appear to yield but contrive to get their own way. In the matter of the electric current she does not know what she is talking about. I do not believe in concealing my opinion. I told her so."

It was at this moment that a door opened at the head of the stairs and Thomasina Elliot appeared. She wore a grey dress which matched her eyes, and she had a most becoming colour in her cheeks. As it happened, she saw Miss Silver before Miss Silver saw her. Since she had known that they would meet, the sight did not surprise her. Her colour deepened a little, but she continued on her way down. She had in fact reached the seventh step, when Miranda exclaimed and Miss Silver looked up. She did not require the information contained in a contralto whisper, but she undoubtedly sustained a shock. Not only was she quite unprepared for the appearance of Thomasina Elliot, but nothing could have given her less pleasure. With commendable self-control she turned to Miranda.

"You said—?"

"Elaine and Gwyneth's paying guest. They have one sometimes, but not generally so young. They knew this girl's aunt in Wyshmere."

Thomasina had reached the foot of the stairs. She was being introduced to Emily, to Peveril, to the little man in a blue blouse who was Augustus Remington, to Miranda, to Miss Silver herself.

"This is our young friend, Ina Elliot. We have delightful recollections of her aunt, Mrs. Brandon."

Miss Silver took her cue. Since Thomasina was being introduced as a stranger, strangers they would be. She said in a reserved tone,

"How do you do, Miss Elliot? Are you making a long stay?"

Thomasina was not insensitive. She was prepared for disapproval, but she had not known that it would affect her so unpleasantly. She had not felt so much in the wrong since her first year at school. It was most dreadfully undermining. She found herself tripping over her words.

"I d—don't know. It d—depends."

Miss Silver continued to look through her. She said,

"Town is, I think, preferable at this time of year, unless there is work that takes one into the country. But that would not be your case."

Thomasina said, "N—no." She had not stammered since she was ten years old. She was furious with herself and with Miss Silver.

Miss Elaine struck in.

"We hope that she will stay as long as she can. Such a pleasure. But she must not find it dull. Now I wonder—" she addressed Miss Silver—"if you and the children are walking tomorrow, whether she might join you. She is so very fond of children—are you not, my dear?"

"If I shouldn't be in the way—" said Thomasina Elliot.

There was a pleading note in her voice, but Miss Silver's look did not soften. She gave a grave assent and turned from Thomasina to meet Augustus Remington, brought up to her by Miss Gwyneth. He was a slender creature, pale and wispy, like a plant that has grown in the dark—hair of the colour called lint-white in Scotland, soft and unsubstantial as a baby's—slender hands, slender feet—rather indeterminate features. He wore blue corduroy trousers and a belted blouse of the same pattern as Mr. Craddock's but without embroidery. He had a whispering way of talking, and used his hands a good deal.

"Miranda has told me about you. She said you were psychic

—or did she—I don't know. Perhaps she said you were not psychic—I have a most distressing memory, and Miranda talks so much. Now, are you, or are you not?"

"I have no claim to being psychic, Mr. Remington."

He threw up his hands in horror.

"Not that formal name! The legacy of ancestors from whom one strives to free oneself! Besides, too, too suggestive of the typewriter! Could anything be more repugnant! What distasteful visions it calls up—rattle, rattle, rattle—click, click, click! Could anything describe me less! No—call me Augustus! It suggests the spacious peace of summer days—mellow pastures—the lap of water—the murmur of bees and of the homing dove. What is your name?"

In the interests of her profession Miss Silver was prepared for many sacrifices, but there were limits. She was not prepared to be called Maud by Augustus Remington. She said primly,

"I prefer to be addressed as Miss Silver."

CHAPTER 15

"You SHOULD NOT have come," said Miss Silver on a note of severity.

Thomasina's colour brightened.

"I just felt I had to."

Ahead of them, Jennifer ran up the sloping path with the other two after her. She was fleet of foot and the boys could not catch her. She had time to stop and wave to them, or hurl insulting names as Slowworm, Tortoise, Dilly-dally. The afternoon was grey, but in the west the clouds had broken to show a stretch of pale faint blue.

Miss Silver shook her head disapprovingly.

"It is most unwise to give way to impulse. Have you considered that Miss Ball may have spoken of you to the Craddocks?"

"Anna never spoke about people."

"Or that they may have seen the advertisement you put in the *Times*— 'Anna, where are you? Do write. Thomasina.' Anyone who had read that might find the juxtaposition of these two names suggestive."

Thomasina could not wait for her to finish.

"But that is just why I am calling myself Ina. Even if Anna had talked—and she wouldn't—Ina doesn't suggest anything, does it? It's quite a different kind of name. And it's not like taking a name that doesn't belong to me. I did think about doing that, but it gave me a rather horrid sort of feeling, and I thought I wouldn't."

If Miss Silver felt that she had to be thankful for small mercies, she could at least be relieved that Thomasina had not presented herself under an assumed name. She said,

"It is all most unwise, but now that you are here we must make the best of it. You will, I hope, limit your stay to a very few days."

Thomasina looked doubtful.

"Well, I don't know. They are rather pets, you know, Miss Elaine and Miss Gwyneth—and I thought I'd like to learn weaving."

"It would be most imprudent."

There was protest in Thomasina's voice.

"I don't see why. The longer I stay and the more I learn weaving, the more it will look as if that is what I have come down for. And it's all quite natural. They did know Aunt Barbara, and they were very fond of her, and I like hearing them talk about her, and I don't see why I shouldn't learn weaving if I want to. And please don't be disapproving, because it spoils everything. Peter was just horrid about my coming here, and if you are going to be angry too—"

Miss Silver was reflecting that the milk was spilled, and that it was no good crying over it. As Thomasina was here, she might as well stay. In point of fact, there was no way of dislodging her. She therefore smiled and said,

"I am not angry."

Thomasina brightened.

"Peter was horrid," she said. "And it isn't his business what I do or where I go. He isn't even a real relation—he is just Aunt Barbara's husband's nephew."

Saying this seemed to put Peter in his place. It produced a glow of satisfaction—very heartening for the moment, but almost immediately succeeded by a horrid feeling that complete independence with no bothering relations and Peter a long way off was rather a chilly business. The glow faded, and she gave the kind of shiver that makes country people say that a goose is walking over your grave. She spoke quickly,

"Oh, I've got a message for you—I was nearly forgetting!"

"From Mr. Brandon?"

"Oh, no—from Detective Inspector Abbott. I went to see Mrs. Moray like you said, and he was there. He seems to know a lot of the sort of people you wouldn't expect a policeman to know."

"He has a great many friends."

"He didn't seem a bit like a policeman when he was at Mrs. Moray's. He asked me out to dinner, and we went to the Luxe and danced. He dances very well."

"I believe so."

"That was one of the things that Peter was angry about. And it wasn't his business. He hadn't asked me himself, so why should he be angry because Frank Abbott did? I enjoyed myself very much. There was a girl called Daphne there who Frank said was his cousin. I liked her."

"He has a great many cousins."

"He said he started counting them once, and when he got up to a hundred he thought he had better stop—but of course that was nonsense."

Miss Silver was unable to deny that Frank Abbott when off duty was given to talking nonsense. She had reproved him for it too often. She smiled indulgently and said,

"He gave you a message for me?"

"Yes, he did. He said it would be safer than writing. He said letters might be opened and I'd better post myself and be careful what I said. And I said I shouldn't be writing to anyone, because after the things Peter said—"

Miss Silver did not permit herself to be impatient. She gathered that Mr. Brandon had not behaved with tact, and that his remarks had considerably stiffened Thomasina's determination to go down to Deep End and stay with the Miss Tremletts. When she had received a graphic account of the ensuing quarrel she said mildly,

"And Inspector Abbott's message? Had you not better let me have it?"

Thomasina came back from some way off.

"Didn't I? Oh, no—I got off on to Peter—I'm sorry. He wants—Frank, I mean, not Peter—he wants to see you. He wants you to meet him in Ledlington. Tomorrow. He says there's a bus from Deeping that gets there just before three, and will you get off at the station, and he'll pick you up in his car. He says you can ask for the afternoon off. If you don't come, he'll know you couldn't make it. But he said to come if you can, because he really does want to see you."

Miss Silver considered all this. To allow any connection between herself and Scotland Yard to appear would be to make her position at Deepe House untenable. She was not convinced that she was accomplishing any useful purpose by remaining there, but Frank Abbott's message did at least suggest that he might have something useful to communicate. Up to the present the only really suspicious circumstance that had come to her notice was the fact that her letter to Margaret Moray had been opened. She very much disliked the idea that it might have been one of the children who had opened it, but it was possible, and she was too honest to disregard a possibility. As regards Anna Ball, she had discovered no more than that there had been some talk about a Mr. Sandrow, a shadowy and insubstantial person glimpsed in the dusk by Mrs. Craddock and seen, perhaps, by one of the Miss Tremletts.

She had reached this point, when Thomasina said,

"And now you won't be angry any more, will you? Because I've got things to tell you. The Miss Tremletts talk all the time you know. They just go on and on and on. As soon as Elaine stops Gwyneth begins. They sat till half past twelve last night doing it—all about Wyshmere and Aunt Barbara, and weaving and folk-dancing, and how wonderful Peveril was. But I don't think they think an awful lot about Emily, though they were quite kind. Just pointing out her faults, you know, and saying what a pity it was for Peveril, and how unrestrained the children were, and of course it would be all wrong to repress them, but some people could manage children and other people couldn't. And they seemed to think you were one of the ones who could. But not Anna or the other girl who only stayed a week."

Miss Silver smiled.

"I have had considerable experience."

"Well, I was just getting to the stage when I was missing quite a lot of what they said, when they got to Anna and that woke me up. Do you know, there really was a man."

"Mr. Sandrow?"

"Oh, you do know about him." Thomasina's tone was frankly disappointed. "Who told you?"

"Mrs. Craddock mentioned him, but I really know very little."

"Well, this is what the Tremletts told me. They said Anna used to slip out quite late at night and meet him, and they didn't think it was at all nice. Elaine went down to post a letter at the gate because it was a fine night and she wanted a breath of air and she was going to be busy in the morning. And there were two people standing very close together just off the drive, a man and a girl. The lodge is empty, so she thought it was odd. She said, 'Who is that?' and the man turned round and walked away out of the gate. Well, she had a torch, and she turned it on, and the girl was Anna. So she said, 'Who was that?' and Anna said, 'Mr. Sandrow.' Elaine had her letter in her hand, but of course Anna and the young man were much more interesting, so she said, 'I will walk up the drive with you. Who is Mr. Sandrow?' And Anna said, 'Oh, just a friend of mine. Hadn't you better post your letter, if that's what you came for' "

"That was not very polite."

Thomasina said earnestly,

"Oh, but Anna *wasn't.* That's what made it so difficult—about her making friends, you know. She used to be rude, and then she would go on about people not liking her. You see, unless she had a crush on anyone she just wouldn't bother."

Miss Silver deplored the expression which Thomasina had used, but she did not feel that this was the time to comment on it. There were points of interest. She said,

"Miss Ball was liable to sudden violent fancies?"

"Yes, but they didn't generally come to anything. People didn't really like it—she was too intense."

"Then she may have taken one of these fancies for this Mr. Sandrow."

"Oh, yes."

"Did either of the Miss Tremletts see him again?"

"Yes, they did. Gwyneth was in Ledlington, and whilst she was waiting for her bus she saw a car go by. She said Anna Ball was driving it, and there was a man with her. She said he had a red beard and red hair. She really was rather offended, because she thought they might have picked her up and given her a lift back to Deep End."

"Perhaps they did not see her."

"She swears Anna did. She has very good sight, and you know, you really can always tell. She says Anna looked straight at her and went by. Of course if I was out with somebody I liked, I don't suppose I should want to pick Gwyneth up." Thomasina's eyes danced for a moment.

Miss Silver repeated the proverb with which Anna Ball had so rudely rebuffed Mrs. Craddock.

"Two is company. But, my dear, all this conversation about

Miss Ball—it sounds a little as if the Miss Tremletts were aware that you had an interest."

"Oh, no—not really. They talk about everyone. Do you know, old Mr. Masters in the cottage with the post-box is as jealous as he can be because the postman's father-in-law is going to be a hundred next year, and he is only ninety-seven or something. And Mrs. Hogbin who lives next door but two has had thirteen children, and they are all alive and doing well. One of them sends her a parcel every week. And Mr. Tupper who works in a nursery garden the other side of Deeping has had two lots of wisdom teeth."

"My dear!"

Thomasina nodded.

"And Miranda is a very pleasant neighbour, and of course there's nothing wrong about it, but they do think it isn't quite *wise* to see so much of Augustus Remington—living next door, you know, and running in and out all the time. And then there is Mr. Robinson. So strange that he should live like that—just one man with a whole wing of the house to himself—no one to cook or do anything for him, and half the windows boarded up. And he won't go anywhere except to watch birds—not even to their parties, which does seem so very strange. They had been going on like that for hours before they got to Anna."

Maurice came running back to them, red-faced and out of breath.

"Jennifer says we'll be in the wood, and if you want us you can coo-ee!"

"That will do very nicely, Maurice."

He ran off again, kicking his heels and waving his arms. Remembering the unheralded flight of all the three children on their first walk together, it was impossible for Miss Silver not to feel some gratification.

When he had gone she said,

"Miss Ball never mentioned a man friend to you?"

"No, never. I thought she told me everything, but—I suppose she didn't."

In Miss Silver's experience no one ever did.

Thomasina went on speaking.

"And there's another thing she never told me. I didn't know that she could drive. I suppose she learned when she was in Germany—she didn't tell me."

"And she never mentioned the name of Sandrow?"

"She didn't mention it, but—I was going to tell you. When

I didn't get any answer to my advertisement, I sent for her box. You know, the one she had forwarded to me when she came down here. It wasn't any use leaving it up there, and I thought I would go through it again, just in case there was anything that would give a clue. I thought there might be something I had missed."

"A most sensible course. And you found something?"

"I didn't think I had—not till Gwyneth and Elaine were talking last night. Now I'm not sure. I'll tell you. One of the things in the box was an old handbag. The clasp didn't hold any more, so I expect that was why she didn't take it with her. Well, I went through it, and it was empty except for a torn-off piece of paper crushed down behind the mirror, and the glass was broken. And there was this bit of paper crumpled up behind it. It was just a piece off one of those thin blocks, with names scribbled on it—Sandro, spelt the Italian way, S A N D R O. And then with a W tacked on—Sandrow. And then spelled a lot of other ways—I can't remember them all—things like Sindrow—Sendrow. I just didn't think anything of it at the time, but now—it's odd, isn't it?"

Miss Silver thought it very odd indeed. She said so.

It was on their way home that she had her first sight of Mr. John Robinson, the tenant of the other wing. The children, who had made friends with Thomasina, were all talking at once. They wanted her to come home to tea with them, and when she said that the Miss Tremletts would be expecting her they took her by the arms and ran with her down the slope and across the unkempt grass.

By the time Miss Silver, at a more sedate pace, came up with them they were in the dank courtyard looking up at the blind and mutilated face of the house. Benjy was saying,

"And there's nothing left inside—only spiders, and dust, and Papa's study what we mustn't never go near because of his book that he's writing, and because of the stones that might fall on us."

His childish voice set up an echo. The word "fall" came back from the enclosing wings. The air still trembled with it as John Robinson came round the corner to the left and stood for a moment on the outskirts of the group.

Afterwards, when Miss Silver tried to formulate a description of him, she found that it would have fitted so many other people as to be of very little value. He was neither tall nor short. He seemed to be of a slim build, but his clothes were so loose and baggy that even this might be in doubt, since a loose raincoat may hide a sagging waist-line. Beneath the raincoat aged flannel trousers and deplorable boots. Above, a long woollen muffler of uncertain shade. And above that a short beard, shaggy eyebrows, and an unkempt head of brown hair just flecked with grey. He stood, he looked—at Miss Silver in her black cloth coat, her elderly fur tippet, and her second-best hat; at Thomasina, glowing from her run; at the children, laughing and whispering with her. He looked, and spoke with a marked country accent.

"Youth at the prow—and Prudence—at the helm," he said, and on this misquotation walked rapidly away, leaving Miss Silver quite a little surprised and not at all sure that she cared about being alluded to as Prudence by a total stranger. Better that, it is true, than the "Pleasure" of the original, but why the quotation at all?

As soon as he was gone the children bubbled over with information about him.

"That was Mr. Robinson."

"Mr. John Robinson."

"He watches birds—he knows an awful lot about them. He goes out all night and watches them."

"And in the day too."

Maurice said, "He's batty!" And Jennifer, "He's always like that if you meet him—he just says something and goes away. Sometimes it's poetry, and sometimes it isn't. In the village they say he's mad because he goes about talking to himself up in the woods and on the common, but old Mr. Masters says, 'Why shouldn't he if he wants to? There's a lot of people that are not so interesting to talk to as what you are yourself.' "

Thomasina went back to the stables, and was ten minutes late for tea with the Miss Tremletts.

CHAPTER 16

Mr. Craddock was present at supper, where he dominated the conversation. During the soup he discoursed upon Alchemy and the Philosopher's Stone, but by the time they were all eating boiled fish he had diverged into a long and very involved dissertation upon Planetary Influences, to which nobody except Miss Silver appeared to pay any attention. Mrs. Craddock occupied herself with serving, and every now and then said "Oh, yes," or "Oh, no," as the occasion appeared to demand. The children ate their fish. Once at least Jennifer's eyes went to her stepfather's face in a long, bright stare. There was anger in it and something else, but when he turned to meet it the dark lashes came down. She reached out, helping herself to salt, and some of it spilled between them. Not a comfortable meal! But then Deepe House was not a comfortable house.

Mr. Craddock's sentences got longer and longer, and their meaning less apparent, until with the arrival of a cold and naked looking blancmange Benjy broke into a roar.

"Don't want it! Don't like it! Won't eat it!"

Mrs. Craddock said, "Ssh!" in a guilty voice, and then, "Mrs. Masters must have forgotten. I did tell her—nobody liked it."

"She likes making it," said Maurice with angry gloom.

Jennifer said accusingly, "If you didn't have cornflour in the house, she couldn't make it."

Mrs. Craddock helped the horrid whiteness with a trembling hand. Mr. Craddock had as yet said nothing, but he looked as if he might at any moment let fly with a thunderbolt. Instead, he merely pushed back his chair and left the table.

Nobody ate the cornflour shape except Miss Silver, but after Mr. Craddock's departure the children partook of hearty slices of bread and jam whilst competing cheerfully as to who could say the most insulting things about the rejected blancmange.

Later on when they were in bed, Mrs. Craddock recurred to the incident. The darning needle shook in her hand as she said,

"I am such a very bad manager, and I cannot cook at all well. Everything seems to go wrong when I try."

"But you have Mrs. Masters to do the cooking," said Miss Silver.

"She despises me," said Emily Craddock in a helpless voice. "She knows that I cannot do the things myself, so she takes no notice of anything I say. I have told her over and over again that Mr. Craddock will not sit at a table with a blancmange, and the children hate it. But it is so easy to do, and when she is in a hurry she will make it."

Miss Silver coughed.

"If you did not have any cornflour—"

"Then she uses sago, and that is worse."

"Perhaps if you did not have any sago—"

"She would find something else," said Mrs. Craddock in a despairing voice. A tear dropped upon a much darned under-garment. "Sometimes I feel as if I couldn't go on. If it were not for you—" She sniffed faintly.

Miss Silver said with gravity,

"You require rest and relief from responsibility. Jennifer and Maurice would be far better at school—even Benjy."

Emily Craddock gave a startled cry.

"Oh, no, *no!* I couldn't! Mr. Craddock wouldn't approve—and I shouldn't feel they were safe. He says it is foolish of me, but I can't help feeling frightened about them when they are away. You see, I very nearly lost them all last summer."

"My dear Mrs. Craddock!"

The tears were running down Emily Craddock's face.

"Such a pleasant seaside holiday, but I nearly lost them all—and Mr. Craddock too. They were all out in the boat, and it overturned. I was having my afternoon rest—and they were nearly drowned—all of them. It took them a long time to bring Benjy round. None of the children could swim."

"And Mr. Craddock?"

"Only a little—just enough to keep himself afloat. He couldn't help them. If it hadn't been for some men in another boat . . . . . It gave me such a terrible shock. I don't seem to get over it." She fumbled for a handkerchief and pressed it to her eyes.

Casting about for a change of subject, Miss Silver recalled the meeting with Mr. John Robinson. It would, she considered, divert Mrs. Craddock from an agitating topic, and at the same time gratify her own strong desire for information about the tenant of the other wing. She introduced the name in a bright conversational manner, adding,

"He came up and spoke to us out in the courtyard this afternoon when we came back from our walk."

Mrs. Craddock had stopped crying. She had a fluttered look. She said,

"Oh—" And then, "Was he at all—strange?"

Miss Silver was putting the final touches to the pale blue coatée. She said,

"He quoted a line of poetry."

"He does—at least I believe—I have heard that he does. You know, I've never spoken to him myself. He is—" she hesitated for a word— "rather strange. Quite solitary, I believe. He has been here for some months, but I have only seen him just once or twice in the distance. It does seem strange, but I am sure he is quite harmless. He speaks to the children sometimes. I used to worry about it, but last autumn— Oh, Miss Silver, they had such a narrow escape—and it was all due to him—so whatever people say about him, I shall always be grateful."

Miss Silver fastened off her thread and ran it in along a seam. It was not until she had completed this task that she said,

"They had an escape?"

Emily Craddock's thin hands were clasping one another convulsively.

"Oh, *yes!* It was when that Miss Ball was with us—and of course she didn't understand that sort of thing at all. They went out to look for mushrooms, and they found some very fine ones up on the edge of the pinewood over the hill. And when they were coming home they met Mr. Robinson, and he said where had they found so many, and when they told him he looked at them and said they weren't mushrooms at all, but some horrid poisonous thing. He said real mushrooms didn't grow near pine trees, but something that looks very like them does, and he made them throw them all out. Of course it wasn't Miss Ball's fault, for how could she know—but it upset me *dreadfully,* and of course I couldn't help feeling so very grateful to Mr. Robinson, because if he hadn't happened to meet them—"

"It was indeed providential," said Miss Silver.

CHAPTER 17

Miss Silver woke up in the dark. One moment there had been a vague but pleasant dream, the next she was broad awake and considering what it was that had awakened her. It was just as if she had stepped from one room into another and closed the door behind her. But in the moment of that passing there had been a sound, and she thought that the sound had been a scream. There was a reading-lamp beside her bed. She turned it on and saw that the hands of her watch stood between one and two. The sound might have come from outside—an owl cry perhaps, but she did not think so. She thought it came from the room next door—from Jennifer's room. There was a communicating door, but it had been locked ever since she came, with no sign of a key on either side. She got up, put on her slippers and a warm blue dressing-gown, and went out into the passage.

Of the five bedrooms in use four were on this side of the stairs—Jennifer next to herself, Mrs. Craddock and the little boys across the way. Beyond the well of the stairs, in the direction of the main building, Mr. Craddock's room looked out upon the courtyard.

The passage was unlit from end to end. Miss Silver stood in the dark and listened. A sound came to her from the room next to hers—something between a groan and a sob. She went quietly to the door and opened it. The room was quite dark, except where the square of the window showed faintly against a denser gloom. Between it and the opened door a light air moved. A curtain stirred, blew out, and fell again. Jennifer's gasping voice said,

"No—no—*no!* Take it away!"

Miss Silver came into the room, turned on the light, and shut the door behind her. Jennifer sat bolt upright, her hands pressing down upon the bed on either side of her, her pose rigid, her eyes wide, her dark hair wild. She did not look at Miss Silver, because she did not see her. What she saw was a picture in a dream, and the dream was horrible.

Miss Silver went over to the bed, sat down upon it, and laid her hand gently over one of those straining ones. At once the pose broke up. Both Jennifer's hands clutched at her, held to her. The blankness went from the eyes. They gazed in terror, then focussed on Miss Silver, not in full recognition but with a piteous effect of groping.

Miss Silver said, at her kindest and most matter-of-fact,

"It is quite all right, my dear. You have been dreaming."

The child's grip was frightening. Miss Silver did not bruise easily, but she kept the mark of those fingers for days. Jennifer said in a horrid whisper,

"It was the Hand."

"It was a dream, my dear."

There was a long, deep sigh.

"You didn't see it."

"It was a dream. There was nothing to see."

This time the sigh became a shudder that shook the bed.

"You didn't see it. I did."

Miss Silver said firmly,

"Jennifer, my dear, there is nothing to see. You have had a

bad dream and it has frightened you, but now you are awake again. There is nothing to frighten you any more. If you will let go of me I will get you a glass of water."

She would not have thought it possible that Jennifer's grasp could have tightened, but it seemed to do so. The thin body shook, the eyes stared. Words came tumbling out.

"You don't know—you didn't see it! Mr. Masters told me—I thought it was just a story—I did—I did! I didn't think it was true!"

"What did he tell you, my dear?"

Jennifer went on staring and shaking.

"About the Everlys—why there aren't any more of them. There weren't any boys. There was old Miss Maria, only she wasn't old then, and there was Clarice, and Isabella—three of them—and there was a man, and he was their cousin, but they couldn't all marry him. Mr. Masters said it was a pity, because then it wouldn't have happened like it did."

Miss Silver coughed.

"A very foolish and improper remark, my dear."

"It wouldn't have happened," said Jennifer—"not if he could have married them *all*. Solomon had a thousand wives, and he was in the Bible. Mr. Masters said one was trouble enough for most, and three to one wasn't fair odds, but it would have been better if the cousin could have married the three of them, because then Isabella wouldn't—" She choked on a caught breath.

"What did Isabella do?" said Miss Silver gravely.

"She killed her." Jennifer's whisper crawled with horror. "He was going to marry Clarice, and she killed her—with the axe—out of the wood-shed. She cut her hand right off—the one with the ring he had given her. They said she was mad—and shut her up. And Maria went on living here all by herself until she died, and there weren't any more Everlys."

"A terrible story, my dear. It was very wrong of Mr. Masters to speak of it."

Jennifer shuddered.

"He had to—it wasn't his fault. I told him about the doors being kept locked into the big house. And I told him I was going in to explore, and he said I mustn't do it, because—" she tripped and stumbled over the words—"because of the hand—because of Clarice's hand."

"My dear—"

"He said people saw it. He said there was a boy—a long time ago—he saw it, and—he never spoke again."

"Then, my dear, how did anyone know what he had seen?"

Jennifer gave an impatient jerk.

"I don't know— Mr. Masters said . . . . . And there was a girl—she got drowned. She used to work here—her name was Mary Cheeseman. She used to say she didn't believe in any such tales, and she found a way to get in. At least I think she did—she wouldn't tell. And she got drowned going home. Pushed down in the bog, Mr. Masters said—'Like as if it was a hand had pushed her.'"

"Mr. Masters is a foolish and superstitious old man. I do not think that any of his stories lose in the telling. I have heard about poor Mary. It was a rainy night, and she missed the bridge and wandered into the bog."

Jennifer sat up straight, her face quite close to Miss Silver's, her eyes unnaturally bright.

"Did she?" she said. "*Did she?*" She let go of Miss Silver as suddenly as she had clutched her. "Perhaps she did. You don't know, and I don't know, and Mr. Masters doesn't know." Her voice dropped to a mere breath. "I know what I saw."

"What did you see, Jennifer?"

The long lashes drooped. From under them something looked, and was gone. Hope—uncertainty—fear? Miss Silver wasn't sure. Jennifer said,

"You wouldn't believe if I told you. People don't—not if they don't want to." Then, without any change in her voice, "I can unlock the door into your room. I hid the key because of Miss Ball. This used to be the dressing-room, you know. If the door is open, I don't expect I shall have another bad dream —shall I? My mother used to let me have a night-light, but he said not to."

"It is more restful to sleep in the dark."

Jennifer was getting out of bed. She turned a scornful glance on Miss Silver.

"Is it?" she said.

CHAPTER 18

LEDLINGTON HAS a good many points in common with other county towns. Some of it is old and picturesque, and some of it is not. In the years between the two world wars its approaches have been cluttered up with small houses of every type and shape. When these have been passed, there are the tall, ugly houses of the late Victorian period with their basements, their attics, their dismal outlook upon the shrubberies which screen them from the road. Still farther on a beautiful Georgian house or two, or, older still, the mellow red brick and hooded porch of Queen Anne's time—comfortable houses in their day, converted now for the most part to offices and flats. Here the road narrows to the High Street, winding amongst houses which were built in Elizabethan days. New fronts have been added to some, incongruous plate-glass windows front the street. A turning on one side, very competently blocked by the quiet hideous monument erected under William IV to a former mayor, leads to the station. Nothing more inconvenient could possibly have been devised, but the answer of course is that nobody devised it. Like nearly everything else in England it just happened that way. Every few years some iconoclast in the council proposes that the monument should be removed, but nothing is ever done about it. A little farther on, upon the oppsite side of the High Street, an even narrower turning conducts to the Market Square, which has a colonnaded walk on two sides, the George Inn on a third, and some really beautiful old houses on the fourth.

Upon this picturesque scene the much more than life-size statue of Sir Albert Dawnish looks down. It had been named by some as the most beautiful statue in the British Isles, but the competition is, of course, very strong. Ledlington owes a good deal to Sir Albert, the originator of the Dawnish Quick Cash Stores. His original shop, the cradle of the enormous Dawnish fortune, was for many years a well-known eyesore at the corner of the Square. It was pulled down in 1935 and re-erected where the High Street widens out, but the statue of Sir Albert most unfortunately remains. Of the some twenty bombs which fell in and around the town, not one inflicted so much as a scratch upon his marble trousers.

The bus from Deep End, coming in by the new by-pass, drew up in front of the station at seven minutes to three—an advance on the scheduled time which enabled the driver and conductor to adjourn for refreshment to an adjacent snack bar. Miss Silver alighted.

At precisely the same moment a man came out of the station. He was of a noticeable and somewhat pitiful appearance, since his head and all one side of his face was heavily bandaged and he leaned upon a stick with a gloved right hand. In spite of his disability and the fact that he was burdened with a small suit-case he got along surprisingly fast and took his way past the Mayor's monument into High Street, where he turned to the left, emerging from the bottleneck, upon the good wide road of Regency times. One of the large houses fronting upon the street is now the County Bank.

At precisely three minutes to three the bandaged man limped up two shallow steps and pushed open the door of the bank. A girl who was coming out held the door for him and stood aside to let him pass. Then she came down the steps, got into a small car which was standing at the kerb, and started up the engine. Rather a striking-looking young person by the accounts of two or three of the people who were passing at the time and who happened to notice her. A baker's boy was able to state the make of the car and give the first two figures of its number—a not very useful piece of observation, since it merely proved the car to have been a stolen one.

Miss Muffin, on her way to the post with old Mrs. Wotherspoon's letters, was more helpful.

"Oh, yes, *very* golden hair. I mean, one couldn't help wondering whether it was natural, though of course—girls do do such things to their hair nowadays—I mean, quite respectable girls. . . . . Oh, yes—*very* much made-up, Inspector. Eyebrows halfway up her forehead—so odd. And the sort of complexion that must take hours to do—if you know what I mean. But quite unnoticeable sort of clothes—just a dark coat and skirt, and a plain felt hat—black, I think, though it might have been a very dark navy—so difficult to tell in a poor light, and the sky was very much overcast at the time."

Since it appeared that she had merely walked past the car with the letters in her hand, and that she had been hurrying because Mrs. Wotherspoon didn't care about being left alone in the house, Inspector Jackson thought she had managed to get a considerable eyeful.

Mr. Edward Carpenter's contribution, though less detailed, was not without value. His eye had not only observed but disapproved. When he was younger he would have known just how to place the lady, but now of course there was no telling—she might be anyone. You couldn't be sure that your own nieces and cousins wouldn't turn up looking as if the less said about them the better.

Young Pottinger, on the other hand, was quite appreciative.

"Some blonde! I'm telling you!— What I could see of her, that is. She got her hand up doing something to her hat as I passed, and you can't just stand and gape—well, can you?"

It was not, unfortunately, possible to obtain a statement from the bank manager or from the young clerk, Hector Wayne, any evidence they might have to give being of necessity deferred to a day of final account. At the moment when the bandaged man shut the door of the bank behind him and came down the two shallow steps into the street one of them was already dead and the other drawing his last few laboured breaths.

Miss Muffin, voluble after the event, was sure that she had heard the shots. The baker's boy had thought there was a motorbike starting up in the Square. Mr. Carpenter enquired how anyone could tell one sound from another in what he termed the damnable babel of High Street. Young Pottinger said there was a brewer's dray backing out of Friar's Cut, which is immediately opposite the bank, and he didn't suppose anyone could have heard anything. And since the bandaged man used a silencer, it is quite probable that he was right.

However that may be, the man, with his suit-case in his hand, walked some ten feet along the pavement and got into the waiting car. The engine was running and they got off without any delay. It was not until an hour later that the car was found abandoned seven miles away in one of the lanes near Ledstow. But nobody had seen a spectacular blonde, and nobody had seen a bandaged man.

CHAPTER 19

Miss Silver, having alighted from her bus, walked back along the approach to the station. Since all her fellow-passengers had also got down, she was by no means the only person who was doing so. One or two of the people who had been in the bus had gone into the station, but for the most part they were making for the High Street and the Market Square.

The station stands a little below the by-pass. She was about half way up the slope, when she noticed the man with the bandaged head. Since he had not been one of the passengers in the bus he must have come out of the station, and since the County Hospital is very conveniently situated not more than a few hundred yards to the right, it was quite natural to suppose that he might be making his way in that direction. She had the habit of noticing anything at all out of the usual. The man excited her commiseration. It was his head that was bandaged, but he had also a pronounced limp, and he leaned upon the stick as he walked. A loose dark overcoat seemed to weigh him down, and he was further burdened by a suit-case. Despite his feeble appearances he passed her and went on up the rise. By the time she reached the by-pass he had crossed it. And then her attention was diverted, because a car drew up a few paces away and Frank Abbott hailed her.

When she was in the front seat beside him and the door was shut, he said,

"I didn't get out—just in case. That being the Deep End bus, I thought we'd better be on the safe side. There might be someone who saw me when I came down before, and we don't exactly want to advertise the connection with the police. What I thought we might do was drive out to a new road-house they've started between this and Ledstow. It caters for courting couples, I am told, and is full of discreet corners and lights turned low. It's not likely to be crowded so early as this."

They slipped smoothly out along the by-pass. They did not therefore hear the shots which killed the bank manager and his clerk.

To Miss Silver's "I am very glad to see you, Frank," he replied,

"And I to see you—I haven't been easy. And now what have you got to tell me?"

"Not very much, I am afraid. Mrs. Craddock is delicate and overworked. The children have been mismanaged and neglected, but they are beginning to respond to more sensible treatment. I do not, therefore, feel that I am wasting my time."

The road being open and empty, he was able to throw her a look of mingled affection and protest.

"And so you are settling down as a nursery governess!"

Miss Silver smiled.

"Not entirely. I hope to persuade Mrs. Craddock to send Jennifer and Maurice to boarding schools. It would be better for them in every way. But that is not what you want to hear about. You know, of course, that Thomasina Elliot is here."

"I did my best to stop her. Fine eyes, but a stubborn temper. I have decided to let her marry Peter Brandon."

"I was at first considerably disturbed by her arrival, but

she is very conveniently placed for hearing any talk there has been about Miss Ball. The Miss Tremletts delight in talk of every kind."

He raised his eyebrows.

"Has there been any talk about Miss Ball? And when you say *talk,* do you mean what usually goes by that name?"

"I think so. There was a man whom she used to slip out to meet in the evenings. Mrs. Craddock informed me that she had seen them together and was not at all happy about it. And Miss Elliot tells me that each of the Miss Tremletts had also seen them."

She proceeded to describe the three incidents as they had been conveyed to her by Mrs. Craddock and by Thomasina, ending up with a description of the paper found in Anna Ball's handbag.

"I do not know how it strikes you, but the impression I received was that Miss Ball in writing down these variants of Sandrow was either trying to recall a name imperfectly remembered, or to decide upon an alias for someone whose real name it was desirable to conceal."

He nodded.

"I expect you are right. So there was a man after all—I ought to have been able to bank on it. When a girl goes missing there always is. And the people who ought to know better come in flocks and tell us that Mary, or Doris, or Elsie never had a boy friend in her life. It looks as if we've been had for mugs."

"My dear Frank!" Miss Silver's tone reproved him.

"Let us say we have been misled. Well, that rather lets the Colony out, doesn't it? She went out meeting Mr. Sandrow at nights, and she left the Craddocks in a hurry before her month was up. It doesn't look to me as if there was much mystery about it, you know. Lonely girl with an inferiority complex meets beguiling stranger and goes off with him. I think we may rely upon it that his intentions were strictly dishonourable, because if they had married she would have tumbled over herself to let Thomasina know."

Miss Silver did not answer immediately. Then she said,

"It might be so. But there are two points which are not explained. In the first place, there is a singular combination of secrecy and frankness. She conceals her meeting with this man at one moment and obtrudes them at another. She slips out after dark without saying anything, but she allows Miss Gwyneth Tremlett to see her driving with the fellow in Ledlington by daylight."

"Well, Anna couldn't have known that she would run into Miss Gwyneth."

"My dear Frank! I can assure you that if one of the Miss Tremletts goes into Dedham or Ledlington, everyone in the Colony will know by what bus she goes in, and by what bus she intends to return."

"Oh, it's that way, is it?"

"Indeed it is. They delight in imparting information about everything they do. I have no doubt at all that Anna Ball was aware that Miss Gwyneth would be waiting for her bus at the time she drove by with Mr. Sandrow."

"You think she wanted to be seen with him?"

"Yes, I think so."

"Why?"

"I do not know. That is my first point—Mr. Sandrow is first concealed, and then obtruded. And one of the things that is obtruded is his name. She gave it to Mrs. Craddock and she gave it to Miss Elaine, and she gave it without solicitation or pressure. It looks as if she wished the name to be known. But nothing more. In each case a most natural enquiry is checked by downright rudeness. And now for my second point. If, as you conjecture, she left the Craddocks to join a lover, why was she overcome by distress?"

"Distress?"

"You told me yourself. When you came down to make enquiries the Miss Tremletts and Miranda informed you that they had seen Miss Ball drive away with Mr. Craddock. She was wearing a red hat which the Craddocks had given her. The stationmaster at Dedham, where she took a ticket for London—"

"Yes, I remember—he said Craddock saw her off—a dark young woman in a red hat. And a bit about her being a good deal upset, and Mr. Craddock telling him she had been having trouble with her nerves and they were glad to be rid of her."

"Yes. Do you remember he said that she was crying?"

"I don't know—I think I got that impression. Let me see. . . . No, I don't seem to get farther than 'a good bit upset.' What is the point?"

Miss Silver said slowly, "If she was crying she would probably have had her handkerchief up to her face. 'A good deal upset' and Mr. Craddock's explanation about nerves does to my mind suggest tears and a necessity to account for them. If she was really crying, what was the reason for those tears? But suppose she was not crying at all. Suppose they were only a pretext for the handkerchief."

Frank whistled.

"You mean?"

"I have wondered whether it was Anna Ball who got into the London train that day."

Frank Abbott swerved to avoid a motor-bicycle emerging with great suddenness from a particularly narrow lane. After a moment he said,

"What makes you think it wasn't?"

Miss Silver coughed.

"I do not go as far as that. I merely wonder whether the young woman who got into that train was really Anna Ball."

"And what has set you wondering?"

"The red hat."

He repeated the words in a tone of surprise.

"The red hat!"

"Yes. From the first I have thought a good deal about that red hat. Anna Ball was not satisfied with the Craddocks, nor they with her. She was slipping out at night to meet a man about whom she told them nothing but his bare name. She had been extremely rude to Mrs. Craddock, her demeanour was reserved and sullen. Why should they go out of the way to give her a red hat? There might, of course, be other reasons, but there is one which has kept on coming into my mind. If for some reason it was desired to create the impression that Miss Ball had gone away by train when she had in fact not gone away at all, or not gone away in that manner and at that time, then the red hat would be of great assistance in producing that impression. When the Miss Tremletts say that they saw Mr. Craddock go by with Anna Ball—when Miranda and Mr. Remington corroborate this—what do you suppose these four people did actually see? They would hear the car coming, and they would look to see who was in it. They would see Mr. Craddock and a girl in a red hat. I doubt very much if they would see more than that. They would all know about the gift of the hat. Do you suppose it would occur to them that the person wearing it was not Miss Ball? If a deliberate deception had been planned, it would be easy enough for the person who was wearing the hat to turn toward Mr. Craddock as if talking to him, in which case all that would be seen by the Miss Tremletts, or by Miranda and Mr. Remington, would be a passing impression of dark hair under a red hat. As to the stationmaster at Dedham, it is most improbable that he knew Anna Ball by sight, but just in case there should be anyone in the station who had seen her at Deep End, the girl in the red hat is upset. She uses her handkerchief to dab her eyes and, incidentally, to hide her face. Mr. Craddock impresses it on the stationmaster that Miss Ball has been having trouble with her nerves, and that they are glad to be getting rid of her. This would serve the double purpose of focussing the stationmaster's attention upon the fact that Anna Ball had left Deep End and returned to London, whilst at the same time accounting for the fact that she avoided observation and kept her handkerchief up to her face."

Frank Abbott turned a quizzical eye upon his Miss Silver. "We do not really know that she did either."

Her reply was in her mildest manner.

"I believe, my dear Frank, that I prefaced my remarks by the word 'if.' '*If* for some reason, it was desired to create an impression that Miss Ball had left by train for London —*if* a deliberate deception had been planned.' I certainly did not commit myself to the opinion that this had been the case. I merely wished to point out that had there been such a desire and such a plan, there would not have been any great difficulty in carrying it out."

"Why should there have been a plan of that kind? To put it bluntly, why should Mr. Craddock desire to make away with Miss Ball? You see, this theory of yours would implicate him up to the hilt. The Miss Tremletts, Miranda, and Augustus Remington and the stationmaster are one thing—Craddock is quite another. Whoever was deceived, he couldn't have been. If the girl he saw off at Dedham wasn't Anna Ball, he must have known that she wasn't."

"Certainly he must have known it."

"Well then, we're back at the question of motive. Why the play-acting?—Why any of it?"

"Yes—that is what I have been asking myself. And more particularly, why the gift of the red hat? I do not say there is not a satisfactory answer to these questions, but up to now none has presented itself."

Frank Abbott said with half a laugh,

"The best answer would come from the girl herself. Pity she hasn't been traced."

Miss Silver answered him gravely.

"And that takes us back to the point from which we started. Where is Anna Ball?"

CHAPTER 20

As THEY turned in at the road-house, a small car passed them, heading for Ledstow. There were two people in it. Frank Abbott noticed a couple of the figures on the number-plate. Miss Silver was aware that the driver was a woman. There was no reason why either of them should have noticed more than that. It was only a good deal later when the car had been found deserted in Miller's Lane that they realized it was the Ledlington bank murderer and his accomplice who had passed them. The car was going very fast indeed.

Inside the café they drank tea and went on talking. The place, as Frank Abbott had said, was well adapted for private conversation. There were nooks, there were alcoves, there were comfortable chairs, and discreetly shaded lights. Having listened to all that Miss Silver had to tell him, he had a contribution of his own to make.

"You haven't asked me how I come to be here."

Miss Silver smiled.

"Are you going to tell me?"

"Yes, I am. Do you remember my talking to you about a bank robbery at Enderby Green a month ago?"

"A very shocking affair. The bank manager was shot dead. But there was a clerk—I hope he recovered."

Frank nodded.

"He was lucky—the bullet just missed everything that mattered. I think I told you he had been rather clever. He was making some entries in red ink at the time, and he managed to get some of it on to a bundle of notes they made him hand over. Well, of course everyone has been warned to look out for those notes. The murderer naturally wouldn't try to pass anything that was badly marked, but what the clerk did was to get a finger in the ink and smear the edge of the packet. If the colour didn't run in beyond the edge, it might have been just possible to shave it off, so all banks were told to be on the look out for this. Well, two notes turned up this week. A young chap called Wayne in the County Bank here spotted them. It was bright of him, because the shaving had been very carefully done. I can't say I'd have noticed it myself if I hadn't been on the look out for it, but under a magnifying glass you can see that the edge has been tampered with, and there is even a trace of the red ink. The Chief sent me down, and we've been in a huddle over it most of the morning."

"And have you been able to trace the notes?"

"Up to a point, yes. Or at any rate one of them. They were paid in separately, and when this fellow Wayne noticed one of them he reported it to the manager and they went through all the lot and found another. Only of course by that time no one could say where it had come from, so except as an indication that someone in the district is passing these notes, the second one is a wash-out."

"And the first?"

"Well, that was paid in by a Miss Weekes who has a fancy work shop at Dedham. Jackson and I went over to see her about it. She hasn't any regular day for banking her takings, because she has relations in Ledlington, and when she comes over she likes to spend the day with them, so it's a matter of mutual convenience. There's a friend who looks after the shop when she isn't there."

Miss Silver smiled.

"Fancy work shops are often run in quite an easy-going way. It is considered a refined occupation by those who have had no business training."

He laughed.

"Miss Weekes is nothing if not refined. I think you've met her?"

"She has wool of a very good quality. I bought some two days ago."

"And you paid—how?"

She said soberly,

"With a pound note. My dear Frank, you are not going to tell me—"

"I don't know—I wish I did. Miss Weekes banked four pound notes yesterday. Of those four she herself took three —one from you. She described you as the lady who is staying at Deepe House, and added that you did a lot of knitting."

"Oh, yes, I was recommended to go to her by Mr. Hawkes, the postman. She is, I believe, a connection of his."

His very fair eyebrows rose.

"Whoever it was who said that one half of the world doesn't know how the other half lives obviously had no experience of an English village. Talk about the fierce light that beats upon a throne—it simply isn't in it with the light that beats on rural England."

Miss Silver coughed.

"I have often thought so. But let us return to Miss Weekes and the four pound notes. One of them came from me. What about the others?"

"She says Mr. Augustus Remington came in for embroidery silks. He is a frequent customer and she knows him well. He came in the same day that you did. His bill amounted to thirty-two and six-pence, and he paid it with a pound note, a ten shilling note, and a half-crown. Later on in the afternoon Miss Gwyneth Tremlett came in for canvas and raffia. She also paid with a pound note. So there are three of them accounted for. But no one seems to know anything about number four. Miss Weekes became quite tearful over it and said her friend must have taken it on Tuesday morning whilst she was out doing the shopping. The friend's name is Hill, and she is a dreep. She has nervous prostration if more than two people come into the shop together. On Tuesday morning there was apparently an avalanche of six, and she became completely disorganized. By the time Jackson and I had finished with her the only thing she was sure about was that she had put all the money in the till, and if there was an extra pound note there, someone must have given it to her, but if it was her last dying breath she couldn't say more than that, and if we were going to take her to prison, she was ready to go, and all she wanted was to be allowed to die quietly of the disgrace and not have to face the neighbours. You know the kind of thing."

"It is extremely difficult to deal with."

"That's putting it mildly. Jackson says he has an aunt like it, and there's nothing you can do. As he put it, by the time they've finished working themselves up they don't know black from white, nor chalk from cheese. So there we are—one pound note from you, one from Augustus Remington, one from Miss Gwyneth, and one from wherever you please. Where did yours come from?"

She said in an expressionless voice,

"Mrs. Craddock pays my salary weekly."

"Oh, she does, does she? And that pound note was part of it—you're sure about that?"

"I am perfectly sure."

"Then three out of the four notes come from the Colony."

Miss Silver coughed.

"It is more than a month since the robbery at Enderby Green, and there has therefore been a good deal of time for the notes to circulate. The one paid over the counter to Miss Weekes may have passed through a number of hands before it reached her. Since I myself cannot be sure that I did not handle it, the same may be the case with regard to Mr. Remington and Miss Gwyneth Tremlett. Any of us could have passed one of the stolen notes in complete innocence."

"But the chances are still three to one that it came from the Colony."

There was a hint of reproof in her voice as she said,

"I think it would be fairer to say *through* instead of from."

CHAPTER 21

As Miss Silver walked down towards the station to wait for her bus she reflected gravely upon the conversation which she had just had with Frank Abbott. It had not clarified anything, it had not led them anywhere, but it had certainly added to the apprehension with which the whole situation inspired her. She had the unpleasant sensation of trying to find her way in a fog. No sooner did a clue present itself than it petered out, any attempt to follow it resulting in confusion. Having started out to discover what had happened to Anna Ball, she found herself involved with Mrs. Craddock's fears for the safety of her children. And now, superimposed upon everything else, there was this business of the notes taken from the bank at Enderby Green. When she referred to what might be called the Craddock problem Frank had not given it very much attention. Three unruly children were enough to upset any boat, and as for the mushrooms—well, there *was* that close copy of the real thing, and anyone might be taken in by it. He remembered a correspondence about it in the *Times*, and the last word of the experts was that there was no certain test, but if you found the things growing near pine trees they were not mushrooms, and that was that. In the matter of the stolen notes, as she pointed out to him, once in circulation, any one of them might pass through a dozen hands before it was paid over Miss Weekes' counter. But whether she regarded the problem of the Craddocks or the problem of the notes, a feeling of apprehension not only persisted but increased.

She was half way down the slope, when she heard footsteps behind her and a whispering voice said,

"Whither away, fair lady?"

Since she knew only one person capable of such a form of address, it was no surprise to find Augustus Remington at her elbow, looking a good deal less peculiar than usual. It could not be said that his clothes were like those of other people, but he no longer wore the blouse and corduroy trousers which he affected in the Colony, and beyond a certain flowing line and the fact that he wore a low-necked shirt, his garments approximated to those of the ordinary man. He was bare-headed, and his long lint-white hair lifted in the breeze.

Miss Silver said soberly,

"I am catching the five o'clock bus."

The slender hands gestured.

"I also. A deplorable necessity. These mechanical inventions defile the purity of country life."

It had never occurred to Miss Silver that life in the country was particularly pure, but she refrained from saying so.

"The smell—" said Augustus Remington, his whisper becoming fainter. "The noise—I am quite terribly susceptible to noise. The ruthless, inexorable grinding of the—ah, gears. I am entirely ignorant of those hideous mechanical contrivances, but I believe I am right in supposing that there *are* such things. As I have just said, a painful convenience, an outrage upon every artistic sense, but a present necessity. You have been shopping?"

"I have been having tea with a friend."

"And I in pursuit of beauty." He gave a little giggling laugh. "But you must not misunderstand me. I refer to that abstract beauty which is the guiding star of art, and in this case it led me to what I have been seeking vainly for many weary weeks. I have been impeded, obstructed, frustrated, but today my struggles have been crowned with success. Without any volition of my own I found myself entering a little shop in the Square. The old beams exuded an aroma of the past—there were strange whisperings in the walls. A young girl served me, blooming and unimaginative as a cabbage rose. She had a hideous accent—she had been eating peppermints. She laid a tray of embroidery silks before me, and there, at last, was the shade I had been seeking—one of those fainting hues which resemble the haunting of a rose that has died in the bud."

They had by this time reached the bus. Since it was not due to start for another five minutes, there was still plenty of room inside, and it was therefore quite impossible to avoid sitting next to Mr. Remington, who continued to discourse in a manner which Miss Silver found very trying to her patience. A little before five o'clock Miss Gwyneth Tremlett got in, and quite at the last minute a large young man with a suit-case stepped on board and, making his way to a vacant seat at the very front of the bus, sat down and stared gloomily at the driver's back.

Miss Silver recognized him at once, and she may be forgiven for an exasperated feeling that he was, in his own person, the proverbial last straw. There was, however, nothing she could do about it. The engine started, the bus quivered and leapt forward. Augustus Remington gave her a running commentary on the sensations which this induced. His voice fell, now fading into inaudibility, and now recurring to a full-blown whisper. Miss Silver had no attention to spare for him. Her eyes were fixed on the back of Peter Brandon's head, and her mind was quite taken up with annoyance that he should have followed Thomasina to Deep End and speculations as to how soon he could be induced to go away.

As they continued their progress in the direction of Deeping, the passengers thinned out, the largest number getting off at Ledhill, once a country village but rapidly becoming industrialized. There being now a vacant seat just across the gangway, Miss Gwyneth Tremlett took the opportunity of moving into it, and was affectionately greeted by Mr. Remington.

"Ah, now—how much better this is! I have been asking myself what have we done that we should be ostracized."

Miss Gwyneth bridled in a pleased sort of way.

"*Really*, Augustus—don't be so absurd! You can't have been noticing, or you would have seen that I took almost the only seat which happened to be empty."

He heaved an ostentatious sigh.

"I have a very sensitive soul. The least breath of coldness

from a friend, and I am not well. Last week when you were vexed with me I had to take three aspirins. And then today I was already suffering. I yield to no one in admiration for our Peveril, and I know that you and Elaine do not like to hear a word against him, but I cannot pretend that I do not feel hurt when he drives his car into Ledlington and drives it back again without so much as thinking of offering any one of us a lift."

Miss Gwyneth sat up rather straight. She wore a shapeless green coat and a great many scarves, one in orange and purple stripes over her head, and two or three others in varying shades about her neck and shoulders. As she talked, the ends kept poking out and having to be tucked in again. She said rather abruptly,

"But Peveril wasn't in Ledlington."

Augustus Remington's whisper took on a purring note.

"My very dear Gwyneth, of course he was. He had parked his car in the Market Square--I saw it at once when I came out of my little dark shop. But you don't know about that. It was Miss Silver that I was confiding in. My dear, at last I have attained the object of my search—the exquisite shade which had eluded me for so long that I had begun to despair of finding it. It glowed like a jewel in the little dark place! And when I came out, there was Peveril's car. Remembering that I had confided my intention of visiting Ledlington this afternoon, I could hardly fail to be wounded. Or do you think I could?"

Miss Gwyneth, aware that she had told Peveril that she was going into Ledlington, could do no better than to say with some bluntness,

"If he had wanted us to come with him, I suppose he would have suggested it."

"Dear Gwyneth! How well you put it! If he had wanted us he would have asked us. So simple, so direct, so entirely to the point! Since he did not ask us, he did not want us. An inescapable inference. The whole wounding truth packed into the fewest possible words. Only those endowed with the supreme wisdom of commonsense have courage enough to achieve such clarity. For myself, I am a creature of emotion. I cannot analyse, I can only feel. When a cold wind passes over me I shrink and I am silent."

Miss Gwyneth's colour had risen. She seemed about to speak but it was some time before he afforded her any opportunity of doing so.

Miss Silver continued to listen to what was being said, and to watch Mr. Peter Brandon. Once in a while a trick of the light would show her his reflection in the glass which faced him. It was not a very clear reflection, depending as it did upon the dark backing of the driver's coat and the angle at which the light struck the pane, but it confirmed her impression that Mr. Brandon was in a very bad temper, a fact which greatly increased the likelihood of his committing some fatal imprudence.

The bus jogged on, and ultimately arrived at Deeping, leaving the passengers for Deep End a walk of about three-quarters of a mile. It was at this point that Peter Brandon addressed himself to Augustus Remington. He asked to be directed to Deep End and enquired whether it would be possible to find accommodation there for the night.

"I have come down to see a relation of mine who is staying here. A matter of business. My name is Brandon."

As these remarks were made in quite a loud, abrupt voice, neither Miss Gwyneth nor Miss Silver could avoid hearing them. It was, in fact, quite apparent to Miss Silver that Mr. Brandon was at one and the same moment issuing a challenge and fishing for an invitation.

Miss Gwyneth's response was immediate.

"Mr. Brandon—I really must introduce myself. Your aunt was our very dear friend, and as you know, your dear little cousin is our guest—mine and my sister's. My name is Tremlett—Miss Gwyneth Tremlett. I do hope there is nothing wrong. We are enjoying Ina's visit so much."

That he boggled at the "Ina" was plain. Miss Silver thought that he would have had a very good face for a silent film—what she would herself have called a speaking countenance. But Miss Gwyneth, whose scarves were being blown all about her, was too much taken up with retrieving them and buttoning them inside her coat to notice anything. As soon as she had dealt with the scarves she was deploring the fact that they had no second spare room and wondering whether Mrs. Masters would take Mr. Brandon in.

"She has quite a nice room, and everything most beautifully kept. And I know that it is empty, because young Goddard who has lodged there for the last eighteen months has managed to get one of the new Council houses at Deeping, so of course he decided to get married at once. He and Mabel Wellstead have only been waiting for somewhere to live. Mrs. Masters was quite adamant about not taking a married couple, and of course Deeping is much more convenient for them, as he works in the Nurseries there. But I don't really know about you, Mr. Brandon. You see, she goes to the Craddocks at Harmony for three hours every morning, and of course she gave Jim Goddard a wrapped lunch, and he had breakfast and supper with her and her father-in-law, who is our oldest inhabitant."

If Miss Gwyneth had been obliged to sit silent in the bus, she made up for it now. Peter felt himself in danger of being submerged. Snatching at the one essential point, he said firmly that he didn't care where he took his meals, and the room at Mrs. Masters' sounded as if it was just what he was looking for.

He had to say it all over again when he reached the cottage, where he found it extremely difficult to get in a word edgeways, Miss Gwyneth being quite extraordinarily informative and diffuse, and Mrs. Masters using the slightest pause to repeat that she didn't know that she wanted to take another lodger, and that she didn't reckon to let to the gentry.

It was Mr. Masters who finally settled the matter. From behind his daughter-in-law's back he crooked a finger and beckoned Peter in. The kitchen was warm with firelight and lamplight, the table was spread for a meal. There was a mingled smell of paraffin and kippers, there was a singing kettle and a purring cat. Old Mr. Masters pointed to a chair and said, "Set down." Then he opened the door a chink and bellowed through it into the darkness.

"You come right in, Maria, and dish up! It's my house, and he's staying!"

It was a good deal earlier than this, not in fact more than ten minutes after the bus had left Ledlington, that Frank Abbott was being ushered into the closed and shuttered County Bank. Inspector Jackson accompanied him, and the Superintendent of the Ledlington police and the Chief Constable of the county were waiting for them. Outside, darkness was closing in upon the winter dusk. Here there were bright lights and hard dark shadows. The lights shone down upon two dead men, men who had been alive and in their full strength when he had talked with them only that morning. They could give no evidence now but the mute accusing testimony of their blood. The manager was a married man with two children still of school age. The clerk was Hector Wayne who had been so quick to detect that one of the pound notes paid in by Miss Weekes had been tampered with. A cold anger came up in Frank as he looked at them. He had nothing to say, and he said nothing. It was the Chief Constable who spoke.

"It's a bad business," he said.

CHAPTER 22

THE PAPERS CARRIED heavy headlines next day—"Another Bank Robbery—Double Murder At Ledlington." Miss Silver came down to find Mrs. Craddock trying to stop the children talking about it. She was not having any great success, and at Miss Silver's appearance Maurice rushed at her, waving a newspaper and demanding in his loudest voice,

"Did you hear the shooting? Your bus must have got in just about the right time! The bank manager was shot, and one of his clerks! Were you near the bank? Did you hear anything? I wish I had! I wish I'd gone into Ledlington with you, because if I had I was going to buy marbles, and the marbles shop is right opposite the bank, so I should have heard the shooting, and I might have seen the man who did it! This paper calls him the Bandaged Bandit! He had his head all done up in bandages!"

"My dear Maurice!"

"He did! All over his head so you couldn't see what he was like! I call that a wizard idea—don't you? Miss Silver, if I'd seen him I'd have had to try and stop him, wouldn't I? I could have kicked him on the shins, couldn't I, and dodged behind the car if he tried to shoot?"

"I would have kicked him too!" said Benjy at his shrillest. "I would have kicked him like this!" He aimed a violent kick at the table leg, hurt his foot, and started to roar.

Maurice went on without taking breath.

"There was a car with a girl in it! Beautiful Blonde is what they call her! She drove him away! Beautiful Blonde and Bandaged Bandit—that's what it says! And they got right away! But the police have got a Clue! Look—it's all here!"

Miss Silver removed the newspaper from his grasp and turned a critical eye upon his nails.

"My dear Maurice, what have you been doing to get so dirty before breakfast? Please go and wash. No, Benjy, it wasn't the table's fault, it was yours. You kicked it—it didn't kick you."

The tears stopped rolling down Benjy's scarlet face. His chin quivered and he began to laugh.

"Wouldn't it be funny if it had kicked me! Wouldn't it be funny if all the tables and chairs began to fight and kick! Wouldn't it be funny if that big old chair was to get up and kick Mrs. Masters!"

Jennifer had not spoken. She had her shut-in look. Now she pounced on Benjy and shook him.

"It wouldn't be funny at all—it would be horrible!"

Mrs. Craddock said in a distressed voice,

"Children—children—*please*—"

And then the door opened and Peveril Craddock came in.

A sudden silence fell. Maurice stopped half way through a sentence, and Benjy in the middle of a roar. Jennifer let go of him and backed away until she came to her place at the table. When she reached it she pulled the chair out with a jerk and sat down. The boys scrambled for their places and began to eat the porridge which had been cooling. Jennifer did not touch hers. She drank a cup of health tea, and presently got up and poured herself out another.

As a rule Mr. Craddock read one of the papers at breakfast and kept the other beside him in case he wished to read that too. This morning he made no attempt to look at either, merely removing them from the table, folding them, and laying them aside. All this in an abstracted and gloomy manner. It was impossible to avoid the conclusion that he had already read the news, and that it had affected him painfully. Miss Silver had not been long in discovering that whilst he constantly proclaimed the right of children to complete freedom in the manner of self-expression, he was in practice extremely intolerant of anything that ran counter either to his opinions or his comfort. That Jennifer both disliked and feared him was apparent, but even Maurice's bold tongue was apt to fail him under a certain portentous look, and when Maurice blanched all the spirit went out of Benjy too. They sat as still as mice and gulped their porridge whilst Mr. Craddock frowned over his coffee, complained of the sausages, and enquired how many times he had stated that he would *not* eat cold toast.

It was whilst Jennifer had gone to make some more that Emily put down her cup and said in a fluttering voice,

"You have seen the papers? This is terrible news, isn't it?"

The Jovian frown rested upon her.

"I do not consider it a suitable topic for the breakfast table, but since you have referred to it, I can only say that I am very much shocked. I was in the bank only yesterday and had a few words with the manager. It is a terrible occurrence, but not, I think, adapted for family discussion. Is it really not possible to obtain better coffee than this, Emily? May I ask how many spoons you put in?"

Mrs. Craddock looked guilty.

"I—I—Mrs. Masters—"

"You let Mrs. Masters make the coffee! After all that I have said! I do not expect that my wishes should carry any undue weight, but I thought I had made a very particular request that you should see to the coffee yourself. Mrs. Masters can see no difference between water that has been freshly boiled and water that either has not boiled at all or has been kept stewing on the stove for hours. This coffee has been made with only half the proper amount, and it has been stewed. My special herbal flavouring, designed not only to improve the taste but to counteract the disastrous effect of caffeine, has been omitted. Is Jennifer merely making toast, or has she to bake the bread as well?"

"There—there—is plenty of bread."

"If it is burned, I will *not* eat it," said Peveril Craddock with a rasp in his voice.

The toast was, fortunately, not burned. When she had placed it before him Jennifer poured herself yet another cup of health tea and drank it in sips, holding the cup between her hands as if she needed the warmth.

The police arrived at just after ten o'clock.

CHAPTER 23

As THEY TURNED into the drive, Frank Abbott said to Inspector Jackson,

"Look here, I want Miss Silver to be there when we question these people, and the only way it can be done is to have them all in together. She knows them, and we don't, and I want her opinion as to how they react. But I don't want to give anything away. I don't know how long she means to stay anyhow, but her position here would be quite untenable if they thought she had anything to do with the police. So if it's all right with you, I suggest we round up all these Colony people and see them together at Deepe House, and if there seems to be any reason for it, we can go through them one at a time afterwards. If I drop you off about here, you can do Remington, and Miranda, and the Miss Tremletts, whilst I collect the elusive Robinson. And you had better bring Miss Elliot along too. She's staying with the Miss Tremletts. I don't suppose any of them will be out."

Inspector Jackson agreeing, Frank Abbott stopped the car and set him down.

He stopped again at the east wing, where he wasted ten minutes trying to make Mr. John Robinson hear. All the windows looking on to the courtyard had been boarded up, and an accumulation of dead leaves and dusty spiders' webs suggested that the front door was no longer in use. The bell was certainly out of order. Having made as much noise as he could with the knocker without producing any result except to awake the courtyard echoes, he walked along the impenetrable hedge which joined the front wall of the house and called, "Hullo!" At the sixth or seventh repetition there was an answering call, and a man's voice said, "Want anything?"

"I want Mr. John Robinson."

"Well?"

"Are you Robinson?"

"I am. What do you want with me?"

"Answers to a few questions. I am Inspector Abbott of Scotland Yard, and I have come over with Inspector Jackson of the Ledshire County Police to make some enquiries. We shall be obliged if you will join the other members of the Colony over at Mr. Craddock's side of the house."

A not unmelodious whistle came from behind the hedge. Mr. Robinson said,

"What's up?"

"A routine enquiry."

"Well, even routine enquiries have to be about something. All right. I'll know more about it when I join the party, won't I? You'll have to put up with my working clothes." His voice receded.

Frank had begun to wonder whether it had gone away for good, when there was a sound of footsteps away on his left and John Robinson hove into view. The working clothes to which he had alluded were of the disintegrating kind—flannel trousers with a good many rents in them and a liberal plastering of mud, a couple of sweaters so carelessly disposed that the under one, which showed traces of having once been blue, stuck out at the neck and sleeves and from gaping holes in the elbows. Above all this, a short beard, a very untidy head of hair, dark eyes under bushy eyebrows.

He nodded affably as he came up, and remarked,

"Go where glory waits thee, but when fame elates thee, oh, then remember me—as Tommy Moore says. And if you have any idea of hailing me to quod on account of something I haven't done, I will merely mention that I have a family of hens, a blackbird with a broken leg, and a tame rat called Samuel Whiskers. He is the only one of the party able to shift for himself, so I commend the others to your humanity—if a policeman has any. It is, of course, rather a lot to expect." He had a soft, agreeable voice and a country accent, more noticeable than it had been from the other side of the hedge.

They arrived at the door of the other wing, and were admitted by Mrs. Masters, who put them in the study and went to tell Mrs. Craddock that there was a policeman there with "that Mr. Robinson," her manner declaring that she always had said there was something wrong about him.

Peveril Craddock came into the study, very much the master of the house and of the situation. He might have been the headmaster receiving a deputation of which he could not be expected to approve. There was a kind of courteous gloom, a magnanimous condescension. His voice took on its richest tones.

The police—he really failed to see—but of course every facility they desired. . . . . The other members of the Colony? . . . . . Indeed? . . . . . Of course if they wished it. . . . . Oh, yes—certainly, certainly. . . . .

He was wearing corduroy trousers of a subdued blue and a belted blouse of the same colour with the merest hint of red and green embroidery at the neck and wrists. Hair and beard were in beautiful order and disengaged a faint odour of what was doubtless a herbal brilliantine. His gaze rested upon Mr. John Robinson's deplorable get-up for no more than a moment, and then withdrew.

Mr. Robinson sustained both the look and its withdrawal with cheerful calm. He went on looking at Peveril, and appeared to be seeking for some quotation which would describe him in suitable terms. He was, as a matter of fact, hesitating between one which might be considered offensive and a milder one which he felt to be inadequate, when the door opened and the two Miss Tremletts, Thomasina Elliot, Augustus Remington, and Miranda trooped in, shepherded by Inspector Jackson. There were greetings. There were a great many questions. The Miss Tremletts were agitated. Miranda, her red head topping the others, frowning and silent, Augustus Remington voluble in protest.

"My morning's work will be ruined! I had an idea—very slight, very tenuous, quite terribly elusive."

He addressed himself to Gwyneth Tremlett.

"Inspired by the exquisite shade of silk I purchased yesterday—treasure trove, my dear, pure treasure trove, but fragile as the bloom on a butterfly's wing. But you will understand me—at this stage a touch, a breath, a current of cold unsympathetic thought, and the nascent idea is bruised, is blighted, is carried away. I hope it will not prove so in this case, but I am quite terribly afraid."

He continued his lamentation whilst Mrs. Craddock and Miss Silver were summoned. With his straw-coloured hair distractedly ruffled and in workaday garments consisting of brown velvet trousers and a grass-green smock, Thomasina thought he looked a good deal like a grasshopper—if you could imagine a grasshopper with straw-coloured hair. She was, however, a good deal too much taken up with her own affairs to do more than spare him a momentary attention. He was mad of course, but then most of the people here, if not absolutely mad, were so odd that there wasn't much in it. She went back to thinking about Peter Brandon and how absolutely enraging it was that he should have dared to come down here—getting Mrs. Masters to take him in and positively pushing himself on to Miss Gwyneth! If the police wanted to arrest anyone they had better arrest Peter. It would just about serve him right.

These romantic thoughts were broken in upon by the entrance of Miss Silver and Mrs. Craddock, the latter as pale and nervous as if she were being ushered into a cage of lions instead of into a room full of people whom she met every day. She took the first chair she came to and sat on the edge of it, looking frightened. Since there was no vacant chair beside her, Miss Silver had perforce to leave her there and cross the room. The seat she found gave her a very good view of everyone. She had the Miss Tremletts and Thomasina beside her, and beyond them Mr. Craddock, with Mr. John Robinson on the other side, hunched up on the window-seat with his back to the light. From across the room Augustus Remington and Miranda faced her, Miranda sprawled in one of the larger chairs, Augustus on a low stool in what she considered a ridiculously affected attitude. The two Inspectors had drawn chairs up to the writing-table.

As soon as everyone had been accommodated Inspector Jackson said in his slow, deep country voice,

"I am taking it for granted that you will all want to be of assistance to the police. Inspector Abbott has come down here from London about some notes that they are anxious to trace. A couple of them have turned up here. One of them was paid into the County Bank in Ledlington by Miss Weekes who has a fancy work shop at Dedham. She says it was part of last Tuesday's takings, and she has mentioned the names of several people who might have paid it over. Three of them are here now, and I would like to ask them whether they can remember anything that would help us—as for instance, the amount of the bill—how they paid it—and if in notes, whether they thought there was anything at all out of the way about those notes."

"I have never entered a fancy work shop in my life," said Peveril Craddock in a calm resonant voice.

Augustus threw out his hands.

"But, my dear Peveril—what a loss to yourself! The rows and rows of woolly bundles like fat contented sheep of some beautiful rainbow variety unknown to the plodding agriculturist—the sheen of silk, shifting and shoaling from one delicious hue to another—the bright plastic needles like spears of light—"

It was not easy to astonish Inspector Jackson. He said in a very definite tone,

"Did you buy anything from Miss Weekes on Tuesday, Mr. Remington?"

Augustus looked vague.

"I might have done. I was searching for a certain shade of silk—a fruitless quest. But when it comes to which day of the week, I fear I cannot help you. I am of those who believe that time is an illusion. Sometimes we drift with it—sometimes it passes us by. I am quite unable to say whether it was on Tuesday that my quest took me to Dedham."

Miss Gwyneth leaned forward. She was wearing a chain of large brown wooden beads, and they made a rattling sound.

"Oh, but it *was*," she said. "Because when I went in in the afternoon they said you had been there. I mean, Miss Weekes did—I didn't speak to Miss Hill. Miss Weekes said she was so sorry she hadn't the colour you wanted."

"One of those fluent shades—" Augustus murmured.

Jackson said firmly,

"Well, Mr. Remington, it was Tuesday. Now can you remember the amount of your bill?"

"Oh dear, no. Money is merely a distasteful symbol—I really do not regard it."

He spoke in a lisping way which gave Jackson a strong feeling that he ought to have been smacked for it when he was young. He had two little boys of his own, and they would have been over his knee and getting six of the best if they had started any such finicky nonsense. He said shortly,

"Miss Weekes says that the amount was thirty-two and sixpence."

"She is probably right."

"And that you paid her with a pound note, a ten shilling note, and half a crown."

"How distressingly observant."

"You agree with her statement?"

The hands were waved as if in supplication.

"My dear man, don't ask me ! I am sure she must be right."

"Then I have to ask you whether you noticed anything at all unusual about the pound note."

It was at this point that Mr. John Robinson was heard to remark that hope sprang eternal in the human breast. Augustus sighed.

"I do not notice pound notes. I have just been telling you so. They exist, but I do not admit them any farther into my consciousness than that."

Inspector Jackson persevered.

"Can you tell me how this pound note came into your possession?"

Augustus shook his head.

"I suppose from my bank. I have a modest account at Dedham. My means are small, but I occasionally cash a cheque."

"Well, we can get the date of your last cheque from them—unless you can remember it yourself."

"Oh, no."

Jackson turned to Miss Gwyneth, who proved voluble and informative. She had bought a yard of canvas in a netural shade, three bundles of blue raffia, and one bundle each of green, red, and yellow. And she had paid with a pound note, which did not quite cover the amount of the bill, but there was a small credit, as she had brought back two bundles of raffia which she had bought in a bad light the week before.

"Not at all the right shade, Inspector, and Miss Weekes is always most obliging. And I paid with a pound note, as I said, but I'm afraid I can't tell you where it came from, because there was a five-pound note that I had put away for some time, and I changed it at the railway station at Dedham the last time I went to London about a month ago, and the note might have been part of the change, or I might have had it by me for some time—I really can't say. But I certainly did not notice anything peculiar."

Too much information can be as disconcerting as too little. Miss Gwyneth went on to recall that she had received a registered envelope containing three pound notes at Christmas, the gift of an aged aunt who had an incurable objection to writing cheques. She also remembered having obliged Mrs. Craddock with a pound's worth of silver for a pound note one day when she had no change for the bus. About a fortnight ago, she thought, but she wasn't quite sure.

Appealed to for confirmation, Mrs. Craddock thought so too. The money was housekeeping money. Mr. Craddock drew a cheque about once a month when he gave her the housekeeping money. Some of it would be in notes, and some in silver. She had run out of silver, and Miss Gwyneth had very kindly changed one of the notes. Oh, no, it never occurred to her that there was anything wrong with it.

She sat drooping in her chair and never raised her eyes. Her words were barely audible. Jackson was reminded of a rabbit in a trap, too frightened to move. And what in the world was she frightened of? That was what he would like to know. He knew fear when he saw it, and here it was, plain enough, and he wanted to know why.

Frank Abbott was making notes. He too was aware of Emily Craddock's fear. Nervous, delicate woman. Might be just nerves—might be she knew something. He listened while Peveril Craddock spoke of having an account at the County Bank in Ledlington, and of the cheque drawn every month for household expenses. They weren't getting anywhere. They had got to go through with it, but there really wasn't the remotest chance of identifying the pound note poor Wayne had spotted with any one of those which seemed to have been drifting in and out of the Colony. It was like looking for a pin in a box of pins. The only chance was that they might get a line on one of these people through some involuntary reaction. He looked up, and got one reaction at any rate. Mr. John Robinson was regarding him with a gleam of critical humour. Sitting as he was, on the window-seat with his back to the light, his features in shadow and a good deal obscured by beard and eyebrow, it was extraordinary how that transient gleam came across. As clearly as he had ever got anything in his life, Inspector Abbott received the impression that the police were making fools of themselves, and that they had Mr. Robinson's sympathy.

Well, at any rate Jackson had finished with the pound note and was now very polietly inviting the company to explain individually just what each of them was doing between the hours of two and seven on the previous afternoon. No one making any demur, he proceeded to go round the circle clockwise.

"Miss—er—Miranda?"

She shook back her mass of dark red hair.

"Miranda," she said deeply. "Neither Miss nor Mrs.—just Miranda."

Inspector Jackson thought this was as odd a lot of people as he had ever come across. He avoided the issue.

"Just so. Perhaps you would not mind telling me what you were doing yesterday afternoon."

"I don't mind in the least—why should I? I went for a walk up over the common. I can't say exactly when I started, or when I got back, but I had to turn on the lights when I came in, so I suppose it was about four o'clock."

"Mr. Remington?"

Augustus heaved a sigh of utter boredom.

"My dear man, how repetitive! Haven't we had all this before? . . . . . No? Well, I suppose I must take your word for it. These sordid journeys—a bus always seems to me to be one of the lower mechanical organisms! I do hope you don't expect me to remember every time I go to Dedham or to Ledlington. . . . . Oh, just yesterday afternoon? Well, I will do what I can." He turned to Miranda. "I suppose I did go into Ledlington yesterday afternoon?"

"Don't be ridiculous, Augustus! You know perfectly well you did. I saw you start, and you came back on the five o'clock bus with Gwyneth."

"Ah, yes—my quest! It was successful. I found the exquisite shade which had eluded me for so long. But these things have no relation to time or space— I am sure you will understand that."

He gazed earnestly at Jackson, who said bluntly,

"What bus did you go in by?"

"Would it have been the one-forty?" He once more appealed to Miranda.

She nodded curtly.

"If you caught it. I saw you start. I didn't see you get on the bus, but you had plenty of time."

He gave a sigh—of relief this time.

"There you are, Inspector! She always knows everything."

Jackson went on grimly, but as might have been expected, Mr. Remington's account of how he spent the afternoon was vague in the extreme. He had walked about and looked at the old houses. He had fulfilled his quest. He had seen Peveril Craddock park his car in the Market Square. Oh, no, he had no idea what time that was. He had had a cup of coffee in one of the shops, but he couldn't say which. He had wandered into a picture shop and spent some time there looking at the work of a young artist who had evolved an entirely new technique—"Not yet fully developed of course, Inspector, but showing a definite aspiration towards the super-sensible."

Inspector Jackson turned with relief to Mr. John Robinson.

"And you, sir?"

John Robinson sounded amused. He spoke with an intensification of his country drawl.

"I'm afraid I must plead guilty to having been in Ledlington too. But I didn't take the bus. I used my bicycle, and—I'm afraid I can't be very accurate about departure and arrival. I went out after my midday meal—but then I just have it when I'm hungry. And I didn't intend to go into Ledlington at all —it was just a sudden whim. I meant to go up into the Rowbury Woods, but there was someone shooting there, so I turned off, and when I found I was getting near Ledlington I thought I might as well fetch up there."

"Can you fix the time at all?"

"I suppose it was round about three. I can't swear to it—my mind was rather taken up."

"Round about three. And what did you do then, Mr. Robinson?"

"I dropped into the Museum and had a look round there. I'm interested in birds, you know, and they have the Hedlow collection."

"How long do you suppose you stayed there?"

"Ah," said John Robinson—"there you have me! I'm afraid I have no idea. Time, you know—very variable, as Remington says." His words took on an imitative inflection. " 'Long lines of cliff, breaking, have left a chasm, and in the chasm are foam and yellow sand,' as the poet remarks. You will, of course, see the application." His eye went round the circle with a mocking gleam. "Museums do rather have that effect, you know—like some of the older Clubs—one passes into a trancelike state practically indistinguishable from death. The danger is that one might just be picked up and buried before one knew what was happening. I hope they would do it handsomely. 'And the little port had seldom seen a costlier funeral.' You will naturally recognize the quotation. One of Tennyson's major lapses. I shouldn't like anyone to think it was mine."

Knowing his Miss Silver's reverence for the great Victorian poet, Frank Abbott expected, and looked for, some mark of disapproval. What he saw was simply a frown, a frown of peculiar intensity. Mr. Robinson sustained it. It was Miss Silver who looked away.

Inspector Jackson continued his interrogation.

Miss Gwyneth was able to give a most meticulous account of her blameless afternoon's shopping. Miss Elaine had remained at home, where, after a brief rest, she had devoted herself to entertaining her young friend Miss Elliot.

Miss Silver stated that she had gone into Ledlington by the bus which arrived there just before three, had met an old friend with whom she spent the afternoon, and returned to Deeping by the bus which left at five. She was asked no further questions.

Mr. Craddock had awaited his turn in dignified silence. Asked now to give an account of his movements, he complied in the grand manner.

"I drove into Ledlington. I did not look at my watch, so I cannot give you the exact time. I was immersed in my literary labours, and did not join the family for lunch—when this happens Mrs. Craddock brings me a tray. When I had completed the passage upon which I was engaged I felt the need of some fresh air. I drove over to Ledlington and parked in the Market Square. I then walked about the town and made a few purchases—stamps at the post office, papers at the station—things like that. After which I picked up my car again and came home."

Pressed by Jackson, he appeared to be quite as unable as Augustus Remington and John Robinson to fix the time either of his arrival or departure. The only thing he appeared to be sure about was that he had reached home before lighting-up time.

"I really have no more than that to say," he concluded. "I might ask, and I think with justice, why we should be singled out for questioning in this manner. I do not mind saying that I resent it very strongly, not only on my own account, but on behalf of the Colony. I must tell you that we are well aware of our rights. We were under no obligation to submit to being interrogated in this manner. But we are law-abiding citizens, and we have nothing to hide."

How much longer he might have continued to deliver himself of these rolling periods cannot be determined, because it was at this moment that Mr. John Robinson laughed. It appeared to be one of those spontaneous outbursts, a very natural, hearty, and uncontrollable laugh. He just threw back his head and let it go.

Emily Craddock was quite differently affected. She straightened up, looked round her in a terrified manner, and slipped down out of her chair in a dead faint.

CHAPTER 24

As ALWAYS, Miss Silver proved herself to be extremely competent. She superintended the removal of Emily to the schoolroom sofa, and sent Jennifer to make her a good cup of tea. She had not been very long at Deep End before discovering that Mrs. Craddock maintained in secret a small store of what she called real tea. When Mr. Craddock was absent they would enjoy it together, at first with apologies on Mrs. Craddock's side, but after the first time or two in a pleasant matter-of-course kind of way. Placing a very decided emphasis on the word good, Miss Silver was assured that Jennifer would not brew her mother's cup of tea from the wrong canister. She kept everyone out of the schoolroom, and was presently rewarded by some gasping sighs and a rush of tears.

"I am sorry—to have been so foolish—"

Miss Silver was brisk and reassuring.

"You are overdone, and it was something of an ordeal. But it is over. You have nothing to be afraid of."

"You—don't—know—"

The words came so painfully that Miss Silver could not be certain of them, yet she remained under the very decided impression that they had been spoken. She laid a kind, firm hand on Emily Craddock's shoulder.

"Pray do not be so troubled and anxious. I believe that all will be well. Jennifer is bringing you some tea, and she will stay with you. Are you warm enough, or shall I pull the rug a little higher?"

By the time that there was a knock on the door and an enquiry from a young constable as to whether Miss Silver could come and speak to the Inspectors she was able to give an affirmative reply. Two cups of tea and a lightly boiled egg had been partaken of, the egg being Jennifer's idea. "You didn't eat a crumb of breakfast," she said in a scolding tone, adding darkly, "I *saw* you." After which Miss Silver felt quite happy about leaving her in charge.

She found the two Inspectors alone in the study. A chair had been placed in readiness for her. When she had seated herself Frank Abbott said,

"Well, how did it all strike you? Did that faint mean anything, or didn't it?"

She took a moment before she replied in a noncommittal voice,

"Mrs. Craddock is in poor health. She ate no breakfast."

"And that was all?"

"No, I do not think it was all."

"It came very pat after Craddock said that they had nothing to hide."

Miss Silver coughed.

"I do not think that too much stress should be placed upon that."

His shoulder lifted in the slightest of shrugs. If they had been alone, he might have taxed her with having something up her sleeve. If she had, it would stay there until she was ready to produce it. He said,

"Well, well—" And then, "Any sinister reflections upon the Miss Tremletts?"

"I do not think so."

He laughed.

"We had them in one at a time—more to give you a smokescreen than for any other reason. Jackson agrees that they have probably never had a stain upon their characters. Plenty to say for themselves, and an earnest desire to be helpful. They would still be here if we hadn't pushed them off. What did you make of Miranda and her wisp of whimsy? She just sticks to what she said about going for a walk. Remington embroiders on his theme-song. He is much too ethereal a being to concern himself with such earthly matters as where he went, and what he did, and how long it took."

Inspector Jackson said,

"We ought to be able to check up on him—he's noticeable enough."

Miss Silver turned to him with a bright birdlike movement.

"But he was not dressed like that yesterday. He was wearing a dark suit with a navy blue raincoat over it. He had, it is true, one of those rather open shirts, but there was a muffler in the pocket of his coat—he may have been wearing it in the town. He was bare-headed, and of course that very light hair would be noticeable, but there could have been a cap in his pocket too."

Jackson stared.

"You saw him?"

"We came back together in the five o'clock bus."

He said, "Well, that fixes something. I know the picture shop he mentioned—Jarrows. It's new, and a bit highbrow. They ought to remember him there. Not that he or any of these people are actually under suspicion, you must know, but that pound note poor Wayne spotted—well, there was a definite connection with the Colony, and the Chief Constable thought we had better follow it up, especially in the light of this business yesterday."

"A most shocking affair, Inspector. And I think I may have some information for you. Of course I only know what I have seen in the papers."

"Well, I don't suppose any of us knows much more than that. What is your information?"

"I believe that I may have seen the murderer. My bus was early. Since I was meeting Inspector Abbott at three o'clock, I consulted my watch. It was just seven minutes to three. I was walking slowly up the Station Approach, when a man passed me. His head was extensively bandaged, he walked with a stick, and he was carrying a small suit-case. Since he was not one of the passengers on the bus, he must have emerged from the railway station. Seeing his bandaged condition, it occurred to me that he might be on his way to the hospital. But this was not the case. Inspector Abbott was early for our appointment. As I got into his car, and before we had driven away,

I noticed that the bandaged man had crossed the road and was taking the turning which leads into the High Street. I am well acquainted with Ledlington, and at the pace he was going he could certainly have arrived at the County Bank just before three."

Both the Inspectors were looking at her with the extreme of interest. Frank Abbott said,

"It was certainly the murderer—there isn't a doubt about that." His notebook came out. "Now everything you can give us—every detail. Height?"

She paused for a moment, calling up a picture of that limping figure.

"I suppose I should have to say medium. He walked with a stick, he limped. That might take off from a man's height, but by creating the impression that he was stooping it might also give one the idea that he was taller than he appeared to be. And he was wearing a loose light raincoat, one of those mass-produced drab garments worn by every second man at this time of year. They are very disgusting to the figure. A thin man may look larger, or a spreading figure a good deal slighter than it actually is. There is no doubt that the bandages were part of a calculated disguise, and they could have been fastened together so as to enable them to be put on and off like a cap. I think we may assume that the effect of the limp and of the loose raincoat was also very carefully calculated."

Inspector Jackson was dark and serious. If his mind did not move quite as quickly as Frank Abbott's, it was both intelligent and thorough. He said,

"Yes, that's right. He would have put on the bandages in the station—maybe the raincoat too. The two-forty-five was just in, and there would be far too many people coming and going for anyone to notice whether a bandaged man went into a waiting room. They would see him come out, but no one would connect him with quite a different looking person who went in, and by the time he did come out there wouldn't be so many people to see him, because the crowd would have cleared. There's no doubt at all that it was all very carefully thought out."

Frank Abbott nodded.

"Very slick timing," he said. He turned to Miss Silver. "Look here, let's go on with this question of size. Just for the sake of comparison, and without any invidious implications and so forth, how would any of the people here fit it? Try for a mind's-eye picture of any one of them in the bandages and the raincoat, plus limp and stick."

Miss Silver's hands were demurely folded in her lap. She had been looking down at them. She now lifted her eyes and said,

"Either you or Inspector Jackson would be out of the question. You are both too tall. You, I think, are six foot, and he must be a little more. So much height could not be disguised by a limp."

Under a surface twinge of amusement Frank applauded her just and temperate mind. If she was to fit caps, there should be no exceptions. He said in a meditative voice,

"Craddock isn't so tall. About five foot ten?"

"I think not quite as much. He is one of those people who look taller than they really are. Those loose blouses give height and width, and the sandals which he affects have those thick wedge soles. And then there is all that hair."

"You don't mean—"

She said with composure,

"You must not read any special meaning into my words. I am merely answering your question to the best of my ability. I had better continue. Elaine Tremlett certainly did not leave Deep End, and neither she nor Miss Gwyneth could pass as a man. Quite a small man looks tall in women's clothes, and a woman dressed as a man appears to lose height. Miss Gwyneth is definitely not tall enough to have passed as the man I saw. Miranda, on the other hand, must be about five-foot-eight. Her immense mop of hair, its noticeable colour, and the flowing garments which she affects make her look even taller, but I think that my estimate of her height is correct. Then there is Mr. Remington. His fragility makes him appear smaller than he really is. His neck is so very thin, and those open shirts display it. His face, very delicately modelled, and that fine hair of his, all add to this effect. He too wears sandals, but instead of having the new wedge soles they are of the old-fashioned flat kind."

Both the Inspectors were looking at her with attention. Jackson appeared somewhat startled. Frank Abbott said,

"In other words, if you built up his head with bandages and put him into shoes which would give him another inch, his five-foot-five or six would become five-foot-seven or eight, and he might be a possible candidate. His shoulders would have to be built out a bit too, I should say, but of course that could be done." He stopped and broke into a laugh. "I'm afraid my mind boggles at the idea of Augustus playing with any weapon more lethal than an embroidery-needle!"

Miss Silver's cough reproved him.

"I must remind you that the question which I am endeavoring to answer referred only to size."

He had reverted to gravity.

"You are perfectly right. How does Mr. John Robinson fit in? He's medium enough—I should put him at five-foot-eight or nine. The bandages would cover up his beard. And that goes for Craddock too. A bearded man has just got to do something about it if he wants to go murdering people. Can you make a picture of Robinson plus bandages and minus beard, and say how it strikes you?"

She appeared to consider this, but not for longer than a moment.

"In point of size there is nothing against it. Mr. Robinson is neither tall nor short. He wears loose and baggy clothes, but I have the impression that he is of a very average figure."

Frank said quickly,

"Did you notice the man's hands?"

"They were gloved. I have no impression as to their size. I saw the gloves—old loose washleather ones. I associated them vaguely with his injuries, and looked away. I am sorry not to be more exact, but motives of delicacy forbid more than a passing glance at someone who is suffering from any physical disability."

As Inspector Jackson said afterwards, "Well, if that's what she can do with a casual glance, I don't know that I would care to be what you might call put under the microscope." At the time he merely pushed back his chair and got up.

"Well, I'll just have a word with Mr. Craddock. We'd better have the number of his car. By the way, it seems he doesn't keep it up at the regular garage where the Miss Tremletts live, though there's plenty of room there. Can you tell us anything about that, Miss Silver?"

"I can give you the explanation that was given to me. Mr. Craddock has his study in the main block of the house, which is quite shut off from this wing, since a good deal of it is not considered safe. His work demands privacy and quiet. I understand that he is engaged in the study of planetary influences upon plant and animal life, and this necessitates many vigils on the lonely commons and in the woods in which this neighborhood abounds, though I believe he sometimes goes quite far afield. In order not to disturb the Miss Tremletts, he has had one of the damaged rooms in the main block roughly adapted to serve as a garage. It used, I believe, to be a garden room, and it is conveniently placed with regard to the north drive, which goes off in an opposite direction to that by which you came in. He can thus come and go at all hours of the day or night without disturbing anyone."

"And without anyone knowing whether he's in or out. Very convenient indeed." Inspector Jackson's tone was rather marked. He moved in the direction of the door, and then back again. "This man Craddock, Miss Silver—you've been living in the house with him. You've had opportunities we haven't got, and can't get. You see him when he isn't putting up a show—trying to impress. Well, how does he strike you? Is he just a windbag, or is there something there? I've met his kind before. Sometimes they've got everything in the shop window, and sometimes they haven't."

Miss Silver's small, neat features had assumed a very serious look, her voice when she spoke had a very serious tone.

"You say, Inspector, that I am in a position to judge of Mr. Craddock when he is not putting up a show or trying to impress. I doubt very much whether there is anyone who is in such a position."

Frank Abbott put in, "You mean you think he's acting all the time?"

"To a very great extent. A picture is being presented. It is possible that he believes in it himself. I am not sure upon this point. He receives a great deal of quite fulsome adulation from the Miss Tremletts. The lady who calls herself Miranda appears to admire him and to have come here on his account. Mr. Remington is, I think, rather jealous of him, but that is in itself a tribute. His wife, who speaks of him always as Mr. Craddock, appears to be in a state of trembling awe. I have never heard her use his Christian name. Their rooms are at opposite ends of this wing. Jennifer, who is the eldest of the three children—she is nearly thirteen—used, I am told, to adore her stepfather. She now hates and fears him. She is a sensitive girl, and she is in a highly nervous state. The other two are robust little boys, and I do not think they have very much feeling for him one way or another. He talks a good deal about self-expression, but if the children get in his way he can be severe. He is greedy about his food, intolerant of opposition, and continually finds fault with Mrs. Craddock."

Inspector Jackson pursed up his mouth as if he was going to whistle, and then thought better of it.

"Well, that's pretty sweeping. But it's not to say he'd rob a bank."

"No, Inspector."

"Any of the children his?"

"No."

"Inspector Abbott tells me there was something about a boat upsetting, and some mushrooms that weren't the real thing. Where did the information come from?"

"From Mrs. Craddock."

"She has money?"

"Yes."

"Tied up on the children?"

"Yes—she told me that."

"Any sign that she thought her husband had a hand in either of those affairs?"

Miss Silver took a little time before she said,

"I could not say. She was distressed and upset. She takes pains at all times to assure me, and perhaps herself, that the children are very fortunate to have such a stepfather. I do not think that I can tell you any more than that."

Jackson said in a meditative tone,

"If he had red hair—"

Frank Abbott laughed.

"Well, he hasn't. And if he had, it wouldn't mean a thing." Then, as Miss Silver looked from one to the other, "The fellow in the Enderby Green hold-up had red hair. You remember, I told you about it. The bank manager was shot dead—the same technique as yesterday's job at Ledlington. But the eighteen-year-old clerk was luckier than poor Wayne—he is just out of hospital. And about the only thing he seems sure about is that the murderer had red hair. Everything else beautifully medium and unobtrusive, but quite noticeable red hair. So if there is one thing that everyone else can feel sure about, it is that the hair was just as much a disguise as yesterday's bandages, and he won't be found wearing it in private life. Then young Smithers says he had a muffler wound twice about his neck and covering him pretty well up to the ears, and he couldn't say whether there was a beard under it or not. I wonder if there was."

Jackson said,

"Well, if he was all that wrapped up, I don't see how the clerk could see that his hair was red."

"I should say it was meant to be seen. Anyhow Smithers says he saw it—says he'll swear to it. And a lot of good that is going to be!" He threw out a hand. "All right, Jackson, you go and try your hand on Craddock. Find out where he was at three o'clock in the afternoon on the third of January—if you can. I'll come along when I'm through."

Inspector Jackson turned to the door again. He said, "Thank you, Miss Silver," and went out of the room.

Miss Silver was reflecting that Miss Gwyneth Tremlett's description of Mr. Sandrow had included red hair and a red beard, and that she had repeated this description to Frank Abbott.

CHAPTER 25

WHEN THE DOOR had shut Frank turned a cool sarcastic gaze upon her.

"Well?" he said.

"Are you asking me something, Frank?"

"I'm asking you what you've got up your sleeve."

"My dear Frank!"

"Oh, I know, I know—you never have anything there, you never pull rabbits out of hats, and you never, never, never keep anything from the police. Or is it a case of hardly ever?"

"Only when it is a theory which has yet to be proved—never in the case of a fact."

He cocked an eyebrow.

"And the borderline between fact and theory? Rather like the European boundary situation, don't you think? So you have got a theory. Are you going to tell me what it is? . . . . No? Well, I've got one too, and I'd like to talk to you about it. Which means of course that I would like you to agree with me. It's about the girl who waited outside the bank whilst the murderer did his job. Beautiful Blonde. And Bandaged Bandit, as the papers have it. I suppose you didn't see her as well as the man?"

His tone was a mocking one, but she replied in a serious manner.

"No, Frank. And whoever may have seen her during the brief period when she was waiting for the murderer, I think it is quite certain that no one will ever see her again."

"You don't mean—" He looked startled for a moment. "No—

I don't think you do. Well, perpend. I'm not going to risk being wrong."

She made a slight negative movement.

"Oh, no, I do not mean that she will have been murdered, but merely that she has never existed. No one would set out to do robbery and murder with a spectacularly blonde young woman well to the fore as his accomplice. She was, I gather, seen by a number of passers by, and it was undoubtedly intended that she should be seen. May I ask just what these people have to say?"

"You may indeed! Miss Muffin, who is an old lady's companion, is a positive fount of information. She says the damsel had '*Very* golden hair. I mean, one couldn't help wondering if it was natural, though of course respectable girls do do *such* strange things to their hair nowadays. And oh, yes—eyebrows half way up her forehead—so odd—*very* much made-up—and the sort of complexion that takes hours to do. But quite unnoticeable clothes—just a dark coat and skirt and a plain felt hat—black, I think, though it might have been a very dark navy. So difficult to tell in a poor light, and the sky was very much overcast at the time.' This is much the best description, though she was also seen by a Mr. Carpenter, a young man named Pottinger, and a baker's boy. The boy was more interested in the car than in the lady, but as it had been stolen for the occasion from the Market Square, that isn't much help. Carpenter and Pottinger both noticed her. Carpenter with disapproval. Pottinger rather sitting up and taking notice, but hadn't seen as much of her as he would have liked, because she had her hand up doing something to her hat as he passed the car. Both agree that she was, as you say, a spectacular blonde. And of course I agree with you that all the twopence-coloured business would be just as much a disguise as the murderer's bandages. So I imagine what we have to look for is a dullish girl whom nobody would turn his head to look at twice—the sort of girl, in fact, who comes nineteen to the dozen in any sizable town and can pass in a crowd without anyone noticing whether she is there or not. Which makes it so beautifully easy, doesn't it?"

Miss Silver inclined her head.

"I think you are right. But there is, however, some valuable material for conjecture. Miss Muffin's description is extremely helpful. I gather that the car was found deserted in a lane near Ledstow. The young woman would have to get away from there, and before doing so she would certainly take steps to alter her appearance. The golden wig would be taken off and the make-up removed. She would then probably put on some kind of coat, preferably a raincoat. Since the sky was overcast, this would be quite natural, and an excellent disguise for the figure. Substitute a head square for the hat, and all chance of recognition would be avoided. But she would have to make her way from the place where the car was abandoned, and as quickly as possible. She may, or may not, have already dropped the man. I think she would do so as soon as she could. But whilst it was highly necessary that they should separate and return without delay to their normal surroundings, neither of them would dare to risk a public conveyance. A motor-bicycle, or a bicycle, here presents itself as a probability. Was there any place in this lane in which the car was found, or in its immediate vicinity, where a bicycle might have been concealed?"

He nodded.

"You've got it. There's a derelict shed just off the track which runs into the lane. A motor-bicycle had stood there—Jackson found traces of oil. The man probably went off that way. You can't beat a cap and goggles as a disguise, and he could have gone on along the coast past the Catherine-Wheel, or into Ledstow, or back to Ledlington. He could have taken the girl up behind him, or she could have had her own pedal bicycle or a car of a different make and gone off in another direction, possibly taking the loot, which amounted to about three thousand pounds. I think myself that they would separate as soon as possible."

"I think so too."

He pushed back his chair.

"Two hearts that beat as one! Jackson and I will now revert to looking for needles in bundles of hay. He is better at it than I am. I get bored." He leaned forward suddenly. "Look here—why did Mrs. Craddock faint like that?"

"She is a delicate woman, Frank."

One of his colourless eyebrows rose.

"Well, I supopse she goes on being delicate all the time, but she isn't always fainting. Why should her delicacy be aggravated to swooning-point just at the moment when Craddock announces that they have nothing to hide? It seems to me a little too dramatic to be quite fortuitous."

Miss Silver coughed gently.

"It was certainly dramatic. But was that all that struck you?"

"Was there anything which ought to have struck me?"

"I just wondered whether anything had. Whether, for instance, you had been observing Mr. John Robinson with any particular attention."

He looked puzzled.

"Well, I don't know. He was playing the fool a bit. There were moments when I had an idea that he was enjoying himself. Of course he might be quite a suitable suspect, if you put it that way. Well established character as an eccentric—nature study and bird-watching, which accounts for his coming and going at any odd hour—boarded-up windows, and a garden which is practically enclosed by a palisade. But then most of this applies to Craddock too. He studies plants under planetary influences. Which sounds a bit like plucking the fifth cinquefoil from the left at three minutes past midnight when the moon is dark and something or other is in the ascendant, as all the best spells have it. And uncommonly convenient for a gentleman who needs a smokescreen. And it was Mrs. Craddock who fainted."

Miss Silver gazed at him mildly.

"Let us return to Mr. John Robinson. When I asked you whether you had paid him any particular attention I was referring to his habit of quotation."

Frank Abbott laughed.

"Oh, *that?* Well, it's hardly an indictable offence. We have been known to do it ourselves. But I remember he first quoted Tennyson, and then made a slighting remark about the quotation, which was, I must say, not one of the higher poetic flights. I looked at you to see if you were going to wield a thunderbolt, but you spared him."

She allowed herself a faint, brief smile.

"He made two quotations. They were both from the same poem—rather a famous one. One was, in fact, the first lines of that poem, and the other the last."

He frowned.

"Something about cliffs. He said—"

Miss Silver supplied the quotation.

" 'Long lines of cliff, breaking, have left a chasm, and in the chasm are foam and yellow sand.' "

He looked at her blankly and shook his head.

"Nothing doing, I'm afraid. But the other one does seem to produce a slight reaction—'The little port had never seen a costlier funeral.' "

Miss Silver made a gentle correction.

"'Seldom', not 'never', Frank."

He burst out laughing.

"Well, seldom or never, I can't place the thing. Are you going to tell me?"

"I think not, Frank."

He got up.

"Well, I must go and find Jackson. I'd love to stop and play quotations with you, but I'm afraid it might give the Colony an idea that you are cast for the part of chief suspect." Then in a moment he was entirely serious. "Look here," he said, "I'm not liking this for you—I never did, you know. There's something uncommonly ruthless about these crimes, and the only clue we've got does point to some link with this place. You'll be careful, won't you?"

Miss Silver smiled indulgently.

"My dear Frank, I am always careful."

CHAPTER 26

MR. CRADDOCK'S HUMOUR was not at its best by the time Inspector Jackson had finished his polite but pertinacious questioning. He might, and possibly did, assure himself that he had throughout maintained a high standard of courtesy and philosophic calm, but to anyone whose mind was not adapted to so partial a view it was obvious that he was in a very bad temper. He came into the workroom, and standing upon the hearthrug rather to the rear of the sofa upon which Emily Craddock lay, he delivered himself of an oration. What, he demanded, was the world coming to, what was happening to society, when a person practically indistinguishable from a member of the Gestapo could walk into your house and demand an account of every moment of your time over a period of weeks, together with a complete itinerary of your walks and drives.

"Where was I upon this day and at this hour! And what road did I take to each place! And how long did I stay! I preserved my calm. I said to him, 'My good Inspector, do you suppose that I keep a minute-to-minute diary of my comings and goings? Could you yourself possibly answer such questions? If you could, I am sorry for you, since it would prove you to be so obsessed with the minutiae of physical life and its earthbound materialism as to be incapable of any higher intelligence. For myself, I live in the realm of thought—I occupy myself with ideas. I am engaged upon an important work on the subject of Planetary Influences, and I certainly cannot tell you just what I was doing at three o'clock in the afternoon on the third of January. I may have been out, or I may have been in. I may have been engaged in my studies, or in writing, or in meditation. I was certainly not in London. It is a place I detest—all noise, and clatter, and disturbing vibrations. The only time I have been to London for months was on the occasion when I made the journey in order to interview Miss Silver, who, as I told the Inspector, will probably remember the date, which was assuredly not January the third.'"

He cast a look of lofty interrogation at Miss Silver, who sat knitting by the couch. Since she faced Emily Craddock, she was able to observe that she appeared to be rather stunned by the reverberations of Mr. Craddock's powerful voice. She was also well placed to intercept his glance, and to reply,

"I believe it was January the eighth."

The brief respite being over, Mr. Craddock resumed.

"The Inspector had literally nothing to say. I believe that, while remaining perfectly courteous, I was able to administer a sufficient rebuke. People on these lower planes are extremely insensitive, but I believe I was able to show him that his impertinence left me quite unmoved." The rolling voice developed a rasp. He addressed his wife. "If it had not been for your lack of self-control, my dear Emily, I should not have been subjected to all this unpleasantness. I cannot imagine what came over you. I state in front of the other members of the Colony and in the presence of two police officers that I have nothing to hide, and you immediately give way to the incredible folly and stupidity of fainting. I really feel that I am entitled to an explanation. If you cannot perceive the invidious conclusions which might be, and undoubtedly were, drawn from this lamentable exhibition, I feel it my duty to point them out to you."

Emily Craddock's white cheek became a shade paler—something of a feat since it already appeared to be quite drained of colour. She put out her hand in a groping way towards Miss Silver, who laid down her knitting and took it in a kind warm clasp. It was cold to the touch, and it trembled.

"Mr. Craddock, your wife is quite unfit for all this. She has had a sleepless night, a trying morning, and no breakfast. I myself informed the Inspectors that she was in delicate health. What she now needs is rest, and I think there is no purpose to be served by continuing to discuss an experience which has not been very pleasant for any of us."

Her eyes dwelt upon him, as in time past they had dwelt upon so many pupils—the nervous, the tongue-tied, the intelligent, the pretentious, the impudent, the recalcitrant, the cocksure. Each had found in it some corrective quality—encouragement where encouragement was needed, rebuke where rebuke was called for, authority for the rebellious, and, in every case, a most penetrating understanding.

Peveril Craddock had a horrid moment in which he found himself with nothing to say. His head was full of words, but they buzzed there like flies, and he could make no use of them.

Miss Silver continued to hold Emily's hand and to look at him. The sweat had come to his brow before she said,

"Your studies have been gravely interrupted, have they not? I will see that Mrs. Craddock has everything she needs."

It was a dismissal, and he was thankful to accept it.

When he had gone Emily Craddock withdrew her hand and put it over her eyes. After a little time she said in a small, weak voice,

"It would be better if I were dead."

Miss Silver had resumed her knitting. The gentle click of the needles came and went with a rhythmic sound. She said in a firm and cheerful voice,

"Oh, no, my dear, that is quite untrue. You have three children to care for. It would be forsaking a post of duty."

"I'm—no good to them—"

The words could hardly be distinguished, but Miss Silver was in no doubt of their meaning.

"That is not true," she said. "It can never be true of anyone who is doing his duty. You have not to count up what you can do, or how much good it will accomplish. That is not your business. You have only to do what you can, one day at a time, without regretting yesterday or being afraid about tomorrow." After a pause she added, "Your children need you very much indeed. Jennifer now—"

Emily Craddock burst out crying.

"She's so like her father!" she said. "I don't mean to look at, but in herself. We quarrelled, and I can't even remember what it was about now—but he went away. He used to, you know, and write articles, and do sketches, and come back again. But this time he didn't. He went to America, and the plane crashed and everyone was killed. And then Francis left me his money and—I married Mr. Craddock—" The words got fainter and fainter until with Peveril Craddock's name she turned her face into the pillow and found no more to say.

There was silence in the room.

CHAPTER 27

RETURNING HOME with the Miss Tremletts, Thomasina was not at all surprised to discover Peter Brandon upon the doorstep. Not quite literally upon the actual step of course, but prowling up and down with the obvious intention of intercepting them. Since she desired nothing better than an opportunity of telling him just what she felt about his following her to Deep End, she accepted an invitation to go for a walk with no more than a single indignant glance. She had her back to the Miss Tremletts at the time, so there was nothing to chill the warm sympathy with which her departure with Peter was regarded. It was as well that Miss Elaine and Miss Gwyneth could have no idea of the really furious antagonisms which were surging up in the two young people whom they followed with so kindly and sentimental a gaze.

They were no sooner screened by an intervening clump of evergreen than Thomasina turned a fiery glance upon her companion. It told her what indeed she had already guessed, that here was no abashed penitent, but a stiff-necked young man in quite as bad a temper as herself. And worse, because she didn't go into black rages, and Peter did. He was in one now, and they always made him very difficult to deal with. She began to review her armoury. A good vigorous attack would at any rate bring things out into the open. And he needn't think she was going to let him get in first, because she wasn't. A fine colour mounted to her cheeks. The grey eyes which at least two young men, undeterred by the limited number of available rhymes, had compared—in verse—to stars were trained upon him.

"Why on earth did you come here?"

Height confers a most unfair advantage. Peter could look

down upon the top of her head. He did this briefly, and countered with,

"For that matter, why did you?"

"Look here, Peter—"

"I haven't the slightest desire to look at you! I haven't got the patience! You stir up this idiotic business about Anna Ball—well, I was against that all along, wasn't I? The girl probably had some perfectly good reason for getting off the map, and if you ever do find her, I've no doubt she won't be best pleased. Well, then you go grubbing round after her—"

"I do not go grubbing round!"

He raised his voice and swept on.

"You hire a private detective, and she has no sooner got on to the job than you come blundering down here, and get in her way, and run yourself into God knows what unpleasantness. That chap Abbott's down here, isn't he? And there's been a bank robbery and a double murder in Ledlington. I suppose you do know that?"

Thomasina put her chin in the air.

"Considering Frank and a Ledlington Inspector are over here about it this morning, I suppose I do."

"And why are they over here about it?"

She said in a voice that was more thoughtful than angry,

"They want to know who spent a pound note in a fancy work shop in Dedham, and whether there was anything odd about it. And they want to know whether anyone was in Ledlington yesterday afternoon—and of course quite a lot of them were."

"Who?"

A gleam of humour mitigated her glance.

"Not me. Disappointing for you, but there it is."

"I said *who*."

"Oh, Miss Gwyneth—but I don't think she'd be any good at robbing a bank—not really, you know. And Miss Silver, and that funny little Mr. Remington, and the bird-watching man who lives in the other wing at Deepe House with all the windows boarded up, and Mr. Craddock. They were all there, but none of them seems to have any clear idea of where they were or what they were doing when the bank was being robbed. Miss Elaine and I have perfect alibis, because by three o'clock she had stopped resting, and was telling me all about her mother making a phonograph record when they were first invented—Edison and all that you know—and how she stopped because she was nervous and gave a little laugh right in the middle of her song, and of course it came out in the record. Well, nobody could make up an alibi like that if it wasn't true, could they? So Miss Elaine and I are safe."

He was frowning very deeply indeed.

"Why do they think anyone here was mixed up in it?"

Thomasina was serious too.

"I don't know whether they do—I suppose they must. It would be something to do with the pound note they were asking about. They didn't say of course, but there was that robbery near London about a month ago—what was the name of the place—Enderby Green. The bank manager was murdered there too, and I've got an idea it had something to do with that. The note they were asking about couldn't be one that was robbed at Ledlington yesterday, because it was part of the takings of this fancy work shop at Dedham as far back as Tuesday. There seemed to be something they could recognize it by, and of course if they thought anyone from here had paid it in, they would naturally want to know what we were all doing yesterday afternoon. But perhaps I had better tell you all about it."

"Perhaps you had." It wasn't said in at all an encouraging sort of voice.

Thomasina was under no illusion about Peter Brandon. Children always know what people are like. Sometimes they forget later on, but she had known Peter when she was in her pram, and she hadn't got a forgetting nature. She knew just how obstinate and opinionated, and odious he could be. She considered that he was exhibiting all these unpleasant qualities in a highly characteristic manner, but as she really did want to tell him about the interview with the police she refrained herself and plunged into narrative. She made it a lively one. By the time she had finished Peter might almost have been there.

"And when Pompous Peveril said they hadn't got anything to hide, Mr. Robinson laughed as if he thought there was something very funny about that, and Mrs. Craddock fainted."

They discussed all the implications of John Robinson's laugh and Emily Craddock's swoon, emerging upon a worse battleground than before, it being Peter's declared opinion that the whole thing was so fishy that it stank, and that the sooner she got out of it the better.

Thomasina re-entered the fray with zest.

"If there's a stink, it's because there's something that wants clearing up, which is a reason for staying, not for running away."

Peter stuck his hands in his pockets.

"You know, I think I should leave garbage to the garbage man—in this case the police. More efficient and less likely to get themselves and everyone else into a mess. There's a train from Ledlington at three-five. Go home and pack your things, and we'll go out by the bus and catch it."

Thomasina told herself afterwards that she had been perfectly calm and dignified. She said,

"If you think you can look up trains and buses that I don't want and make me take them you had better start thinking all over again, because I'm staying here."

She did admit in the privacy of her own thought that she ought to have left it at that. It was calm, it was adequate, and if Peter wasn't set down by it he ought to have been. Unfortunately, instead of stopping she went on. She wasn't quite sure what she actually said, because her feelings overcame her, but she did remember that she had stamped her foot, and that there had been an access of angry tears when she came to the part about Anna. Because, somehow or other, that was where they had got back to—Anna Ball, and why had she disappeared, and where was she now?

"And don't you see, Peter, if there really is someone here who is going round robbing banks and shooting people—don't you see that something perfectly dreadful might have happened to Anna? Just because of that. You called her a Nosey Parker yourself—you know you did. And she *was!* She always wanted to know everything. I used to be sorry for her about it and think it was because she hadn't got a family or any affairs of her own to be interested in. But don't you see, if she was like that—and she *was*—don't you see, might have got her into finding out something—something dangerous. Don't you see that she might have given someone a dreadful reason for getting rid of her?"

Peter took his hands out of his pockets and caught hold of her wrists.

"Suppose it's true—suppose she did get herself murdered. I don't believe it for a moment, but just suppose she did. What do you propse to do about it—go poking your nose in where you're not wanted, and get yourself murdered too? You might, you know. If you tried hard enough and if there really is a murderer camouflaging himself in this barmy Colony. I suppose you expect me to stand by and let you do it. Well, I'm not going to, and that's flat!"

"Let me go!"

She might just as well not have spoken.

"It's a job for the police, and you know it! There's nothing you could do if you stayed here for a month of Sundays!"

"Well then, there is!"

"As what?"

If she had been a little cooler, or if he hadn't been holding her, she might not have gone on, but the things that were bubbling up in her were too hot and angry. They came pouring out.

"Someone has got to find out about Anna. It's nearly five months, and perhaps she's dead. Or shut up. It keeps coming over me. Suppose she found out something and they've got her shut up in the ruined part of the house. No one goes in there except that Craddock man. It's kept locked off because it's not supposed to be safe for the children. Those old houses have cellars. Suppose Anna is there, locked up—how can I go away? I think about it in the night. Suppose she was locked up in one of those cellars, and everyone said like you do, 'Oh, well, she just doesn't choose to write.' I keep thinking about that, and about our all just getting up in the morning, and having our meals, and going out and coming in, and nobody bothering about her or—or caring whether she is dead or alive. Peter, it's no use—I've got to do something about it. And—and—there's someone coming—let go of me at once, or I'll scream!"

"And give me in charge for assault?"

She said in a quick different voice,

"It would serve you right. Peter, let go—there *is* someone coming!"

John Robinson came up through the wood. He did not watch birds for nothing. He was instantly aware that he had interrupted a quarrel. He observed the traces of Thomasina's angry tears, the brightness of her eyes, and the very becoming colour which deepened at his approach. He observed a broken twig and a crushed leaf about midway between her and the tall frowning young man, and deduced without difficulty that he had just stepped back from—no, not an embrace. Miss Thomasina Elliot was rubbing her wrists. The fellow had been holding her, and he had stepped back. It became necessary to discover whether this was a case of damsel in distress. He therefore checked a little in his walk, allowed a smile to filter through his beard, and addressed Thomasina.

"Taking the air after our grilling by the police? There's quite a good view at the top of the hill. Have you been up there yet?" His voice was slow and pleasant, the country accent much less marked than it had been at Deepe House.

Thomasina was rather pleased with the way she managed to smile and say,

"Yes, the children took me. I haven't time to go on this morning. Peter and I have to be getting back."

So the young man was a friend. Mr. Robinson acknowledged the half introduction with another smile and went on his way whistling melodiously.

Thomasina set off at a brisk pace down the hill without looking round to see whether Peter was following her. She wouldn't run, because if she did, he might run after her. She would just walk as fast as she could and not look round, and whether he overtook her or not, she did not intend to say another single word.

But when, within sight of the Miss Tremletts' cottage, she broke her resolution and looked back, there was no sign of Peter Brandon.

CHAPTER 28

IN THE AFTERNOON the Miss Tremletts took Thomasina to tea with Miranda. Having met the assembled Colony once already that day, it was rather a relief to find that they were the only guests. Even Peter wasn't there. There really was, of course, no reason why he should have been, since it was most improbable that he and Miranda had met. It was therefore completely irrational to feel a little lowered in one's spirits.

Miranda's exuberant welcome did nothing to raise them. She embraced Miss Elaine and Miss Gwyneth as if they had been parted for months instead of a few short hours, and held Thomasina by both hands for quite a long time. Warmth to which one cannot respond has a depressing effect. Thomasina did not in the least want to have her hands held by an astonishing red-haired woman in a flowing violet robe. She hoped that Elaine and Gwyneth would not think it necessary to stay for hours, but she was very much afraid that they might. People did in the Colony.

It was during tea that Thomasina realized how fortunate she was to be boarding with the Miss Tremletts, and not with anyone else. Devoted adherents of Peveril Craddock's they might be, but they remained obstinately faithful to quite ordinary things to eat. There was no health tea in their cottage, no special brand of coffee which was made out of something quite different, none of the cereals which so strongly resemble little packets of chopped straw. There was brown bread, it is true, and there was porridge, but after that the line was firmly drawn.

Miranda had a health tea of her own of a pale greenish colour, and it had lemon in it instead of milk. Thomasina found it quite incredibly nasty. There were also home-made biscuits with a good deal of charcoal in them, a conserve of rowan and elderberry which combined mawkishness with acidity, and a savoury cake which tasted strongly of sage. It was not an inspiring meal, and the dreadful thing was that Miranda was quite overwhelmingly hospitable, and not only told them exactly how everything was made, but continued to press her horrid handiwork upon them in such a manner that it could not be refused.

"I really think my best batch of preserve! Augustus said not enough sugar, but it is keeping remarkably well. And the cake—an experiment, and really quite a striking success, I think, and I am sure that you will too. Elaine, you are eating nothing. . . . . . No, Gwyneth, I really cannot take a refusal—you must positively try these sandwiches. Quite a new filling, and I'm not going to tell you what it is, because I want you to guess. . . . . Oh, no, it is not one of Peveril's. Advanced as he is in some ways, he is inclined to be unprogressive in the matter of food. Experiment must go before experience. We cannot always see where the next step will take us. Miss Elliot —or may I say Thomasina—these forms are so meaningless, do you not think so—you have positively nothing to eat. Now, which is it to be—the cake, the sandwiches, or the biscuits?"

The sandwiches seemed the smallest. Thomasina took one, and found that two more were being pressed upon her plate.

"Something quite new, and I am sure that you will like them."

They were quite incredibly nasty, with several lingering flavors which she found it impossible to resolve. She did refuse a second dose of pale green tea, but her cup was filled and she had to go on sipping from it. The one stroke of luck was being able to slip the two extra sandwiches into the pocket of her coat, where the filling oozed and left a horrid stain upon the lining. She would not have been able to do it if it had not been for the unheralded appearance of Augustus Remington, who wandered into the room in a pale blue smock with a tambour frame in one hand and an embroidery needle connected with it by a strand of orange silk in the other. Since the heads of all three ladies were immediately turned in his direction, she snatched the opportunity and dealt with the sandwiches.

A sad protesting voice rose above the welcoming twitter of the Miss Tremletts and the hospitable insistence of Miranda.

"No—no—not a thing. Charcoal in those biscuits is a mistake—a mere dissonance. And I always told you there wasn't enough sugar in that conserve. No—no—I won't take anything at all. And certainly *not* herbal cake. Nor sandwiches. They remind me too, too painfully of that horror of childhood's days, the picnic—spiders down the back of the neck and earwigs in the milk. Besides, I have no appetite at all. This morning's rude intrusion! Too shattering to the vibrations! I did not come here for food, but for companionship. I heard voices in my solitude, where I was endeavouring to compose myself with my embroidery, and my feet brought me here." He waved the tambour frame at Miss Gwyneth and dropped his voice to a low and confidential tone. "My latest composition."

"What is it, Augustus?"

Both the Miss Tremletts peered at the fine stretched canvas upon which there was depicted a dark grey cloud tinged with pink, a human eye surrounded by three sunflower heads, and a twining plant with scarlet berries. The eye had been completed, but only one of the sunflowers and part of the trailing plant. The cloud was in a fairly advanced state. As an example of the embroiderer's art it stood high, a fact immediately pointed out by Miranda.

"I told you he did the most exquisite needlework"—she addressed Thomasina—"No, it wasn't you, it was that Miss Silver. But he does, doesn't he?"

"What does it mean?" repeated the Miss Tremletts, both speaking together.

Mr. Remington appeared to wave the question away.

"That surely is for you to say. I conceive the idea—I endeavour to give it form and substance. It is not for me to supply the perceptive intelligence as well. Beauty is given to the world—it is for the world to receive it." He flung himself into a chair as he spoke, put a couple of stitches into one of the sunflowers, and murmured in a languid voice, "The inspiration fails. After this morning I am not yet attuned."

Thomasina had already heard so much about the morning that she could not imagine Miss Gwyneth and Miss Elaine having anything more to say about it. But in that she was wrong. Not only they but Miranda and Augustus appeared to have an endless store of speculation, supposition and comment to offer. And they all appeared to be very much taken up with Mr. John Robinson.

"Such a strange person."

"All those windows boarded up."

"No one knows anything at all about him."

"We have never even spoken to him. He seems positively to avoid us"—that was the Miss Tremletts.

"Distressingly secretive."

Sometimes they all talked at once, sometimes Miranda's deep ringing voice bore everyone down. Thomasina remembered the story of the Scapegoat. She thought it would be very convenient if the police could be induced to fix their attention upon Mr. John Robinson, who though in the Colony was not really of it.

"Of course," said Miss Gwyneth, "we are all quite sure that this horrid affair can have nothing to do with us."

"Peveril was wonderful!" said Miss Elaine. "Such dignity—such composure. But that he should be subjected—that any of us should be subjected to being questioned by the police!"

Miranda looked over the tops of their heads and said,

"He stands too high to be touched by it."

Augustus Remington pushed away his tambour frame in rather a pettish manner.

"Dear Miranda, how true! And so, I hope, do we all. Yet innocence should be vindicated. It has occurred to me that you might contribute to this end by your art. As you know, I am somewhat of a sceptic as to the—no, I will not say authenticity, since that would imply a doubt of your integrity which I would of course never for a moment entertain."

Miranda lapsed into her blunter manner.

"If you will say what you mean, Augustus, and stop wrapping it up!"

He closed his eyes for a moment.

"I cannot be hurried—it disturbs the thought process. I was about to say that if I were somewhat of a sceptic as to the practical uses of the crystal, I would suggest that you should employ it in order to clear this matter up."

Miss Gwyneth brightened.

"Miranda sees things in the crystal," she explained to Thomasina. "If she were to look into it she might see something about Mr. Robinson or—or—anyone." She turned eagerly. "Miranda, have you tried?"

Miranda waved a noncommittal hand.

"It has all been dark—"

"But it mightn't be today—with all of us here in sympathy!" Miss Elaine's voice was eager too.

Augustus made a slight negative gesture.

"I am half a sceptic. You must not rely on me."

Thomasina had been brought up to be polite to her elders, or she would have added, "Or on me."

But it became apparent that opposition had merely roused Miranda's spirit, and that with or without any further urging she proposed to accede to the Miss Tremletts' request. The tea-table was cleared and a square of black velvet laid upon it, the crystal, a large round ball on an ebony stand placed exactly in the centre, and all the lights turned out except for one which cast a single dazzling ray. It was all very odd, and something in Thomasina didn't like it. She didn't know why, and she didn't care, because what she felt had nothing to do with reason. It harked right back to the child or the savage who is afraid of the dark. And what that child or that savage wanted to do was to hit right out at the crystal ball and to break it, and then run screaming from the room. Naturally the civilized person who was Thomasina hadn't the slightest notion of doing any such thing.

She watched the ray of light which came slanting from a hooded lamp and made the crystal ball look like a bubble of light floating on dark, deep water. You couldn't see the table, or the velvet, or the ebony stand—only the ball with the light swirling round in it. Because that was what it seemed to do. It swirled like water—no, like mist—like cloudy thoughts in a dream. And then they cleared, and as plainly as she had ever seen anything in all her life, she saw Anna Ball's face looking at her out of the crystal. It was there for a moment, and then it was gone again. But she had seen it, and nothing and nobody was ever going to persuade her that she hadn't. She drove her nails hard, hard against the palm of either hand.

Miranda gave a long, deep sigh, and leaned right back against the cushions of her chair. The ray and the bright crystal were between her and Thomasina. When she leaned back like that she went into the darkness. Her voice came out of it, very deep and low.

"Anna, where are you?"

All the words were on the same deep muted note. Then the voice lifted. It became another voice, faint and far away.

"Not—here—"

Then the deep voice again.

"Where are you?"

"A—long—way—off—"

"Where?"

"I—don't—want—her—to—know. Tell her. . . . . happy. . . . . no good—to—cling—to the past. . . . . Broken links—cannot—be replaced. . . . . This is—final."

There was another of those deep sighs. Miranda moved, put up a hand to her head, groaned distressingly, and sat up.

"What happened?" she said in her natural voice. She sounded bewildered. "Did anyone see anything? I didn't. I went into the trance—or did I? I feel awful. Here, for pity's sake put on the lights, Augustus, and switch off that ray—it's blinding me!"

As the lights came on, Miranda could be seen to be pale. Between the dark red of her hair and the violet of her robe this pallor had a greenish tinge. But the room was consolingly ordinary again. The remnants of the tea, hastily bundled on to a side table, were reassuringly domestic. The crystal on its ebony stand was just a big glass ball. The black velvet square upon which it stood had a worn place on it, and the edges had begun to fray.

Miranda blinked and said,

"I don't remember a thing. What happened?"

Elaine was twittering with excitement.

"You went into a trance!"

Miranda ran a hand through her hair.

"But I was going to look into the crystal—"

"Oh, but you didn't! You just leaned back, and of course we knew it was the trance. And then you began to talk."

"What did I say?"

"You said, 'Anna, where are you?' " Thomasina spoke in a voice which she only just kept from being an angry one. "Why did you do that?"

"I haven't the least idea. Did I say anything else?"

Augustus Remington gave his odd high laugh.

"Oh, yes, my dear, you did indeed! First you said, 'Anna where are you—' "

"And then your voice was quite different, and you said, 'Not here—' "

"And then—"

They tumbled over one another to tell her what she had said—breaking sentences, jumbling up the words, correcting one another. Only Thomasina took no part in it. She looked at Miranda and she held her tongue.

" 'Anna, where are you—' Well, I can't make head or tail of it," said Miranda. "Can anyone?"

Miss Gwyneth was frowning.

"That Miss Ball's name was Anna, wasn't it?"

Miss Elaine gave a little sniff.

"I don't know, I'm sure. She wasn't at all friendly—no one called her by it. And she went away almost at once."

"And why should you get a message from her?" said Gwyneth. "So—so irrelevant."

Augustus Remington had picked up his tambour frame. He held the needle poised and took a delicate stitch.

"How too, too true! The irrelevance of these communications intrigues me. Why wander in from the void to make perfectly banal remarks?"

"But there was a message," said Miss Elaine.

"Oh, a definite message," said Miss Gwyneth.

They spoke as if taking part in a duet.

" 'I don't want her to know—' "

" 'Broken links cannot be replaced—' "

Then, both together,

"But what does it mean? Who is the message for?"

Augustus took another stitch. His glance mocked them. "That, alas, we cannot tell."

Miranda closed her eyes.

"Well, all I can say is that it means nothing to me, except that it's given me a headache. But then that's often the way with messages like this—they don't mean a thing to me. I am only the medium." She raised her hands above her head and stretched magnificently. "Well, that's that, and I'm going to have another cup of tea."

When your hostess has confessed to having a headache it is not in very good taste to linger upon the scene. Miss Elaine and Miss Gwyneth made their farewells. The embraces were on the languid side, and Thomasina got off with quite an ordinary handshake.

As they walked the short distance to the converted stables, Miss Elaine remarked with some acerbity that she thought

Augustus should have had enough sense to come away when they did, instead of settling down on Miranda with his everlasting embroidery. Upon which the sisters started an argument as to whether Miranda would have preferred him to leave, and whether it was really true that he spent every evening there and did not go away until after midnight. Nothing but Thomasina's youth and innocence prevented either or both of them from adding, "*If then!*"

CHAPTER 29

THOMASINA WENT UP to her room and began to take off her things. When she had unfastened her coat she slipped a hand into the pocket, because she knew she had put a handkerchief there and she remembered about the sandwiches. She didn't want it stained to the bone with Miranda's horrid filling. Her hand went down, and came up again all clammy. The sandwiches were there, and the handkerchief wasn't. She opened the window, threw them out, and wiped her hand, all rather vigorously.

And then she remembered having the handkerchief before she put the sandwiches in her pocket, because a drop of that horrid green tea had fallen on her dress, right in front where the coat opened, and from the way it tasted she thought it might leave one of those lingering stains, so she had got out her handkerchief and dabbed it. And then—what had she done with the handkerchief? There was no pocket in her dress, and it wasn't in the coat. She must have just left it lying in her lap and forgotten it when they got up to go. She did up the buttons of her coat again and ran downstairs.

Neither of the Miss Tremletts was in the sitting-room. She would be able to run along the path to Miranda's and get her handkerchief without having to explain how she had come to leave it there. Elaine and Gwyneth were dears, but they did love to talk anything to shreds, and the sandwiches made it all a bit delicate. She shut the door softly behind her and melted into the dark.

As soon as her eyes were accustomed to it she could see quite well. There was a light in Miranda's sitting-room. The curtains didn't quite meet, and a long bright streak showed between them. She came up to the door and found it ajar. That would be Miss Elaine, who never managed to latch a door. She held on to the handle too long, and Miss Gwyneth was always telling her about it.

In ordinary circumstances Thomasina would not have walked into anybody's house without knocking. But they had only just left, Miranda was there, and the door was open. She came just inside the little hall and was going to call out that she had come back for her handkerchief, when the sitting-room door moved. Someone was opening it. It moved a couple of inches and stopped, as if the person who was coming out had turned back for something.

It was Augustus Remington, and he had turned back to say, "You really did that very well, Miranda. You got it across all right."

With a little more practice in eavesdropping Thomasina might have done better than she did—she might have heard what Miranda said in reply. She didn't hear anything at all. The blood drummed in her ears, and she found that she was out of the house and running away as fast as her feet would take her. Some instinct kept her on the grass. There was a path, and there was a rough grass verge. She found that she was running on the grass. Even if someone came to the door and listened, they wouldn't hear her now.

When she got back to the Miss Tremletts' the sitting-room was still empty. She had only been a few minutes away, and no one would ever know that she had been away at all. She went up to her room, locked the door, and sat down on the edge of the bed. She had no doubt at all as to the meaning of what she had heard Augustus Remington say. The whole scene with the crystal was a fake. Miranda had done her part well, and Augustus Remington was commending her. The two of them had played a scene, and Miranda had "got it across all right." That the words could have any other meaning just never entered her head.

But she herself had seen Anna's face in the crystal.

A bright ball with the light shining on it—that was one way of hypnotizing people. She had felt her thought slipping as she looked at the swirling light. It didn't really swirl of course. She just saw it like that because she was slipping into a dream.

And then she saw Anna's face.

She saw it because someone wanted her to see it. Someone was trying to hypnotize her, and to make her see Anna's face in the crystal. A burning anger came up among her thoughts.

She was to see Anna's face, and then there was to be a fake message. "Anna, where are you? . . . . . A long way off. . . . . I don't want her to know. . . . . No good to cling to the past—broken links cannot be replaced—this is final." The short sentences stood out black and clear against the anger. It burned steadily.

It showed her quite a lot of things. Someone wanted to get her away from here. Someone wanted to stop her looking for Anna. Why? The answer stood out too. She was to be got away because Anna was here, in this place. Or if not Anna herself, something that would give her a clue as to what had happened to Anna. Somebody was afraid, somebody wanted her to be gone. Somebody wanted her to think that Anna had made this break deliberately—that she didn't want to have anything more to do with her. If Thomasina believed that, she would go away and not give any more trouble. And this meant that her being here was a trouble to somebody.

She threw up her head with a jerk.

What was the good of all this "somebody"? She knew perfectly well that it was Miranda who had just played a trick on her. And Augustus Remington had told her that she had done it very well and got it across all right. If she hadn't gone back for her handkerchief and heard what he said, it might almost have been true. Almost, but not quite, because of one little thing. She had seen it, noticed it, and put it away to think about. She hadn't had time to do that thinking, because of missing her handkerchief and having o go back. But now she had the time, she thought even that one little thing would have told her she had been tricked—even if she hadn't heard what Augustus Remington said.

It really was a very little thing. Just a smear of powder on the front of Miranda's violet robe, high up towards the shoulder. A little smudge of powder showing up against the purple when the lights came on—just ordinary face powder with a greenish tinge. Anyone might have a smudge of powder on their dress. But it hadn't been there when Miranda held both her hands in that exuberant welcome. And it wasn't there when she plied her with those sandwiches and the savoury cake at tea, or when she laid the black velvet square on the table after it had been cleared and set the ebony stand and the crystal ball upon it. Thomasina was prepared to swear to that, and to seeing Miranda put up her hand to her head when she was pretending to wake from that faked trance. She had looked so ghastly when the lights came on—quite green—

and it had all added to the effect. And of course too easy to look green if you have a pad or some cotton wool in your hand with the right powder on it. She remembered exactly how Miranda had brought up her hand in a kind of sweeping movement right across her face, her eyes, her brow. And of course it looked absolutely natural, because it is just what you do when you are sleepy, or have a headache, or when you first wake up. But Miranda was getting that greenish powder on to her face, and a little of it had dropped and marked her dress.

Thomasina's hot anger had burned down to a steady flame. When you are too angry you can't think, and she needed to think.

After she had been thinking for some time she felt quite clear in her mind. They wanted her to go. They had taken the very words of her advertisement, "Anna, where are you?" She had used only Anna's Christian name, and she had signed only "Thomasina." Someone who read the advertisement had known that "Anna" was Anna Ball, and that "Thomasina" was Thomasina Elliot. It looked as if that someone must be Anna herself. By what means had they made Anna tell them what she knew? There were terrible ways of making people speak. Her own words, said on the spur of the moment when she was quarrelling with Peter, came back to her—"Those old houses have cellars." Suppose Anna was there, locked up in one of those cellars? Anger sets a match to your thoughts. The words had just flashed into her mind because she was angry. Now they came up in quite a different way—a slow, cold, considering way which was much more frightening.

Suppose it was really true? There must be some strong reason for the trick that had been played on her. If Anna really was shut up in the ruined part of Deepe House or in the cellars under it, that would be a reason. If she was there, would she be still alive? Or was she dead and buried under one of those ruined floors? If she was alive, every moment must be like an hour. How was it possible to eat and drink, to lie down at night and get up in the morning, and not know whether all those minutes or hours were not dragging by with a torturing slowness for Anna Ball?

She went on thinking.

CHAPTER 30

If the Misses Tremletts had been less conversational themselves they might have observed that Thomasina had very little to say for the rest of the evening, but they always had so much to say, and were in such close competition for the opportunity of saying it, that it really was just as well that she had nothing to contribute. Nothing could have suited them better than a guest who sat in attentive silence.

First of all they naturally desired to discuss Miranda's trance and the enigmatic communication which it had produced. They had not liked Anna Ball—"Not that we really knew her, and she had a very rebuffing manner, but one would not like to think that anything had *happened* to her—"

"And if anything *had*, why should she wish to communicate with *us?*" said Miss Elaine.

"Very puzzling indeed," said Miss Gwyneth. "Because she couldn't possibly have met you, my dear Thomasina, and since she said *her*—'*I* don't want *her* to know'—the message couldn't have been intended for Augustus."

"So that only leaves myself and Gwyneth."

"And really, as I said, we hardly knew her."

"But these communications do so often seem to be quite irrelevant. Now I knew a case where a Miss Brown—or was it Jones—I can't remember which, but she was a niece, or a cousin, or a friend of a Mrs. Hawkins who was at Wyshmere when your aunt was there. She went to a medium in London because a young man she was half engaged to had stopped writing a month or two after going to South America and she was afraid something had happened to him. She told the medium all about it, and she looked in the crystal and said she saw a ship coming into a foreign port—and of course that was quite all right, because he wrote once or twice after he got there. And then she said there was a dark woman, and a kind of a cloud. And right at the end she said she saw a funeral. Well of course Miss Jones—if it was Jones and not

Brown, and I really can't remember which it was—well, naturally she was very much upset and made up her mind the young man was dead. But he wasn't, because she heard quite a long time after that he had married a Chilean and they had four children. So you see the crystal was quite right about there being a dark girl, but the only thing the funeral could possibly have referred to was that old Mrs. Pondleby who lived over the way from them did die about three weeks later. But she was over ninety and had been an invalid for a great many years, so that it wasn't a surprise to anyone. And, as I said, it just *shows*—"

She did not explain what it showed, because the moment she stopped to take breath Miss Gwyneth broke in with the story of a young man who was connected by marriage with that very charming Mrs. Hughes who was a connection of Lord Dumbleton's. It appeared he had dreamt three times that he saw a grey horse win the Derby, and in the dream he knew the horse's name and the jockey's colours, but when he woke up they had gone.

"And all he knew was that he had seen a grey horse win the Derby. So he went to a medium who was being a good deal talked about just then, and the first thing she wanted to know was whether there was a grey horse running, and of course it was most unfortunate, there were two. So she looked at his hand, and she said he was on the threshold of a great opportunity and everything would depend on what he did next. And that was quite true, because he had to decide whether he would go out to South Africa and join the Cape Mounted Police or take a post in a Birmingham bank—and of course if he was going to win a lot of money on the Derby he wouldn't do either. So she looked in the crystal, and she saw a grey horse all right, but it wasn't winning the race that she could see. It was just galloping along with a lot of other horses, and it was gone in a flash, and she couldn't see the jockey's colours, or what he was like, or anything, only she had a strong impression of the letter H. And as soon as she said that, Mrs. Hughes' nephew got quite excited and said he had that too. But it didn't really help them, because one of the grey horses in the race was "Humboldt," and the other "Herring's Eyes," so she tried again, and she couldn't see anything but a cloud of dust. And in the end one of the grey horses was disqualified, and the other came in last but one. So the poor young man went out to South Africa, and I never heard what happened to him, because Mrs. Hughes left Wyshmere for the Channel Islands."

They went on telling stories like this for a couple of hours. Thomasina didn't mind as long as they kept away from the subject of Anna Ball. She had only to look attentive and make a kind of murmuring sound every now and then. None of the stories seemed to prove anything very much except the readiness with which people will believe whatever they wish to believe.

At ten o'clock they all drank tea and went to bed. That is to say, the Miss Tremletts went to bed. Thomasina did not. She turned her light low and sat down to wait, and to count the strokes when the wall-clock in the living-room chimed the quarters. She had made up her mind to wait until half past eleven, and it seemed a long, long time. It grew cold, and colder. The house gathered its silence about it like a cloak. Every time the clock struck, the sound was more startling. Thomasina found herself waiting for it and dreading it. It was like expecting the sudden flare of a magnesium light.

The time dragged unbelievably as quarter followed quarter on the old wall-clock in the living-room below—half past ten—a quarter to eleven—eleven o'clock—a quarter past— She put on her coat and made sure that the battery in her torch was all right.

As the two strokes of the half hour came upon the air, she opened her door and went softly down the stair.

CHAPTER 31

PETER BRANDON was quite as angry with Thomasina as she was with him. There were moments during the afternoon and evening when he found himself disliking her to such an extent that he would have turned his back on Deep End and shaken its soggy clay off his feet for good and all if he hadn't been unalterably convinced that she would get herself into some really horrible mess if he wasn't there to restrain her. He had been fond of Thomasina for a great many years in the casual, unemotional way of family relationship. He had teased her, criticized her, and quarrelled with her, all without heat, but it was only in the last six months that he had committed the

folly of falling in love with her. He hadn't had the slightest intention of doing it. Somewhere between thirty and thirty-five he intended to marry and have children—not less than two and not more than four, and preferably two boys and a girl. He proposed to be a good husband and father, and to have the kind of pleasant calm affection for his wife which made no demands upon the emotions and conduced to a tranquil atmosphere in the home. The wife had remained a quite nebul
mosphere in the home. The wife had remained a quite
nebulous figure—she bore no resemblance whatever to Thomasina. And then he had to go and fall in love with a creature whom he had known in her pram.

When the fact came home to him he told himself that it was a temporary aberration. He had been summoned to Barbara Brandon's deathbed, and his emotions were not under the usual control. He saw Thomasina being incredibly brave, and when everything was over he saw her heartbroken and desolate. She wept on his shoulder. They were both quite taken out of themselves. But when he went back to London he couldn't get her out of his head. He told himself that it would pass, but it didn't pass, it got worse. He began to write her long letters and to look out for the answers. And then all this damnable business about Anna Ball blew up, and when Thomasina came south he could do nothing but quarrel with her.

It ought to have put him out of love with her, but it didn't. It is quite extraordinary how angrily you can dislike a person with whom you are in love. Peter had moments of cold fury in which he told himself that he never wanted to see her again. As these persisted side by side with a complete inability to stay away from her, his mental state was naturally an extremely uncomfortable one, and as far as possible removed from the placidity of his hypothetical courtship.

When he had walked himself tired he returned to his room at the Masters' cottage, where he read doggedly by the light of an oil lamp until summoned by old Mr. Masters to the evening meal. Mrs. Masters being absent on an errand of mercy—a neighbour having scalded her hand—they sat down to a tête-à-tête.

"And she may be long, or she mayn't, there's not saying with scalds, but I shouldn't be surprised if it wasn't all a much about little, seeing it's Louie Gregory that's been known from a child to be one to cry out afore she's hurt. Six children she's had, and was a-going to die with every one of them, and there they all are a-flourishing like weeds, and Louie trying to make out what a time she's had a-bringing of them up."

They had scrambled eggs, and Mr. Masters claimed with justice that he made them better than his daughter-in-law did. He was in high feather, and by the time the meal was over and he had lighted his pipe he had got going upon his repertory of old stories, and by way of that to the history of the Everlys.

"And I wouldn't tell it, not to anyone but you, Mr. Brandon, because it isn't a thing that ought to be spoken of. There's those that would come here and ask their questions, but they'd never get no answers out of me. All happened a long time ago and best forgotten, that's what I say, and that's what I told him when he came asking, that there Craddock up at the House. And he says, 'What's the story, Mr. Masters?' And, 'What story?' I says. And he says, 'Is it anything about a hand?' And I says, 'Lord—who told you that! Have you been a-seeing things?' I says. Well, he says he might have been. But I didn't tell him nothing, because it wasn't none of his business. Stands to reason, if there's hauntings going on, those that's doing it wouldn't want no up-starting strangers a-coming in. Very high-up people they was, the Everlys—kep' themselves to themselves, very proud and haughty, as you might say. And the three Miss Everlys that was the last of them, they weren't no different from the rest. I knew them all when I was a lad—Miss Maria, Miss Isabella, and Miss Clarice. . . ."

He dawdled on through his tale of three lonely women in a decaying house and the cousin who came to stay and was going to marry Miss Clarice.

"Only Miss Isabella, she wouldn't have it. Seems she wouldn't bear to have her younger sister put over her, and she went out of her head with spite, and it come to murder between them. So when Miss Clarice was dead and Miss Isabella was shut up for mad there was only Miss Maria left, and she lived on there alone in the shut-up house until she died. And they say it's Miss Clarice that haunts the house with her cut-off hand."

"Her cut-off hand?"

Old Mr. Masters screwed up his face into a thousand wrinkles and nodded.

"That's what Miss Isabella did—cut off her hand with the ring on it."

There was something about the casual way he said this that

added to the horror. It was as if it had been repeated so many times as to become a mere shadow of a tale long told. The old voice going on in the old room with the lamplight spilled in a patch of brightness and the shadows black beyond all heightened the effect. Peter had a sense of the stark facts of human nature against the peacefully flowing current of village life. This horrible thing had happened, and the village had gaped and accepted it, but it seemed they kept away from the place where it had happened. Old Mr. Masters was saying so.

"I won't say I'm afraid of ghosts, not if they was my own folk and such that'd died lawful in their beds, but I wouldn't go up round Deepe House in the night—not in that middle part of the house where the murder was, not for a young weight of gold I wouldn't. There was a boy that lost his wits and never spoke after, and there was others. Stands to reason Everlys don't want no one prying in on them, nor I wouldn't be the one to pry." He dropped his voice to a croaking whisper. "There was a tramping chap thought he'd get in and sleep there the way they do where there's an empty house. They say he got up to the window—all cracked it was after the bomb, and he thought he'd pull out a bit of the glass and get in. But when he put his hand to it there was another hand come out of the dark to meet him, and he upped and ran for it through the courtyard and down the drive, yelling his head off."

There might have been more to say, or there might not. Whether there was or no, old Mr. Masters did not get the chance of saying it, because that was where his daughter-in-law came in, a good deal put about and with views of her own to air on the subject of people who didn't know enough to tie up a scalded finger without sending for someone else to do it for them.

"And that's Louie Gregory all over, if it's the last word I spoke. And her mother the same before her. So long as there's someone else to do a thing, you won't never need to do it yourself—that's the way they looked at it, and that's the way they acted it out. Whether it was borrowing sugar and forgetting to pay it back, or leaving you to bath the baby whilst they had a nice comfortable faint on their beds, that was them!"

Old Mr. Masters looked up with a twinkling eye.

"Been bathing the baby, Sarah?"

Mrs. Masters' cheeks, already flushed with vexation and

fatigue, became a rich shade of plum. She stared angrily at her father-in-law.

"More fool me!" she said. "*And* washed up the dinner things which no one hadn't thought to do, and given the children their tea which they was crying for, and cleared up the worst of the muck in the house! And that poor fool of a Louie setting there crying over her finger!"

"What do 'ee do it for?" said old Mr. Masters.

Sarah Masters was slapping plates together as she cleared the table.

"Because I'm a fool, I suppose! Go on—tell me so!"

Old Mr. Masters told her so with a sardonic chuckle, adding as a crowning insult that she'd got too soft a heart, and it would get her into trouble one of these days if she didn't look out. After which she banged out of the room, and could be heard clattering plates and dishes in the scullery.

Peter went back to his room and tried to write. It was not a great success. His pen travelled, but just what part of his mind prompted it, he did not know. Not a very intelligent part, because when he came to read over what he had written it didn't seem to mean anything at all. Thomasina's name had got into it twice. When he had torn it up and started all over again he did manage to keep some control over what went down on the paper. And at the end of it a duller lot of tripe he had never read in his life. It joined the other torn pages in the wastepaper basket. If he couldn't get away from thinking about Thomasina he had better do it in an orderly and intelligent manner. To start with, what was he in such a stew about? It wasn't the first time they had quarrelled, and it wouldn't be the last. It wasn't the quarrel that was worrying him.

Well then, what was it? The moment he began to think about it he knew very well what it was. He had taken up the attitude of the confirmed sceptic in this matter of Anna Ball, but there was just a chance that there was something in it. Girls did get murdered, and Anna was just the aggravating kind who might have asked for it and got it. And if she had—then there was no saying what kind of a mess Thomasina might land in. He didn't like Deepe House, with its rickety bomb-damaged rooms and its boarded-up windows. If it wasn't anything else it was probably insanitary. He didn't like old Mr. Masters' story about the Everly sisters. Like a surprisingly large number of people, he didn't believe in haunted houses, but he didn't like them. They linked up with old horrible things that ought to be forgotten. And at this point he knew very well what was making him afraid. It was the idea of Thomasina going off by herself on some crazy search for Anna Ball in that old dilapidated house.

He remembered what she had said about the cellars. Suppose she took it into her head to go looking for Anna Ball in that crazy place in the dark. She was certainly capable of it. She was angry, she was stubborn, and quite disastrously brave. And she might stumble into almost anything, from a hole in the floor to whatever it was that had sent old Mr. Masters' tramp running hell-for-leather down the drive yelling his head off.

A picture came up in his mind, small but horribly vivid—not Thomasina riding her high horse, proud, angry, sure of herself, but a girl with all the courage scared out of her screaming in the dark. He looked at his watch. It was twenty minutes past eleven. He had been too long over his writing, over his thoughts. Anything might have happened, or be happening now, up there at Deepe House. Here the Masters were in bed and asleep, old Mr. Masters by nine o'clock, and Sarah as soon as she had finished her angry clattering and clearing up. He opened the window, hung by his hands from the sill, and dropped. Since the downstairs rooms were a bare eight foot from ceiling to floor, it was easy enough, and when it came to getting in again—well, he thought he wouldn't be the first to use the old pear tree as a ladder.

The night was damp and chill but not really cold. He had no plan except to go up to the Miss Tremletts' and see whether any light burned there or not. He had no further thought or purpose, and it came to him that it was a senseless one, because if the windows were all dark, it might mean that Thomasina was in bed and asleep, or it might mean that she was out and away. And if there was a light in her window, it could mean that she was awake. She could be reading in bed. She could be doing any one of the things you do when you don't want to go to sleep. Or she could be out in the dark, with the light left in her window to guide her home.

He came up to the cottage and found all the front of it dark. What had been the stable yard now had a little paling round it painted green, and a gate with one of those fancy latches which are equally difficult to open or shut. It was shut when Peter came up to it, and he made a bad job of getting it open, pinching his fingers and swearing under his breath. Inside, most of the cobblestones had been left, but some square beds had been dug and filled with bulbs. In the dark they were soggy traps through which you blundered.

When he got round to the back, there were three lots of windows, and only one of them showed a light. The dark windows looked as if they were open, but the lighted window was shut, which meant that somebody was up, since you don't open your window on a February night until you are ready to dive into bed and pull the clothes about you.

Well then, someone was up. But there was nothing to say that it was Thomasina. It might be Gwyneth, or it might be Elaine. And Thomasina out of the house and well away on a fool's errand! He stood looking at the window and fighting down a rising fury and a rising fear.

There are states of mind in which time flies, and others in which it lags. Peter hadn't the slightest idea how long he had stood looking up at the light filtering through curtains which gave it a blueish tinge, when he suddenly felt that he wasn't doing any good. If Thomasina was here she was all right. But if she wasn't here she was up at Deepe House, and the best thing he could do was to go and find her.

He blundered into another flower bed, shut the gate without bothering about the latch, and set off in the direction of the house. He had a torch, but he didn't want to use it, and once away from the cottage, the path lay across the open park and was not really hard to keep. The mass of Deepe House showed up against the sky, first as mere density, then as a black rectangle with its two wings foreshortened.

He came into the courtyard between the wings and stopped to look and listen. Here it was absolutely dark, the skyline lost. And absolutely still. Not a breath, not a whisper, not the slightest, smallest sound. Since he had seen the place by day, he knew that the windows to the right were curtained and those on the left boarded-up. While straight ahead—now there he couldn't remember whether the whole front was eyeless, every window nailed up against wind and weather, or whether here and there there was still glass in some of the windows.

He moved across the courtyard, his hands out before him. There was a door—he remembered that there was a door with some kind of canopy over it. Yes, that was it, a canopy with pillars. His hand touched one of them and felt a cold slime upon it. There were two steps, smooth and shallow, and beyond the steps a heavy door. He remembered seeing it in the daylight, with a scar on it where the knocker had been wrenched away, he supposed for salvage. His left hand found the place and felt it now. Quite a deep hole where a nail had been driven in. The nail, the scar, just touched his thought and was flung off it by the sudden realization that the surface he was touching was a slanting one. It should have been flat, and it wasn't flat. It should have been steady, and it wasn't steady. It slanted and it moved. The door was ajar.

CHAPTER 32

WHILST PETER BRANDON stood looking up at her window Thomasina was following the footpath across the park. Like Peter, she had a torch but she didn't want to use it. She could manage, because all you had to do was to get away from the trees, and then there was enough diffused light from a hidden moon to show the direction of the big house and to help you to follow the path. All the same, she was not half way across the open park before the thought of the lighted room she had left behind her was tugging at her. She had to keep on thinking about Anna, and how infuriating Peter had been, and that only the most despicable kind of coward started out to do something and then turned back because he was afraid.

With these useful thoughts to spur her she got as far as the courtyard. Her feet came upon the slippery winter moss which furred the stones. You could walk without making any noise at all, but where you bruised it in the dark a faint smell of decay came up and hung in the air.

Insensibly she kept a little to the right, because behind the curtains of that right-hand wing there were people—six of them—Mr. and Mrs. Craddock—the three children—Miss Silver. The rooms would have had fires in them, and lights, even if they were dark now and growing cold. If she called out, someone would hear.

Why on earth should she call out? And why, if you please, had she come here at all? Not to stand in the dark and wonder if Miss Silver would hear her if she screamed. She had come to see whether she could get into the deserted part of the house and stop the horrid, growing thought that it might be hiding some dreadful secret about Anna Ball. This possibility, which had seemed quite strong and vigorous an hour ago, now dwindled to the merest wraith. The house was an empty ruin. The damp deserted smell of it came seeping through the rickety boards which blinded its shattered windows. It came to her that if she stood there for another single moment she wouldn't be able to make herself go on, and that if she didn't go on she would never stop despising herself.

She turned her back upon the inhabited wing, and had taken a single step forward, when something moved, away to the left. She couldn't have said that she saw even so much as a shadow, or that she heard anything at all. Only something had moved. She stood where she was. The movement came from outside the courtyard. She had a sense of its continuance. She thought someone or something was coming in from outside. She couldn't see, and she couldn't hear, but she thought that something went by in the dark.

And the next moment she was sure. A foot slipped on one of the shallow steps which went up to the door, a torch flickered, the door moved, and someone went in. She couldn't see at all who it was, but she meant to find out. That thread of light from the torch had just touched the edge of the door and gone out. But it had taken with it nine-tenths of Thomasina's fear. Silence, and darkness, and decay—these are the things which sap courage at the very roots of the race. Man has always been afraid of the enemy whom he can neither see nor fight. Thomasina certainly wasn't going to let herself be afraid of an ordinary everyday object like an electric torch. That single flicker of light brought the whole thing down to a common human level. Somebody with an electric torch had just gone into the house, and she was going to make it her business to find out who that someone was. Ordinary visitors come up to a door and knock or ring. If they have got a torch they put it on. The person who had just gone into the house didn't want to be seen or heard any more than she did herself.

She came quite silently up to the door and tried it. Since she had heard no click of the latch, no sound of a key being turned or a bolt slid home, she was sure enough that it would move under her hand. But when it did so she had a faint stirring of fear—it opened upon so total a darkness and released so damp and mouldy a smell.

It takes too long to tell. Thought is so much quicker. It really was only a moment since that she had seen the flicker of the torch and the door slide back from it to let a shadowy somebody into the house. As she came in herself she was aware of a footstep going away and a single brief lightening of the darkness as the torch flashed on and off again in some passage which ran out of the hall. It served to show her where she was—on the threshold of a lobby leading into the black cavern of the hall. No detail, just a black cave running back into the house, and the impression of a stairway—all very vague and formless, and then in an instant swallowed up again by the dark.

She began to walk in the direction from which the light had seemed to come, hands stretched out in front of her and feet that felt their way. There was no second flash of light. By the time she had taken about twenty of those slow steps she was no longer sure of the direction from which the light had come. As she stood at the entrance, it had been somewhere away to the right, but she did not know whether she had kept a straight line as she walked towards it. It is a very hard thing to do in the dark. Some people pull to the left, and some to the right. It is the hardest thing in the world to keep a straight course.

She ought to have left the door wide behind her. It would not have let in any light, but looking back, there would have been just enough difference between the outdoor darkness and the enclosed gloom of the house to show her where she was. But she had left the door as she had found it, no more than an inch or two ajar—it had seemed safer somehow. The person she was following might have turned and looked back, or someone else might have come, and then that open door would have given her away.

She stood where she was, looking back and listening. There was a sound—or was there—she wasn't sure. An old empty house has sounds of its own. This sound wasn't in the house. It came from the other side of the door which she had left ajar. Or she thought it did—she couldn't be sure. But if anyone was coming in, she mustn't stand there and be caught. She must get away.

She had put out her foot to take the next step, when, with a blinding shock, imagination passed into actual happening. She had come farther than she knew and she had veered to the right. If her foot had taken that next step, her hand would have touched the panel of a door. But before there was time for the step to be taken the door was wrenched inward and the beam of a powerful electric lamp struck her full in the face.

CHAPTER 33

IT WAS A little earlier than this that Frank Abbott switched out the overhead light in his room at the George in Ledlington and having adjusted the shade of a bedside lamp and arranged his pillows to his liking, took up the second-hand volume of Lord Tennyson's poems which he had that day discovered at Bannerman's in the Market Square and turned over the pages. Since Mr. John Robinson had made two quotations, one from the beginning, and the other from the end of a poem, and since Miss Silver considered this to have some significance as to which his own mind was a total blank, he felt that it was up to him to solve the riddle which, it seemed, she had been pleased to set him. He began to go through the book, looking at the first lines of every poem until he arrived at "Enoch Arden"—masses and masses of Enoch, in Victorian blank verse. And here was the first quotation:

> "Long lines of cliffs, breaking, have left a chasm,
> And in the chasm are foam and yellow sand."

It had meant nothing to him at the time, and it meant nothing to him now.

He began to wade into the story of Enoch, faint but pursuing. In the absence of his Miss Silver, he dared to find him insufferably dull. Astonishing to think that these long narrative poems had ever had a vogue. And then quite suddenly there was a gleam. He began, metaphorically speaking, to sit up and take notice. So that was it, was it? Nothing really to do with the case of course. He could hardly reproach her with keeping back material evidence. But interesting—oh, very definitely interesting.

He followed Enoch to his death-bed, and to Mr. John Robinson's second quotation:

> ". . . . . and the little port
> Had seldom seen a costlier funeral—"

He closed the book, put it down beside the lamp, and was presently sliding in an agreeable manner down the smooth inclines of sleep.

Meanwhile Miss Silver was sitting up in her bedroom. She had undressed, performed her evening ablutions, read her usual chapter, and set the door ajar between her room and Jennifer's. All this completed, she hesitated a little, and then put on her warm blue dressing-gown with its handmade crochet trimming and sat down by the electric fire. Mr. Craddock's foresight in putting in so powerful a plant passed through her mind as a subject for commendation. So labour-saving, so clean, so comfortable a mitigation of the cold and damp of these winter months in the country. She gave the subject quite a little thought before passing to another topic.

The day had been not only interesting, but very completely filled. Mrs. Craddock's indisposition had persisted. She had not fainted again, but she had continued in a very weak and tearful condition, and had not attempted to leave the sofa, or to occupy herself in any way. When it was suggested that she would be better in bed she made no demur. Peveril Craddock's reaction to all this was a mood of gloomy displeasure. No one who had spent even a few days in the house with him would have expected him to be helpful, but he showed so much resentment over his wife's collapse that it really was the greatest relief when he announced that he would be working late and removed himself and a supper-tray to his study in the main block.

There were then the children to feed and get to bed, Emily Craddock to be tended, cheered, and induced to partake of the good milk soup which Miss Silver had prepared for her. After which there remained that general clearing-up which is perhaps the most thankless and least rewarding of all household tasks. It is therefore no wonder that this was Miss Silver's first opportunity of reviewing the events of the last two days.

If there was a connection between these murderous bank robberies and the Colony of which Deepe House was the centre, there must at one time or another have been small clues as light and apparently aimless as those floating threads of gossamer which fill the air just after dawn on a summer morning. They are not to be seen, their origin is not to be traced, they are no more than an insubstantial touch just felt and gone again. But what has once been felt may be recalled. Without pushing the metaphor too far, it was Miss Silver's purpose to empty her mind of speculation and recall certain episodes, conversations, pictures. In the past she had found that memory, unquestioned and left to produce its own images, would often provide some detail not consciously noted at the time. Sitting quite still with her eyes closed and her hands folded in her lap, she went back to her interview with Mr. Craddock in town, her arrival at Deepe House, the first contact with each member of the family, each member of the Colony. First impressions she had always found to be of a particular value. They had to be corrected by experience, but even then something could be gained from them.

She went over her first meeting with Emily Craddock, a simple and pathetic case of a woman dominated to the point of will and judgment being completely in abeyance. Or almost so. There were moments when the hypnotized creature stirred and half woke up to unimaginable misery and fear.

Jennifer was not hypnotized. She had adored Peveril Craddock. She now hated and feared him—a dumb hatred, and a dumb fear. Something had happened to cause these things, and to drive them down into the darkest and most secret places of her thought. Miss Silver had not handled children for twenty years without discovering that if a child is very badly frightened it will never speak of what has frightened it.

The Miss Tremletts, Miranda, Augustus Remington, Mr. John Robinson—there had been a first meeting with each one of them, and in every case a definite and distinct impression had been made. The pictures came into her mind and passed out of it again.

When she had done with them she made room for the one which she had reserved to the last, her brief passing contact with the bank murderer. She saw herself moving along the gangway of the bus and stepping down to the ground. Only two people went towards the station, elderly women with shopping-baskets. The other seven or eight passengers made off in the direction of the High Street. She had let them get away before making any move herself, since she had no desire that anyone should notice that she had come to meet a good-looking young man with a car. She had occupied herself with opening her handbag and scrutinising what might very well have passed for a shopping-list. It was not until the last of the passengers was clear of the station yard that she began to walk up the incline towards the entrance, and it was when she was about half way that the bandaged man had passed her. The scene came back distinctly—the limping step, the gloved hand upon the stick. There was a very small triangular tear between the index finger and the one next to it. She had not remembered it till now, but it was there in the picture. A few stitches of the seam had come undone, to leave a triangular gap. There were three loosened stitches to the left of it, and a little end of thread. It was the left hand which leaned upon the stick. The head had a caplike bandage covering all the hair and most of the right side of the face. The collar of the old loose raincoat was turned up. Since he passed to her left, it was only the right side of his face which presented itself. The right side of his face—a mass of bandages—the collar of the raincoat hiding the neck and the line of the chin—a loose sleeve, and a bandaged hand. The hand held a small suit-case. So much for the side that was turned towards her—the right-hand side. And on the left, folds of the bandage passing about the head and out of sight, the collar of the raincoat standing up about the neck, the sleeve hanging loose, and a gloved hand resting upon a stick. She had seen no more, she could recall no more. The picture was there in her mind, but it gave up no further detail.

She began to consider the stick. It was of the commonest type—a plain crook for the gloved hand to rest on—a plain dark stick. Only nowadays very few men carried a stick at all. But since the murderer was posing as an injured man, the stick went very well with his disguise. Yet for that stick to be available it must have been, and probably still was, in his possession. Because it was an old stick, worn and rubbed about the ferrule. It had not been bought for the occasion, it was a possession. Then he probably had it still. Anyone might have such a stick. It was of too common a type to be a danger. It was of too common a type to offer any certain means of identification. At the very most it could add some slight reinforcement to other and stronger evidence.

What evidence? She went on looking at the picture in her mind, and all at once there came to her an echo from no more than a couple of days ago—Maurice and Jennifer squabbling.

"He always wears gloves."

"He's afraid of spoiling his hands."

And Benjy, "I'm not afraid of spoiling my hands." With Maurice bursting into a loud rude laugh and a "You haven't got anything to spoil!"

It was quite irrelevant. A fragment heard by chance and no name mentioned. Just someone who wore gloves. A man.

The gloves in her picture of the bandaged man, the glove upon the left hand which rested on the crook of the stick—an old wash-leather glove, worn and old like the stick itself—stretched with use until the stitches parted between the two first fingers. The thread which curled up from the small triangular tear was torn and dirty. The glove was an old worn glove. If such a glove and such a stick were to be found in anyone's possession—

She had reached this point, when the picture and the silence broke together to the muffled sound of a shot.

CHAPTER 34

In the country it is no uncommon thing to hear a shot, even in the middle of the night. If Miss Silver had been country born and country bred she might have thought very little of that muffled sound. She might not have thought about it at all. But it came near enough to the subject of her thoughts to be arresting. She was a town-dweller, but she had often stayed in the country, and while not accepting a shot with the indifference born of custom, her ear was fine enough to prompt the thought that this shot had not been fired in the open. It had lacked sharpness and clarity. She thought that it had been fired within the four walls of one of the rooms of Deepe House. She opened her door and stood there listening.

A faint light burned on the landing at the head of the stair. Beyond it the passage which led to the main block was deeply shadowed. And there was silence over all.

And then the second shot.

This time there was no doubt of its direction. It came from beyond the dividing wall between this wing and the deserted house. There was a movement behind her, and Jennifer's hand on her arm. She said in a quiet, firm voice,

"Go back to bed, my dear. Your mother is asleep."

The hand gripped hard.

"That was a shot."

"I expect it was Mr. Robinson. He is often out at night, is he not?"

"He doesn't shoot." There was scorn in the whispering voice. "He doesn't *kill* things, he watches them. That shot came from the house. What are you going to do?"

"I am going to see whether anything is wrong."

Jennifer said with a sort of hushed vehemence,

"You can't get in. He locks the door. He keeps it locked. I've got a key. I found it. He left it sticking in the lock. He never knew where it had gone. I went in—once."

The hand that gripped Miss Silver's arm was as hard and cold as ice. It was too rigid to shake. Very slow and chill, Jennifer's voice said,

"I—saw—the—hand." And then again, "Clarice's hand—the one that was cut off—I saw it."

"If you have a key, will you get it for me, my dear? Quickly."

In the same strained tone Jennifer said,

"He thought he must have dropped it out of his pocket. He asked me if I had seen it, and I told a lie."

"My dear, the key! And I said *quickly!* You must not delay me now!"

The grip on her arm relaxed. Without a sound Jennifer was gone, and without a sound she was back again. She held out the key and said,

"You can't go in!"

Miss Silver took it from her.

"Oh, yes, I can, my dear. And I want you to help me. Will you slip into your mother's room and just stay with her until I come back. It would not be at all good for her to be disturbed. Pray do not leave her alone. And take an eiderdown to wrap round you, so that you will not be cold."

She fetched the eiderdown herself, opened Mrs. Craddock's door, and saw Jennifer inside. There was a night-light on the washstand, and a small electric fire. The room was warm and quiet. Mrs. Craddock slept her exhausted sleep. Miss Silver shut the door, crossed the landing, and went down the dusky passage to the door which led into the deserted house. She had in the pocket of her dressing-gown the excellent torch which she always took with her when she went into the country. In these old places the current sometimes failed at such extremely inconvenient moments. She would certainly take no risk of meeting with an accident in a bomb-damaged house.

She turned the key in the door and went through, leaving it open behind her. There was no light-switch, but her torch showed a short passage leading to a small landing and a descending stair. As she went down, her felt slippers making no sound, she was aware of dust and dilapidation everywhere

—walls where the paper hung in strips, gaps in the plaster, and a smell which suggested damp and spiders and mice. She had a firm spirit and a good deal of cheerful courage, but she had no affection for spiders. There were several very large ones upon these damp disintegrating walls, and as she left the last step and advanced along one of the ground-floor passages, something squeaked and scuttered. She hoped very much that it was only a mouse.

The passage came out into a hall. There were other passages. There were doors. She put out her torch and stood looking into the darkness. At first it seemed absolute, a black curtain before the eyes. Then a slight, a very slight, thinning of the gloom. She was facing the back of the hall, and there was a place where the darkness thinned. A faint glow was coming from one of the passages which ran away to the right. Since the floor had appeared to be perfectly solid, she made her way towards this glow, her finger on the switch of her torch.

She had about twenty steps to take before she reached the entrance to the passage. The glow, at first very faint, became a little stronger, the light more concentrated. She took another step, and saw what caused it. There, half way down the passage, was a faintly luminous shape. It hung in the air, and it moved. It had the shape of a hand—a groping hand.

Miss Silver pushed down the switch of her torch and turned its light upon the floating hand. Her own hand was firm and steady.

The light came on very white and clear. It showed a stained ceiling and dirty walls. It showed the hand hanging from the ceiling by a flex—a hand shaped in some translucent plastic stuff and lighted from within. A clever piece of work—the fingers drawn back a little as if groping and ready to clutch, the lighting very skillfully contrived to suggest more than it revealed. A very clever piece of work and perfectly calculated to maintain the Everly legend and frighten away intruders.

Examining the whole thing more closely, she saw that the flex was plugged in at floor level and then carried up the wall, and so to the hook from which it depended. The whole thing could therefore be moved to any part of the house where there was a point. She wondered where Jennifer had encountered it.

These thoughts were present in her mind without any passage of time. It was, in fact, no more than three minutes since she had closed the door of Emily Craddock's room. She looked down the passage now and saw a door on the left.

Behind that door someone moved. She switched off her torch again, went forward, and turned the handle.

She had promised Frank Abbott that she would run no risks. It did not really occur to her that she was running one now. Afterwards, when reproached on this head, she merely remarked soberly that she had not thought of it in that light.

"Then you were not being as intelligent as usual."

"My dear Frank!"

"Well, what did you expect to find behind that door? Logically, it could only be one person—the murderer."

At the time, though this probability was certainly present to her mind, it did not occur to her that it constituted a risk. She felt completely confident and able to deal with anything she might encounter.

She turned the handle and opened the door upon a lighted room. There was a writing-table, there were chairs, there were books. There were comfortable curtains, a good carpet, and a warm electric fire. The carpet showed a spreading stain of blood.

The blood came from the body of Peveril Craddock. It lay in front of the writing-table. A chair had been pushed over. There was a revolver beside the outflung right hand.

Mr. Peter Brandon was stooping over the body.

CHAPTER 35

When that blinding light struck her in the face Thomasina gasped and flung up a hand to shield her eyes. Most girls would have screamed, but she had a good deal of self-control. A scream might have been heard, but not that choking gasp.

She flung up her hand, and at once someone caught her by the wrist and pulled her into the room. The person who was holding the electric lamp turned it away from her eyes and kicked the door shut. It slammed, and with the sound, sharp in the empty room and echoing from the empty walls, there came another sound, sharper, more definite, more horrifying—the sound of a shot.

At the time Thomasina did not disentangle the sounds. She was startled out of any capacity for thought. She stared, and caught her breath, and exclaimed,

"Anna!"

The grip on her wrist tightened.

"Quick—quick—we haven't a minute!"

She was being pulled towards a door on the other side of the room. There was dust everywhere—its muffling softness under their feet, a choking cloud of it upon the air, the lamp dazzling upon a million floating specks—Anna's voice in her ears, Anna's hand on her wrist.

Just for a moment her mind was shocked into numbness. She had come here to find Anna Ball, and had found her. It ought not to have been a shock, but it was. Afterwards she knew that she had not really thought that Anna was at Deepe House—she had not really expected to find her. She had quarrelled with Peter because he wanted her to go away. And because she wanted to stay she had built up a ridiculous imagination about Anna being shut up in a cellar. And then she had dared herself to come and see if it was true. She had taken the dare, but she hadn't expected to find anything.

And now it was true. Not the cellar part of it, but Anna—Anna hurrying her along—Anna's voice hard and urgent.

"Quick—quick—we can't talk here! We haven't a moment! We've got to talk!"

And then another dusty room, a passage, a door that was opened and slammed, and they were in Peveril Craddock's garage.

Anna Ball put down the electric lamp and switched on an overhead light. They had come out of the dilapidation and decay of the house into what might have been any suburban garage—a cemented floor, fresh whitewash on the walls, a bench with tools, tins of petrol and lubricant, a couple of spare tyres, a small ordinary car. Nothing could have been more commonplace.

But when Anna turned from switching on the light everything changed. Because this was an Anna whom she had never seen before. It wasn't only the clothes—and Anna in slacks and a flaming jersey was something very unlike anything that came to her out of the past which they had shared—it was Anna herself. The heavy, sallow, drooping creature who had hung on Thomasina like a weight was gone. Here was a taut young woman vibrant with energy, her hair standing out in a bush from a recent perm, her face made up to a smooth pallor, her mouth as scarlet as a pillar-box, and her eyes blazing. Anna's eyes had always been her best feature. Peter had libelled them when he said they had a cast. They were good dark grey eyes with strongly growing lashes and a rather brooding way of looking at you. They were not brooding now. The thing that had smouldered in them was flaring. And it was hate—sheer ungovernable hatred.

It is one of the things which nobody can mistake. For a moment Thomasina felt nothing except surprise. Anna to look at her like that! When they had always been friends! When Anna had never had any other friend at all! She had carried the weight of being Anna's only friend through all the years of being at school and college with her, through all the self-pity, the hurt feelings, the jealousies, the emotional scenes which were Anna's idea of friendship. But that Anna should look at her like this! And for what?

She was to know. Insensibly she moved back until she stood against the wall. Anna stood where she was, a yard or two away, with the hatred in her eyes. She spoke now with something in her voice which Thomasina had never heard in it before. Enjoyment. Anna was enjoying herself—enjoying hating her, enjoying telling her about it. Because that was what she was doing.

"I always hated you—always—always—*always!* Why? Are you really such a fool as not to know? You had everything, and I had nothing—except your damned charity! You had all the things I wanted, and every now and then you would toss me one of them—a dress you were tired of, or a hat you didn't want! And thinking all the time how generous you were—how grateful I ought to be!"

Thomasina lifted her head and met those hating eyes.

"No, Anna! Oh, *no!*"

Anna Ball laughed.

"Of course you did! It's a lovely part to play. And it doesn't cost too much—just a few things you don't want, and there you are, on the top of the world, feeling ever so noble and magnanimous! 'Poor Anna—I must be kind to her.' Do you think I haven't seen you thinking that a thousand times? And how nice to be poor Anna whom nobody cares about, and have rich, fortunate Thomasina being kind to you!"

"Anna—*please!* You don't know what you are saying."

Anna gave that horrid laugh again.

"My dear Thomasina, I know very well what I'm saying! I've had it saved up for a very long time, and I'm enjoying every minute of it! You're going to listen to me now! I've had to listen to you often enough—preaching and talking pi!"

Thomasina said in a low shocked voice,

"I didn't mean to preach."

"Oh, no, of course not—you only did it! Now it's my turn! It never occurred to you that poor Anna might make something out of her life after all—that she might have a lover and a life that was really worth living—excitement, adventure, and a man who could give them to her!"

"Mr. Sandrow," said Thomasina gravely.

"I suppose that poor fool Emily Craddock talked!"

"Anna, we thought you were dead. Why did you let me think so? Why didn't you write?"

"Because it didn't suit me. Because Mr. Sandrow—" she gave the name a mocking twist—"Mr. Sandrow and I were having a very good time, and didn't want you muddling and meddling in my affairs. I've got clothes of my own now, and money of my own, and a man of my own. Do you think that I didn't know that you used to ask your friends to dance with me? If I forgave you for all the rest of it I'd never forgive you for that!" Her face was distorted by fury. Then the triumphant look came back to it. "But you see, you're not *wanted* any more!"

It was at some time during this speech that there came the sound of the second shot. Anna heard it. It was then that her triumphant look returned. She lifted her head and let her voice ring out.

Thomasina heard it too, but she did not think about it. Not consciously. She heard it, and a cold breath touched her, but she did not think about it yet. It was a shot. She did not relate it to herself or to Anna. To Anna—her whole mind was taken up with Anna. She had been shocked in the quite literal sense of the word. She was not afraid. How could she be afraid of Anna Ball whom she had known so long and so well?

She had never known her at all. Under the dumb, sulky surface where she had thought there were sore places into which she had poured all she knew of kindness and healing, there had been a ravening jealousy and resentment. She was not afraid—not yet—but she knew now that there was something to be afraid of. She said soberly and quickly,

"I'm sorry, Anna—I didn't know. I'll go."

She put her hand behind her to find the handle of the door. There was an instinct to stay facing Anna, not to turn round.

Anna's hand went into the pocket of her slacks, and came out again with a revolver—one of those little things that look like a toy and hold half a dozen men's lives. She pointed it at Thomasina and said,

"No, you don't! If you touch that handle, I'll fire! I won't kill you, because, I haven't finished with you yet. I'll just break your shoulder. I'm a dead shot—which is one of the things you didn't know about me. I learnt in Germany, which is where I met Mr. Sandrow. He taught me—that, and other things. I'm going to tell you some of them. If the world kicks you in the face, get up and kick it back. If you haven't any money, take it. If anyone gets in your way, shoot him down. It's quite easy to learn when you've been hating people all your life. Well, I came back to England and waited while he made his plans, and then I came down here. Of course Emily Craddock was the most tiresome bore—and those awful children! But I used to slip out and meet Mr. Sandrow." She let her voice twist on the name again. "And then, as you know, it wasn't for long. We staged a very good disappearance, didn't we? Me in a red hat, going off from Dedham, and practically the whole Colony to see me go by in the car with Peveril. And then at the station I was so agitated and distressed that the stationmaster couldn't help noticing me, and Peveril was able to explain how neurotic I was, and how glad they were to get rid of me. I didn't go very far, you know. I just stuffed the red hat into my suit-case, tied a handkerchief over my head, and changed at the first junction. I shan't tell you where I went, but it wasn't a hundred miles from here. Mr. Sandrow and I had it all planned. And now, I suppose, you would like to know who he is. You'll be surprised! But I'll give you three guesses. It's someone you know. There—I've given you a lead! Someone you know very well. Come along, Thomasina—surely you're going to have a try!"

Thomasina's lips said, "No." Her mind said, "She wouldn't tell me these things if she was going to let me go."

When she had groped for the handle of the door she had not found it. She was near enough to the wall, but too much to one side. If she moved or tried to reach for the handle now, Anna would shoot her down. Even without being a dead shot she could hardly miss. There was nothing to do but play for time.

There was no help in that. She was alone with Anna in this deserted place, and no one knew that she was here. She thought about Peter, and he seemed like someone who had happened long ago and very far away. It seemed a silly, trivial thing that she had quarrelled with him.

Anna's voice broke in.

"If you are not going to guess, I shall have to tell you. Someone whom you know very well indeed. Did you know what a good shot he was, or did he keep that dark? There were quite a few things you didn't know about him, I expect. You thought you could have him any time you wanted him, didn't you? He pretended he didn't like me. One of the things you didn't know was that he was such a good actor, and another was that he was mine. Not yours, my dear Thomasina, but mine—mine—mine."

Thomasina thought, "She's mad. It's all frightful, but she's mad—she doesn't know what she is saying." She said,

"Anna, please do stop! You are making my head go round. I don't know what you are talking about, and I don't believe you do either. It's frightfully late. I'm going home to bed."

Anna came a step nearer. If she would come nearer still, there might be a chance of catching her by the wrist, knocking the revolver out of her hand.

But Anna took only that one step. She said in a warning voice,

"Oh, no, you don't! You'll do just as you are told, and when I am finished with you—when I'm quite finished with you—you shall have your sleep—your good long sleep." She laughed and changed her tone. "I was telling you about Mr. Sandrow, wasn't I? You ought to be pleased, because you were trying to find out about him. And so are the police. They'd give their eyes to know the things I'm telling you, but you won't be able to repeat them. Mr. Sandrow is a very clever man, and he is going to be a very rich one. He can get a few thousand pounds any time he wants to just by walking into a bank and asking for it. And do you know, they never refuse him—he's too quick a shot for that. And we drive away together with the money—you didn't know I was such a good driver, did you? He gets into the car and off we go, with nothing for those stupid police to track us by. That first time at Enderby Green I was a boy, made up very dark with a green muffler and a black hat. And at Ledlington I was a dazzling blonde—it's a lovely wig. And there was a young man went by who would have liked to know me better. That was when I was waiting outside the bank. I didn't really let him see my face of course. I had my hand up pretending to do something to my hair. And to show you how good my nerve is, it didn't shake in the least. And then Mr. Sandrow came out of the bank, and we drove away. Come now—haven't you guessed who he is—not yet? Do you know, I don't believe you can be as stupid as all that. Why, he's Peter—Peter—Peter Brandon—whom you thought you had got in your pocket! And, oh, how we've laughed at it together, he and I! Well, now it's your turn to laugh. It's a good joke, isn't it? Laugh, Thomasina—laugh—laugh—*laugh!*"

CHAPTER 36

At the sound of the opening door Peter Brandon let go of the wrist he was holding and straightened up. He saw Miss Silver in her blue dressing-gown with the white crochet trimming, her hair very neatly arranged under the strong silk net which she wore over it at night, and a look of grave enquiry on her face. As he turned, she spoke in a serious, level voice.

"What are you doing here, Mr. Brandon?"

He could very reasonably have asked the same question, but it simply did not occur to him to do so. He might have been eight years old again, raiding the jam cupboard. He said,

"I was looking for Thomasina."

"Is she here?"

"I don't know. I was afraid she might be."

Miss Silver coughed.

"We will speak of that later. Is Mr. Craddock dead?"

"I think so. He wasn't when I came, but I can't feel any pulse now."

She came forward into the room, knelt down, and took hold of a wrist where the pulse would never beat again. After a moment or two she said,

"No, there is nothing. He is dead. How long have you been here?"

"I came to find Thomasina. She said something this afternoon about Anna Ball being here, locked up in a cellar. I said it was all nonsense, and we quarrelled. I wanted her to go away. I thought—"

"Mr. Brandon, I asked you how long you had been here."

He stared at her.

"I came up to look for her, and the door was ajar. As soon as I got inside the hall there was a shot. I couldn't tell where it came from. I tried two passages before I found the one with that play-acting hand. I was looking at it when the shot went off, right in here. I wasn't a minute opening the door, but there was no one here except Craddock. I had to see if there was anything I could do for him. I tried to stop the bleeding with my handkerchief."

Miss Silver had already noticed the handkerchief. Peveril Craddock had been wearing one of those smocks which he affected, of a deep blue in colour. It had been torn open down the front, and Mr. Brandon's handkerchief pushed between it and the vest which was worn underneath. Since the handkerchief was of a dark red colour, the extent to which it was stained did not immediately appear. She said,

"Was he conscious? Did he speak at all?"

He shook his head.

"There was just a bit of pulse. He wasn't quite dead, but as near as makes no difference."

Miss Silver had looked at her watch at the sound of the second shot. She had glanced at it again before opening the door of this room. On his own showing Peter Brandon had been alone with the dead or dying man for just under three minutes, during which time he had been occupied in a reasonable and humane attempt to stanch the wound or wounds. On his own showing—

He might or might not be speaking the truth. There had been two shots. He might have been here when the first shot was fired, and for some time before that. She suspended judgment. And meanwhile she surveyed the scene.

From the way in which the writing-chair had fallen it looked as if Peveril Craddock had been sitting at the table. Upon the far side of it there was a second chair, pushed back at an angle. It looked as if someone had sat there and talked with Mr. Craddock. They had talked, and then something had been said or done which turned two men talking in a comfortable room with a table between into a murderer and his victim. Both had sprung up, Peveril Craddock with so violent a backward thrust as to send his chair flying. And the other man had shot him down. If he had fallen at the first shot, the murderer must have come round the table and stood over him to see whether he was dead.

She weighed in her own mind the time between the first and second shots. She had been startled. She had listened. She had risen from her chair, slipped her torch into her dressing-gown pocket, and gone to the door to stand there and listen again. Just what had been happening in this room whilst she was doing these things? Peveril Craddock had fallen. The murderer must make sure that he is dead. He comes round the table to make sure. There is still some life, some movement. He fires a second shot. Yes, it would be that way. If Mr. Brandon was the murderer, the weapon must be here in this room. If he was the murderer, she could conceive of no reason why he should have lingered on the scene or have been endeavouring to stanch the wounds. Again these thoughts passed so quickly that there was hardly a noticeable pause before she said,

"I see there is a telephone on the table. The police must be informed immediately."

It was the number of Frank Abbott's hotel that she called. He woke from a deep and dreamless sleep to the maddening iteration of the bell right there beside his bed. His "Hullo?" sounded only half awake. To this drowsy state Miss Silver's voice came like a splash of cold water.

"Is that Inspector Abbott?"

He was startled broad awake.

"Miss Silver! What is it?"

"Peveril Craddock has been shot—here in his study at Deepe House—the main part of the building. The front door is ajar, and when you come into the hall you will see a lighted passage on the right-hand side. The study is at the end of it. Mr. Peter Brandon is with me. There is urgent need for haste. Inspector Jackson should arrange for a search warrant for all the houses in the Colony. A plain stick with a crook and a left hand wash-leather glove with a small triangular tear between the first and second fingers should be looked for. But someone should come here at once. I am ringing off."

Replacing the receiver, she turned, to see Peter Brandon looking at her with a good deal of attention.

"Why did you tell him I was here?"

"Because you are here, Mr. Brandon, and I think the police will want to know why."

"I have told you why. I came here to look for Thomasina."

"Have you any real reason to suppose that she is here?"

The farther he got in his attempt to explain, the less probable it all sounded, and the more apparent did it become that reason had really nothing to do with it at all. He found himself thinking, "If anyone pitched me a tale like that, I'd say he was a liar and a fool—"

The words dried up on his tongue. Miss Silver was gazing at him in a thoughtful manner.

"You felt anxious about Miss Elliot because you were afraid she might take it into her head to explore Deepe House during the night, so you climbed out of your window and walked up to the Miss Tremletts', where you found that one of the bedrooms still showed a light. After watching it for some time you came on to Deepe House."

Put like that, it sounded even worse than he had supposed. An idiot child could have produced a better story. He felt as if Miss Silver was looking right through him. The blood rushed to his face. His ears felt as if they had suddenly become red hot.

She said in a tolerant tone,

"It will be quite easy to find out if she is at home. We can ring the Miss Tremletts up."

It was Miss Gwyneth who answered the call. She sounded both flustered and cross.

"Oh, dear—what is it? . . . Miss Silver! Has anything happened? It's the middle of the night. . . . Miss Elliot? Thomasina! . . . Why of course she is! Where else should she be at this hour? Really, Miss Silver. . . . Well, of course, if you insist. But I must say—"

It did not get said, because Miss Gwyneth here let go of the receiver, groped for her slippers, clutched her dressing-gown angrily about her, whisked along a passage, and flung open the door of Thomasina's room.

She found it empty.

The bed not slept in. No sign of the clothes Thomasina had been wearing. No sign of her outdoor shoes. No sign of her coat.

It was a very frightened voice which came along the line to Miss Silver, waiting in the study at Deepe House.

"Oh, Miss Silver—she isn't here! Her bed hasn't been slept in! Her coat isn't there—she must have gone out! Oh dear, oh dear—what had I better do?"

Miss Silver said firmly,

"Pray do nothing at all, Miss Tremlett." After which she replaced the receiver and turned to Peter. "She is not there."

He was at her elbow.

"I know—I heard. This place is like a rabbit-warren—she may be anywhere."

The words "She may be dead" presented themselves. They clamoured to be admitted. He slammed all his doors upon them, but he had seen them and they could not be forgotten.

Miss Silver said,

"Since you say you heard the second shot when you were just upon the other side of the door, there must be some other way out of this room. How long was it before you came in?"

"Oh, no time at all. I suppose half a minute. A thing like that takes you aback. I switched on my torch, and found I didn't need it."

Miss Silver had turned from the writing-table. The room had a deep bay at one end of it. The windows were screened by warm brown velvet curtains. On the left-hand side they extended beyond the bay. It occurred to her that there might be a door in that part of the wall which the curtains concealed. The man who fired the second shot would have had very little time to get away. He must have been aware that he had a line of retreat, and he must have been quick to avail himself of it. He could have slipped behind those curtains in time to avoid being seen. If there was a door there, he must already have made his escape. If there was no door, he might still be there behind the heavy velvet folds, pressed close against wall or window and hearing all that passed. In this case they were, of course, in some considerable danger.

Before Peter Brandon had the least idea of what she was going to do she walked to the window and drew the left-hand curtain back.

CHAPTER 37

THERE WAS A door. The last folds of the velvet slid past it and left it bare. But it was not the door that riveted Miss Silver's attention. She said quickly, "Put out the light, Mr. Brandon!" As the switch clicked and the room fell dark, they could both see the jutting front of the garage and the glow that came from it. The garage doors were closed. The light came from a window on either side.

Miss Silver put her hand to the curtain and drew it close again.

"It would seem that he went that way, and that he is still there. We will have the light again, Mr. Brandon."

When it had been switched on she said soberly,

"I expect you noticed that there was a door. There is no doubt that it leads to the garage. If the man who shot Mr. Craddock is still there, he will without doubt be both desperate and dangerous. We cannot count upon the arrival of the police for nearly half an hour. I think we must decide upon what we are to do next."

"Miss Silver, what I have to do is to find Thomasina. You must see that."

She laid her hand upon his arm.

"Pray take a moment for consideration. Miss Elliot may already be on her way back to the Miss Tremletts'. Mr. Craddock is dead, and the person whom you disturbed, and who is probably the murderer, is in the garage. We do not know why he has delayed his escape. He may be destroying evidence, or he may be waiting for an accomplice to join him. But however he is engaged, it is improbable that he has any time to spare for Miss Elliot. If she is not in the garage she is safe. I think we should make certain that she is not there, and at the same time endeavour to discover the murderer's identity."

Peter nodded.

"The windows aren't any good—at least I shouldn't think they were. The light wasn't coming through them clear. There are blinds."

Miss Silver coughed gently.

"Yes, I noticed that. I think we must see where this door will take us. Let us hope that it is not locked."

It would have been if the murderer had had the time. The key had actually been taken from the lock on this side but had dropped on the far side of the door. The need for haste had been as great as that.

They stood on the threshold and looked into one of those empty dilapidated rooms. Miss Silver's powerful torch showed how thick the dust lay everywhere, except on the narrow trodden path which led to the garage door. She turned the light this way and that.

"Look, Mr. Brandon," she said in a low voice.

A yard from where they stood there were tracks in the dust going away to the left—footprints, quite plain and easy to see, going away to a door in that left-hand wall.

Peter said,

"He didn't go to the garage. That door goes back into the passage with the hand. He must have got out that way as soon as I was safe in the study. But if he did, who is in the garage?"

"That, I think, is what we had better find out."

Inside the garage Thomasina stood against the wall. Anna Ball was still talking. She could have talked for an hour and hardly have begun to tell Thomasina just how clever she and Mr. Sandrow had been, and just how much they hated and despised all the stupid people whom they had so easily taken in.

"He had to see Peveril Craddock, because Peveril was turning yellow. He puts on an act, you know—he hasn't really got a lot of nerve. Mr. Sandrow had made up his mind he would have to deal with him. I expect those were the shots we heard. He was going to arrange it to look like a suicide, but if he couldn't do that—and he says it's very difficult to get the fingerprints really convincing—on the gun, you know—then we were going to get him into the car and stage a crash on Quarry Hill. The car would of course be quite burnt out—a can or two of petrol would fix that all right—and Peveril out of the way for good. I don't suppose Emily would cry her eyes out. He was trying to get rid of the children, you know. But so inefficient—no real nerve. Now if Mr. Sandrow had taken it in hand, there wouldn't have been any hitch, but he said it wasn't his business and Peveril could do his own dirty work."

"*Anna!*"

It was when Thomasina said, "*Anna!*" that Peter Brandon turned the handle of the door and edged it open. It wasn't the door behind Thomasina, but the one on the other side of the garage. He had stood behind it with Miss Silver and heard the angry rise and fall of a woman's voice. Then, as the handle turned and the door slid, he heard Thomasina say Anna's name on that note of horror and protest. His heart turned over. Because he had been afraid—he had been very much afraid.

The first thing he saw was Anna Ball in slacks and a red jersey standing with her back to him, and, past her, Thomasina against the opposite wall. Her hands were pressed against it, and all the colour was gone from her face. Her eyes were wide and dark, and she stared at the revolver in Anna's hand. Because that was the really unbelievable thing

—Anna Ball was holding a revolver and pointing it at Thomasina. He heard her say,

"He'll be here any minute now, and then you can join Peveril in the car. Swoosh over the edge of the quarry, and a blazing bonfire down below—that's what's waiting for you, Thomasina, *dear!*"

Peter walked into the garage, and she turned her head. In that moment Thomasina snatched the torch from the pocket of her coat and threw it with all her might. She had a strong wrist and a good eye. Peter had taught her to throw fast and straight. She threw now for his life and her own. The torch caught Anna full on the side of the head as she turned. Not a serious blow, but a startling one. It took her off her balance as she swung about. She screamed and stumbled, a shot went wide, and Peter had her by the wrists.

Thomasina came forward and twisted the revolver out of her hand.

CHAPTER 38

THOMASINA WAS NEVER quite sure which was the more dreadful, the last half hour when she had stood facing Anna's hatred and her revolver, or the next when they were waiting for the police to arrive.

They went back to the study and waited there with Peveril Craddock lying dead and the stain of his blood on the floor. There were comfortable chairs in the room. Anna sat in one of them with the cord of Miss Silver's dressing-gown holding her there. She sat quite still, quite dumb, her eyes half closed, only every now and then the lids lifted to show the burning hatred there. It was like some horribly bad dream, and, like the things that happen in a dream, it couldn't be measured by time.

Thomasina did not look at Peter, and he did not look at her. The people you love don't belong to that kind of dream. You don't want to see them there. You want to wake up and know that none of it has ever happened.

Miss Silver had taken one of the upright chairs. Her hands were in her lap. Her face was resolute and composed. Her dressing-gown, deprived of its girdle, hung in severe blue folds.

Nobody spoke. The silence was so complete that the sound of the police car coming up the drive startled them all.

And then in a moment the empty derelict house echoed with the tramp of feet and the sound of voices, and there came in on the hushed room with the dead man in it Inspector Jackson, Inspector Abbott, the Police Surgeon—

The routine of investigation began.

Miss Silver was able to get away for long enough to make sure that all was well in the Craddocks' wing. Looking in upon Emily Craddock's room, she found it warm and peaceful. Emily herself still slept that deep, exhausted sleep. Jennifer in the big armchair slept too, her head pillowed on her arm, the eiderdown falling away a little at the neck, her breath coming slow and steady. It was all very far removed from the scene in Peveril Craddock's study. Miss Silver shut the door and went back to it.

Anna sat dumb. Through Miss Silver's statement, through Peter Brandon's, through Thomasina's, through the arrival of the police photographer and the fingerprint man, she sat silent and did not move. The cord of Miss Silver's dressing-gown had been restored to its proper use. Her arms were free, but she held herself as stiffly as when they had been bound. It was not until she was told that she would be taken to the station and charged with being an accessory that she turned her eyes on Inspector Jackson—smouldering eyes, with the lids only half raised.

"And you don't want to hear what I've got to say? There's quite a lot I can say if I choose! Some people won't like it, but that isn't going to stop me saying it!"

He told her that she could make a statement, and cautioned her that what she said would be taken down and could afterwards be used in evidence. She laughed in his face.

"If I'm an accessory I've got to have a principal, haven't I? Why don't you go ahead and arrest him? I didn't shoot up the banks, you know, I only drove the car! And I didn't shoot Peveril Craddock either!" She jerked her head in Thomasina's direction. "She knows that, because we were together when both the shots were fired!"

Thomasina said, "Yes." Just the one word in a deep mournful tone.

Anna flung up her head.

"There! You hear that? Well, there you are! Why don't you get on and arrest him? I'm not going to prison alone!

And I'm not going to stand in the dock alone—I'm going to have my lover with me! She told you about Mr. Sandrow in her statement, didn't she? Well, why don't you get on and arrest him? There he is!" This time the jerk of the head was for Peter Brandon, who stared back at her in angry amazement.

Thomasina got up from the chair where she was sitting and walked over to stand beside him. She slipped her hand inside his arm. They did not look at one another.

At the writing-table Inspector Abbott surveyed the scene in silence. Nobody could have dreamed that just half an hour before he had entered this room he had been in bed at the George in Ledlington. His dark suit was, as always, immaculate, his tie perfectly knotted, his fair hair mirror-smooth. He held a pencil negligently between two fingers. His light, cool eyes watched Anna Ball. He had just passed a note to the sergeant who stood at his elbow. Now he watched Anna Ball.

Inspector Jackson was watching her too. He said,

"You are making a statement to the effect that it was Mr. Brandon who was concerned in the robbery at the County Bank yesterday in the course of which the Bank Manager and a clerk were murdered, and that you were waiting for him with a stolen car and afterwards drove him away. Is that what you really mean us to understand?"

She gave him a hard mocking look and laughed, mimicking his formal way of speech.

"How clever you are, Inspector! That is just exactly what I do mean you to understand! How did you manage to guess? But of course the police are all brains! Inspector Jackson—Mr. Sandrow—Mr. Peter Brandon Sandrow. Peter, darling, we're for it. Meet the police!"

"Well, Mr. Brandon?"

Peter's shoulder lifted.

"Red herring," he said briefly.

Miss Silver said in a quiet but decided voice,

"It would not have been possible for Mr. Brandon to be the bandaged man who passed me on the Station Approach. He is too tall and too broad, and he takes at least two sizes larger in shoes."

Jackson said,

"Where were you during yesterday afternoon, Mr. Brandon?"

"I was on my way down from town. I reached Ledlington

at a quarter to five and took the five o'clock bus out to Deep End. Miss Gwyneth Tremlett, Miss Silver, and Mr. Remington were in the same bus."

"But not the same train."

"No. But there was a man in the carriage with me all the way from London. He told me he had a book-shop in the Market Square. A tall, thin man with glasses and a stoop, full of odd bits of information about the country. We were talking quite a lot, so he ought to remember me."

"That would be Mr. Bannerman," said Inspector Jackson. "He sits up late—I think I'll give him a ring."

Mr. Bannerman, it appeared, had not yet gone to bed. The call was answered promptly, and a brief tantalizing interchange took place, Inspector Jackson leading off with, "I believe you were in town yesterday afternoon," and continuing with intervals when the telephone made odd noises, amongst which a thin, far voice came and went. Only Frank Abbott sitting next to the instrument could hear that Mr. Bannerman was giving an accurate description of Mr. Peter Brandon, finishing up with, "A very agreeable young man—a writer. I have read his books with interest."

Inspector Jackson hung up the receiver.

"Mr. Bannerman confirms your statement, Mr. Brandon. As a matter of form, I will ask him to identify you later."

As he spoke, there was a faint stir of relief in the room. Anna Ball sat dumb. Miss Silver very slightly inclined her head. Thomasina drew her hand away from Peter's arm and went back to her seat. When Anna had accused him in the garage it had all been part of the nightmare. When she repeated the accusation here in front of all these people a rush of passionate protest had taken her to his side. Now she came back to her seat again. Her mind had been violently wrenched. She felt empty and weak.

Inspector Jackson was saying,

"Now, Miss Ball, do you wish to make a statement, or do you not? It is no use your accusing innocent people or trying to throw dust in the eyes of the police. We are here to investigate the death of Mr. Craddock. If you know who shot him—"

Anna interrupted him with a fierce laugh.

"Of course I know! But I'm not going to tell you! Why should I?"

As she spoke, the door from the passage was opened by a police sergeant and Mr. John Robinson was ushered in. He stood for a moment looking about him—at the two Inspectors, at Thomasina Elliot and Peter Brandon, at Anna Ball, at Miss Silver in her blue dressing-gown, and at Peveril Craddock's body lying on the study floor. He did not start because he did not allow himself to start. There was an obvious effort at control, a visible stiffening. After a moment he said,

"Craddock! Who did it?"

Frank Abbott said in his almost casual manner,

"Well, we were rather wondering whether you could help us about that."

"*I?*"

"Yes, you. Your name is not really John Robinson, is it?"

"What makes you think so?"

"Oh, just a quotation or two. You shouldn't have risked them, you know—Miss Silver has her Tennyson by heart. You gave yourself away when you quoted from *Enoch Arden,* I'm afraid. I bought a second-hand Tennyson yesterday afternoon and tracked him down. He was a sailor who was supposed to have been lost at sea. By the time he came home his wife had married somebody else, and he had to make up his mind whether to upset the apple-cart or not. And that, I take it, has been your position. What I don't happen to know is just what your real name is."

Mr. Robinson shrugged his shoulders and said,

"Oh, well, I was through with the game anyway. The name is Verney—John Verney."

"And you are Mrs. Craddock's husband?"

"Yes, poor soul."

"In which case you had quite a strong motive for killing Craddock."

John Verney shrugged again. Everyone was looking at him now, but he appeared extremely cool. When he spoke, the country drawl had been dropped.

"I?" he said. "Why should I kill him? If he had made Emily a decent husband, I'd have cleared off. I came here to find out how things were. I was in a plane crash in the States. The plane was burnt out and everyone with it—as they thought. I don't know how I got clear, because I don't remember a thing about it. It was in one of those remote districts—very inaccessible. I must have wandered for miles, and the next thing I knew, it was six months later, and I was officially dead. Some people had taken me in—I'd been chopping wood and doing chores for them. I don't remember anything about it. Well, I thought Emily would be better off without me, so I stayed on. I got interested in birds and creatures. I did a book with illustrations. It caught on, and I made a little money. The next one was a freak best-seller, I haven't the least idea why. It went like a forest fire, so I thought I had better come over here and see how Emily and the children were getting on. Well, I found she had come into money and married again. I didn't think it was my business to butt in if she was doing all right, so I came here to find out. Of course anyone could see that Craddock was a pompous ass, but they all said she adored him. I had rather a jolt in the autumn when I found the children taking home poisonous fungi under the instructions of this young woman—it is Miss Ball, isn't it?"

Anna Ball laughed angrily.

"If you're going to take that line, I'm through! 'Is that Miss Ball?' indeed!"

He stared at her and said, "Are you mad?"

She laughed again.

"Mad? No, I've come to my senses! You'd throw me off, would you—pretend you've never had anything to do with me—pretend we haven't been lovers!"

"My good girl!"

"Listen to him!" She whirled round on Jackson. "Innocent, isn't he! Who had a motive for killing Peveril Craddock if he hadn't? Think of having to give up Emily—*and* her money! And he may be John Verney—I don't say he isn't—but he's my Mr. Sandrow too, and you'd better ask him where *he* was yesterday afternoon! Doing some quiet nature-study in a wood? Or bandaged up and robbing the County Bank!"

It was in the minds of both Inspectors that Mr. Robinson had had no pretence of an alibi for yesterday afternoon. According to his own statement he had meant to go up into the Rowbury Woods, but turned off when he found that someone was shooting there, and fetched up in Ledlington, where he spent some time in the County Museum looking at the Hedlow collection of birds. Well, he might have been there, or he might have been rolled up in bandages shooting up the bank manager and his clerk. Only if he were the bank murderer, it did seem an odd thing that he should choose this moment to allow his feelings as a dispossessed husband to get the better of him. There had been months when he could have murdered Peveril Craddock with so very much less risk to himself. And actually, why murder him at all? He had only to declare himself and walk off with his wife and her fortune. If his book was really a best-seller, even the money motive didn't count, and that apart, would anyone in their senses do murder for poor Emily Craddock's sake?

John Verney appeared to be very completely in his senses. He might have been following their thoughts—perhaps he was. He indicated Anna, and said bluntly,

"She's talking through the back of her neck. Emily and I were a pretty detached couple. She needed someone who would look after her, and if Craddock was making a good job of it, I hadn't any grudge against him. But I had to find out. The toadstools could easily have been a mistake. Then one of the children mentioned an escape from drowning. That might have been an accident too. I only saw Emily in the distance—she looked ill. The boys were all right, but Jennifer wasn't. I had just made up my mind to come out into the open, when Miss Silver arrived on the scene. She was so obviously competent and trustworthy that I thought I would wait a little longer. Now I wish I hadn't. But all that stuff about my robbing the bank is just damned nonsense."

Anna's eyes taunted him.

"Then who did rob it? I'm the only one who knows, you see, and I say it was you."

"Just now you said it was Mr. Peter Brandon," said Inspector Jackson.

She jerked her head round and stared at him.

"Oh, that was just my fun. I owed him something for the way he used to look at me when I went out with him and Thomasina—as if I wasn't good enough to be looked at—as if I was something that ought to have been drowned when I was a baby! Pity nobody thought of doing it, isn't it?"

Frank Abbott gave her a long hard look.

"And what have you got against Mr. Verney? Did he look at you in a way you didn't like, or—didn't he look at you at all?"

A dull red colour ran up to the very roots of her hair, swamping the lavish make-up. She almost screamed back at him.

"Of course he looked at me! I tell you he was my lover! I tell you he was Mr. Sandrow! I tell you he robbed the bank! I tell you he shot Peveril Craddock! I'm the only one who knows, and I tell you he did it—Mr. Sandrow—Mr. Verney Robinson Sandrow! If it wasn't him, who was it? Who—" She stopped on the word, because the door was opening again.

And this time it was Augustus Remington who came in, shepherded by one of the Ledshire constables. He had a fretful expression on his face, and was wrapped in a large shawl-like cape which he immediately discarded. Under it he wore a violet smock and a pair of black velveteen slacks. He gazed about him, shuddered at the body of Peveril Craddock, and recoiled with a hand before his eyes.

"No—really—this is too much! What has happened? Is he dead? How extremely shocking! I should have been warned. I am entirely allergic to violence of any kind—the vibrations are alarmingly disturbed. Perhaps a glass of water—" He sank down upon the nearest chair and closed his eyes.

Jackson said sharply,

"I'm afraid we have none here. Pull yourself together, Mr. Remington! Are you sure that this is a shock to you?"

A murmured "Terrible!" came from the parted lips. The violet smock heaved in a succession of painful gasps.

The constable advanced to the table and laid something down upon it.

"Burning them, he was," he said briefly, and fell back.

On the green leather which covered the table there lay a pair of soiled wash-leather gloves. The two Inspectors bent an enquiring gaze upon them. Everyone looked in the same direction. Anna sat dumb and staring, her mouth half open as it had been when she checked on her last word.

Frank Abbott took hold of the left-hand glove and spread it out. It smelt of the fire, and there were marks of singeing. Part of the little finger was burned away. There was a small triangular tear between the first finger and the one next to it. The seam had come undone, and an end of the broken thread stood up beyond the gap.

He said, "Miss Silver—" and she came forward to stand between him and Inspector Jackson.

"Anything here that you recognize?"

Looking down at the glove, she said,

"Yes."

"Could you swear to it?"

She said, "Yes," again. She turned to go back to her seat. The moment of tension was over—the moment when everyone had been looking at her and at the wash-leather glove and no one had been looking at anything else. At anything or at anyone. Now that the strained attention had been released it turned inevitably to the man who had tried to burn the glove.

And he wasn't there.

Only a moment before he had been gasping for breath in his chair beside the door. Now he wasn't there any longer. The violet smock was gone, and so was Augustus Remington, and no one had seen him go. The door beside him may have been ajar, or it may not. It was ajar now, and he was gone.

CHAPTER 39

Miss Silver did not join in the search. She remained in the study with Thomasina and the sergeant who had been put in charge of Anna Ball. Another of those dreadful times of waiting.

Anna had not moved at all. Looking at her rigid face, Miss Silver felt a stern compassion. So thwarted, so twisted a creature, and now in so much pain. And at the root of it all the dreadful poisons of jealousy and envy. How necessary to guard against them in the child, to correct them in the developing thought. For how much unhappiness, how much crime, were they not responsible?

Thomasina had her thoughts too. She remembered so many things. She had tried to be kind to Anna. The kindness that has to try isn't enough. It doesn't reach people. She felt humble and ashamed. She had been pleased with herself. She had thought pretty well of Thomasina Elliot. If she ever felt like that again she would remember Anna Ball.

The time passed. It was not really very long. Frank Abbott and Peter Brandon came back. Frank said,

"He's got away. The girl had a car. We got out through the garage in time to see his tail-lights go off down the north drive. Jackson and Thomas have gone after him in Craddock's car. It would have taken too long to go round the house for one of ours, and they would have lost him."

Anna drew a long deep breath and said,

"He's gone—he's got away! He's too clever for you! He's always been too clever for you—he always will be!" The triumph went out of her voice. It broke half way and dropped. "He's gone—" she said.

Her voice whispered and stopped. She looked all round the room in a hesitating, bewildered kind of way, her hands twisting in her lap. She did not speak again.

There was coming and going. An ambulance arrived, and the body was removed. The sergeant sat at the desk and was busy with the telephone. Calls went out to all stations with a description of Augustus Remington. As to the car in which he had gone, there was no description available. Anna, questioned, did not even reply. She twisted her hands in her lap and stared at them. In the end they took her away with the policewoman who had come out from Ledlington in the ambulance.

Peter took Thomasina back to the Miss Tremletts', and Miss Silver returned to the Craddocks' wing. The study was left with a couple of constables in charge.

Thomasina and Peter walked across the park in silence. When there is too much to say it is easier to say nothing at all. They did not speak. Thomasina was alive, and she might so very easily have been dead. There could have been two bodies in the ambulance now on its way to Ledlington. As often as Peter wrenched his mind from this thought it swung back again.

Thomasina did not think about how narrowly she had escaped. She thought about Anna Ball. Those twisting hands, and the cold misery in her voice when she said, "He's gone–"

Coming to the Miss Tremletts' was like coming into another world. They wept, they talked, they were avid for every possible detail, they were instant with cups of tea. By the time they had reached the second brew they were beginning to be quite sure that they had always thought there was something odd about Augustus Remington.

Mr. John Verney had a word with Miss Silver before he too went back to his own wing.

"You'll tell Emily–"

"About Mr. Craddock's death–yes. As to your identity, Mr. Verney, I think you must be aware that she recognized you, and that that was why she fainted. Your disguise was a very good one. The loose untidy clothes, the beard, the country drawl–all these were a most efficient barrier to recognition. But when Mr. Craddock was speaking you broke into quite spontaneous and natural laughter. She recognized your laugh."

"He was being so pompous–"

"It has been a very great shock." Miss Silver's tone held a note of reproof. "Mrs. Verney is not at all strong. She is going to need care."

"I know, I know. I've been a deplorable husband. That

was why—I wanted to be sure— You'll do your best for her, won't you?" He took her hand, held it very hard for a moment, and then dropped it abruptly.

They went their way to their separate wings.

CHAPTER 40

IT WAS AUGUSTUS REMINGTON's violet smock that gave him away, in spite of the coat with which he had covered it and the dark wig which concealed his pallid hair. He had to stop for petrol, because Anna hadn't done what he had told her to do. She was not going far, and she had either forgotten to have the tank filled up, or she had not thought it necessary. When the gauge showed how low the petrol was, there was nothing for it but to chance the first all-night station. And when he stretched out a hand to pay, a long pointed end of violet cuff came out of the coat sleeve and hung there dangling.

Since all petrol stations had been warned, it was enough. The man in charge was a brawny fellow. He put a hand on Augustus Remington's arm and said, "Just a moment, sir," and the game was up. There never was a chance to use the revolver which was found in that coat pocket.

Frank Abbott dropped in to see Miss Silver a few days later.

"Of course he never intended to make a get-away, or he wouldn't have been wearing those ridiculous clothes, and he wouldn't have let himself run out of petrol. It was Anna Ball who was to disappear, but she wasn't to go far, so I suppose she didn't bother. He had to have her up at Deepe House in case he couldn't stage a convincing suicide for Craddock. I don't know what had passed between the two men, but there's no doubt that Craddock had become a danger and was to be eliminated. Anna Ball's pleasant little monologue in the garage makes that clear, and if Augustus couldn't make it look as if Peveril had shot himself, they were going to put him in the car and run him over Quarry Hill with enough petrol to make sure that there wouldn't be any clues. And of course Augustus couldn't have shifted the body by himself. Anna had to be there to give a hand—she's quite a hefty wench.

And when it was all over Augustus was going to fade back into his art needlework, whilst Anna put in time somewhere not too far away. He seems to have trusted her completely. All the notes from the Ledlington robbery and about half the Enderby Green ones were stowed away in the car. There were false backs to both the cubby holes in the dashboards, as well as one in the boot. That's where they found Anna's golden wig. There was a red one too and a beard, which is what Augustus wore for the Enderby Green affair, and when they gave the Sandrow story a build-up by letting Miss Gwyneth see them in Ledlington. Anna drove the car at Enderby Green. She was dressed as a boy. We found the whole outfit."

Miss Silver said soberly,

"Then she did know him before she came down here."

"Oh, yes, a long time before that. Some of it's guesswork still, but we're getting it straightened out. Cables to Major and Mrs. Dartrey out east—you remember she was with them in Germany. Telephone calls to the British Occupation Zone, and quite a lot of interesting stuff to hand. We're pretty sure it's going to link up with a couple of sensational jewel robberies in Germany. Anna Ball was on the spot—and who was going to suspect Mrs. Dartrey's English governess? What we haven't tracked down, and perhaps never will, is just where Augustus came in. He may have been the frail old Frenchwoman who was trying to trace a missing grandson and who took such a fancy to the Dartrey child. Or he may have been somebody else. He is certainly an adept at disguise. What is significant is that very shortly after the second robbery Mrs. Dartrey paid a short visit to France to her great-aunt, the Comtesse de Rochambeau. She took the child, and Anna went along. What would be easier than to have got that jewellery over the frontier, packed among the little girl's things? We shall never be able to prove it, but that's how I believe it was done. And then the Dartreys go out east, and it's time for a change of scene. I don't know if Augustus had worked with Craddock before, but I expect he had. You don't fix that sort of thing up on a half hour's acquaintance. Craddock had been doing a small business in forging notes—getting his hand in, as you may say. He had the idea of taking over a derelict country house and setting up something more ambitious there. Mrs. Verney and her money came in very handy. He made a great parade of his occult studies and the Colony he was going to found, and put in the powerful electric installation which immediately attracted your attention."

Miss Silver was knitting a useful pair of socks for Maurice. Her needles clicked briskly as she said,

"Mrs. Verney remarked on it to me—quite innocently of course, poor thing."

"Oh, yes, she and the children were very good camouflage. And so were the Miss Tremletts—perfectly respectable spinster ladies with a streak of the crank and a disposition to admire the egregious Peveril. Then there's Miranda—we haven't been quite sure about Miranda, but I don't really think she knew anything. She's a bit of a charlatan of course. She owned to faking a trance in order to get Thomasina off the map, but she says she only did it because Augustus said she disturbed his vibrations—and I'm afraid she is pretty fond of Augustus."

"Yes, I am afraid so. I have been to see her. She is very unhappy."

Frank leaned forward.

"Most esteemed preceptress, you know everything. Can you tell me why at least two women should fall for that miserable little rat? And I rather think Miss Gwyneth has a soft corner for him too."

"Not now," said Miss Silver. "She is too much shocked. As to Miranda and Anna Ball, it is, and always has been, quite impossible to account for the violent attraction which some criminals appear to exercise. The victims are as a rule lonely women who have failed to make other ties. It is a tragic spectacle, and one which would be avoided if these people would realize that their craving for affection defeats its own ends. If they were willing to give instead of merely wishing to receive, they would form genuine ties of friendship and not fall a prey to the first adventurer who plays upon their vanity."

Frank received this with respect. What in an irreverent moment he had been known to allude to as Maudie's Moralities never failed to delight him, but under the mockery there was not only affection but a very real respect. Because Maudie was herself a Case in Point. She not only preached, but she practised. Going out into the world as a penniless governess, a position so undefined as to be exposed to the condescension of the employer and the formidable dislike of the domestic staff, she had won her way to a comfortable independence, and in the course of doing so had acquired a very large circle of admiring and devoted friends. And this had been done by the exercise of intelligence, courage, and devotion to duty. She had thought of others before she thought of herself, she had sought justice and loved mercy, and walked humbly in the sight of what she called Providence. She had her reward, not because she had sought it, but because it had been earned. He smiled at her and said,

"Miranda will get over it. She strikes me as having a fundamental streak of common sense. She didn't mind obliging Augustus with a fake trance, but she would probably always have drawn the line at forged notes, and the bank murders have really shocked her to the core."

Miss Silver continued to knit placidly. She said,

"The Verneys will return to Wyshmere. It is indeed fortunate that her house there was only let and not sold. She told me that she could not bear to part with it as all her children had been born there, and since her tenant wishes to return to London she can go back whenever she likes. Mr. Verney has shown much good feeling. She needs kindness, and he will supply it. The children are already devoted to him, and Jennifer is a different creature. The Miss Tremletts would also like to return to Wyshmere, and I gather that they will be able to arrange to do so. Deep End is really not at all congenial. Miss Elaine has missed her classes for folk dancing, and both are longing to see their friends again. They have a chance of securing a larger and airier cottage, and I believe they will avail themselves of it."

"And Thomasina Elliot?" said Frank. "Do you know, I feel sorry for Thomasina. She took the bit between her teeth and ran head-on into a good deal more than she expected."

Miss Silver's needles clicked.

"She acted from the most conscientious motives."

Frank cocked an eyebrow.

"I know. It is invariably fatal. Consider the consequences. Instead of remaining quietly in town, a course commended by both of us, accepting the benevolent counsel of a rising police officer, dining out with him discreetly and, who knows, making steady progress in his affections, she rushes violently into the middle of a murder case, very nearly gets herself bumped off, and will probably end by marrying that chap Brandon."

Miss Silver smiled benevolently.

"They will suit one another very well," she said.

CHAPTER 41

THOMASINA WAS VERY UNHAPPY. She would have liked to put four hundred miles between her and Deep End. Or, failing Scotland, she would have liked to bury herself in London and not see anyone she knew for a very long time. Most particularly she did not want to see Peter Brandon. He had said, and everyone else had said, that she would get herself into a mess if she insisted on coming to Deep End, and now there was nothing to stop any of them—or Peter—from saying, "I told you so." Except their kind hearts. And she was just as certain as she could be of anything that Peter hadn't got that sort of heart at all. He would not only say, "I told you so," but he would probably go on saying it for the rest of their lives, and she couldn't bear it. But whether she could bear it or not, she would have to stay at Deep End with the Miss Tremletts till after the inquest on Peveril Craddock. That would be only a day or two now. After it was over she could go back to town, but when the trial came on she would have to give evidence.

The thought was a nightmare. Augustus Remington would be tried for the bank murders and the murder of Peveril Craddock, and Anna Ball would be tried with him. You couldn't let murderers go free, but when you knew people they weren't just murderers, they were people you knew. The only comfort she had was that she would be able to pay for Anna's defence, and perhaps it might be possible to prove that she was insane. Because of course she must be. Nobody who said the things Anna had said in the garage could be anything but mad, and if she was mad they wouldn't hang her. She shuddered away from the word.

The Miss Tremletts were much concerned. The bright bloom which they had admired was gone. Dear Thomasina got up pale and heavy-eyed in the mornings, and they were sure that she did not sleep. She refused to be tempted with Gwyneth's breakfast scones or Elaine's Olde Tyme marmalade.

"And it stands to reason that a cup of tea is not enough to take you through the morning even if you eat a good lunch, which she doesn't—just goes on saying not to give her so much and pushing it under her fork. We are very much distressed, Mr. Brandon—" Miss Gwyneth broke off to consider that Mr. Brandon also looked as if he had not been able to face his breakfast.

Miss Elaine echoed her sister.

"We are very much distressed."

"But she won't see you," said Miss Gwyneth. "It's no use, Mr. Brandon, she really won't."

"She has locked her door," said Elaine.

They sat side by side in the quietest of their smocks. The absence of bead necklaces proclaimed the deference due to a tragic occasion. They gazed earnestly at Peter, but they had no help to give him. Thomasina was locked in her room, and she wouldn't come out.

This went on for three days.

On the fourth day the inquest was to take place, and immediately after the inquest Thomasina was going back to town to see a solicitor and arrange about Anna's defence.

On the evening of the third day, having reconnoitred and observed that there was a light in Thomasina's window, Peter walked into the house without ringing, took the stairs as cautiously as any burglar, and came in upon Thomasina, whom he found in the act of changing her dress for the evening meal. As the folds of soft grey wool happened to be entirely covering her face and head, she had no means of knowing why the door had opened and shut again. The dress was beautifully warm, and quite comfortable when it was on, but it was always a devil to get into, and it chose this moment to stick. She was still wrestling with it when a firm hand pulled it down on either side and her head came through the opening.

Peter gave the folds a final pull. Then he stepped back and said in his most aggressive voice,

"I can't imagine why women wear such insensate clothes."

Something that had been cold and sick in Thomasina warmed a little. The warmth was anger—at least she thought it was—but it was better than the cold sickness. She found herself saying,

"They don't! And at any rate we don't have all those buttons and things!" And then, "Go away, Peter!"

He retreated to the door, set his back against it, and said,

"Not on your life!"

"Peter!"

"It's not the slightest bit of good. I've been coming up here three times a day, and you won't see me. You won't see me! I never heard such a pack of damned nonsense in my life! I don't know how much longer you expected me to go on standing for it, but I'm through! You are seeing me now, and you are going to go on seeing me until we've had this out!"

When Thomasina's face came through the opening of the grey dress Peter had found himself suddenly angry. She looked as if she had been out all night in the rain—and cold February rain at that. He was now a good deal braced by the fact that her natural colour had returned. Her eyes did not exactly sparkle, but they looked as if they might be going to do so at any moment. A secret and horrid fear that something irrevocable had happened between them, he didn't quite know how or why, just faded out. If this was going to be a row, he was all set for it. They always had had rows, and he supposed they always would. And they didn't matter a bit, because under all the sparring there was something enduring and strong—very, very strong. They clashed because they were both proud, and independent, and honest, and because they knew it didn't really matter. A bout between them was not a duel, it was a fencing-match. At any moment they could drop their points and go off hand in hand. But this time—this time he had been afraid. Now he wasn't afraid any more. He stood with his back to the door and said,

"Tamsine, don't be a fool!"

All this time he hadn't called her Tamsine once—all this horrible time at Deep End. It did things to her, and she was betrayed. The proud anger in her melted, and when Peter stopped propping the door and came over and took her in his arms she could do nothing but cry. And, like everything else she did, Thomasina didn't cry by halves.

Miss Gwyneth, who had been standing outside the door for some time, was alarmed to the point of opening it. Not wide of course, but just far enough to make sure that nothing *dreadful* was happening. She saw Thomasina weeping vehemently on Mr. Peter Brandon's shoulder, and she heard her say between sobs, "Oh, Peter, I'm so unhappy!" To which Mr. Brandon replied, "Darling, what you want is a hanky. Here, take a good blow and you'll feel a lot better." This reassured her so much that she closed the door and withdrew, followed by Miss Elaine, who had been looking over her shoulder.

When they were at a safe distance she said in the tone of one who admired some unaccountable phenomenon,

"Men always do seem to have a handkerchief. I suppose it is all those pockets!"

Miss Elaine turned an indignant face upon her.

"How can you be so unromantic, Gwyneth? Handkerchiefs, indeed—when you ought to have been thinking of *orange blossom!* Oh, I do *hope* they will ask us to the wedding!"

PYRAMID BOOKS

Printed in the USA
CPSIA information can be obtained
at www.ICGtesting.com
LVHW020817230923
758935LV00047B/733